C# GAME PROGRAMMING: FOR SERIOUS GAME CREATION

DANIEL SCHULLER

Course Technology PTR
A part of Cengage Learning

COURSE TECHNOLOGY
CENGAGE Learning

Australia • Brazil • Japan • Korea • Mexico • Singapore • Spain • United Kingdom • United States

COURSE TECHNOLOGY
CENGAGE Learning™

**C# Game Programming:
For Serious Game Creation**

Daniel Schuller

**Publisher and General Manager,
Course Technology PTR:**
Stacy L. Hiquet

Associate Director of Marketing:
Sarah Panella

Manager of Editorial Services:
Heather Talbot

Marketing Manager: Jordan
Castellani

Senior Acquisitions Editor: Emi
Smith

Project Editor: Jenny Davidson

Technical Reviewer: James E. Perry

Interior Layout Tech: MPS Limited,
A Macmillan Company

Cover Designer: Mike Tanamachi

CD-ROM Producer Brandon Penticuff

Indexer: Broccoli Indexing Services

Proofreader: Sara Gullion

For product information and technology assistance, contact us at
Cengage Learning Customer & Sales Support, 1-800-354-9706
For permission to use material from this text or product,
submit all requests online at **cengage.com/permissions**
Further permissions questions can be emailed to
permissionrequest@cengage.com

Visual Studio 2010 Express Web installer is a registered trademark of Microsoft Corporation in the United States and other countries. TortoiseSVN is a trademark of CollabNet, Inc. sfxr was created by DrPetter. NUnit is a copyright of NUnit.org. Bitmap Font Creator is a copyright of andreas jönsson.

All other trademarks are the property of their respective owners.

All images © Cengage Learning unless otherwise noted.

Library of Congress Control Number: 2010922097

ISBN-13: 978-1-4354-5556-6

ISBN-10: 1-4354-5556-8

Course Technology, a part of Cengage Learning
20 Channel Center Street
Boston, MA 02210
USA

Cengage Learning is a leading provider of customized learning solutions with office locations around the globe, including Singapore, the United Kingdom, Australia, Mexico, Brazil, and Japan. Locate your local office at: **international.cengage.com/region**

Cengage Learning products are represented in Canada by Nelson Education, Ltd.

For your lifelong learning solutions, visit **courseptr.com**

Visit our corporate website at **cengage.com**

Printed in the United States of America
2 3 4 5 6 7 12

This book is dedicated to Garfield Schuller and Stanley Hyde.

ACKNOWLEDGMENTS

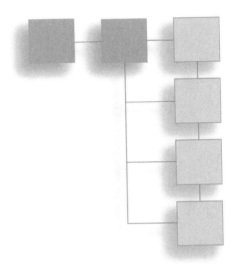

Many thanks to everyone who has helped with this book and to everyone who developed the wonderful libraries and tools that it uses. Thanks to Jenny Davidson, the book's project editor, for all her help making my writing clearer and ensuring that everything was finished in time. Thanks to my technical editor, Jim Perry, who caught my many coding mistakes and provided valuable suggestions and advice. I would also like to thank my family and coworkers for their support and helpful input.

About the Author

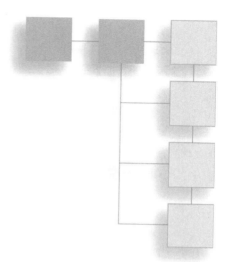

Daniel Schuller is a British-born computer game developer who has worked and lived in the United States, Singapore, Japan, and is currently working in the United Kingdom. He has released games on the PC as well as the Xbox 360 and PlayStation 3. Schuller has developed games for Sony, Ubisoft, Naughty Dog, RedBull, and Wizards of the Coast, and maintains a game development website at http://www.godpatterns.com. In addition to developing computer games, Schuller also studies Japanese and is interested in Artificial Intelligence, cognition, and the use of games in education.

Contents

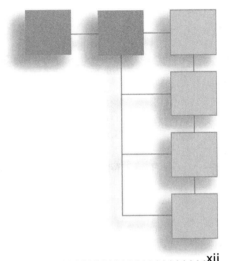

INTRODUCTION

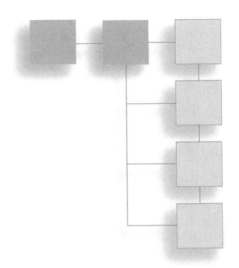

I want to help you make your game.

Everyone has a great game idea, but the path from initial idea to finished product is not a clear one. There are an intimidating number of programming languages, libraries, and production methods. Even experienced game developers often fail to realize their vision. Without a good solid architecture, game code may become so complicated that a developer drowns in the complexity. The more complex the code, the harder the game becomes to change or continue developing.

This book shows how to write simple, clean, reliable code by developing two basic games. These games are built using the C# programming language and OpenGL. C# is a modern, high-level programming language, so writing code is faster, with fewer programming warts to avoid. OpenGL is as close as the game industry has to a standard way to display graphics. When the book is finished, you'll have an excellent code base to develop and grow, pursuing your own ideas.

In the first part of the book you'll find a broad overview of the methodologies and libraries used to build great games. The second part introduces how to use these libraries and how to create your own reusable game library. You'll also learn how to develop a simple scrolling shooter game, and then you'll be provided with some suggestions and tips for developing your own great game idea. The included CD has everything that you will need to start developing games. Every code snippet in the book has the full source code and program included on the CD. There are also some simple game assets and a collection of links to useful game development and graphics websites.

CD-ROM Downloads

If you purchased an ebook version of this book, and the book had a companion CD-ROM, we will mail you a copy of the disc. Please send ptrsupplements@ cengage.com the title of the book, the ISBN, your name, address, and phone number. Thank you.

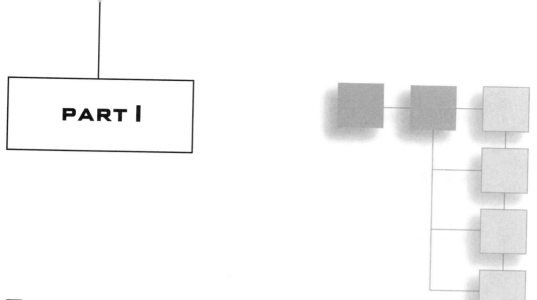

PART I

BACKGROUND

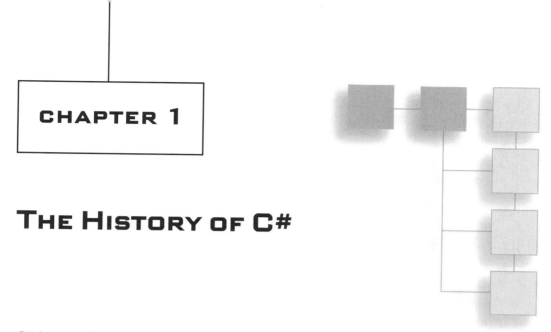

CHAPTER 1

THE HISTORY OF C#

C# is a modern object-oriented language developed by a Microsoft team led by Anders Hejlsberg. The Common Language Runtime, or CLR for short, is the virtual machine on which C# runs. Many languages run on the CLR and this means they can all be compiled and used on Windows PCs, the Xbox 360, and the Zune. The CLR is owned and developed by Microsoft, but there is also an open-source version of the CLR called Mono. Using Mono, C# programs can be run on Macs, Linux, or any other system for which Mono can be compiled.

In the game industry, we use C++, but it's not because we want to. C++ is a sprawling language with lots of areas that can trap an unwary programmer and many areas that are simply undefined. C# is much friendlier than C++ and it's far more fun to use for writing games.

C# Basics

C# was first announced in July 2000 at the Microsoft Professional Developers Conference in Orlando. At the time it was a little like the Microsoft version of Java, but it rapidly developed into something much different. C#'s most recent updates are very innovative and exciting.

Modern languages like C# and Java make programs that run on virtual machines. Older language like C++ and C make programs that run directly on the hardware of a specific machine. The hardware that runs the program is called the central processing unit, or CPU for short. This is the brain of the computer.

Modern Macs and PCs generally have an x86 CPU; the XBox 360 has a Xenon CPU; and the PS3 has a Cell CPU. All of these brains are slightly different but share the same basic purpose—to run the programs programmers write. Programs are just lists of instructions. The instructions a particular CPU understands are called machine code. Machine code for one CPU is unlikely to be understood by a different type of CPU.

Compilers take human-readable source code, written in a language like C++ or C, and compile it into machine code. For example, the PlayStation 3 C++ compiler compiles source code into machine code that can run on the Cell CPU. To run the same C++ code on the Xbox 360 Xenon CPU, it must be compiled again using the Xbox 360 C++ complier. C# doesn't work like this. C# compiles down to an assembly language called the common intermediate language or CIL. CIL is then run on a virtual machine that generates the machine code for the particular system. In the PlayStation 3 case that would mean to run C# on the PlayStation, it would need a virtual machine that could take CIL code and output machine code that the Cell CPU understands. This difference between languages using virtual machines and languages that compile directly to machine code is shown in Figure 1.1.

C#s virtual machine, the CLR, has many advantages. The biggest advantage is you only need write the code once and it will run on every CPU that supports the

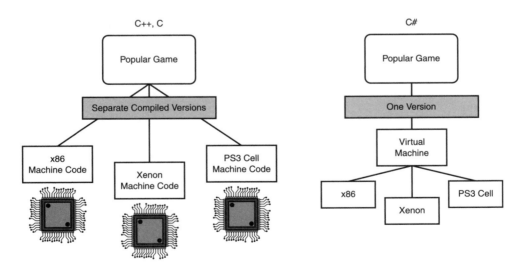

Figure 1.1
Virtual machines and directly compiled code.

CLR. It's very hard to crash the system using C# because the system is insulated by this virtual machine. The virtual machine can catch errors before sending them to the real hardware. Also you don't need to worry about allocating and freeing memory as this is done automatically. Programming languages can be mixed and matched provided they all compile to the CLR; languages such as F#, IronLisp, IronRuby, IronPython, and IronScheme can all be used in a single program. As a game programmer you could write your AI in a high-level, AI-friendly language and your graphics code in a more procedural C-like language.

Versions of C#

C# is regularly updated with new functionality and improvements. Even if you have programmed in C# before you may not be aware of all the new features added to the language in recent updates.

C# 2.0

C# version 2.0 added generics and anonymous delegates. It's easiest to explain these new features with examples.

Generics

Generics are a way of writing code to use some general object with some general properties, rather than a specific object. Generics can be used with classes, methods, interfaces, and structs to define what data type they will use. The data types used with generic code are specified at compile time, which means the programmer no longer has to be responsible for writing test code to check that the correct data type is being used. This in turn makes the code shorter because test code doesn't need to be written, and safer because it reduces type mismatch errors at run time. Generic code also tends to be faster because less casting between data types has to be performed.

The following code is written without the use of generics.

```
ArrayList _list = new ArrayList();
_list.Add(1.3); // boxing converts value type to a reference type
_list.Add(1.0);

//Unboxing Converts reference type to a value type.
object objectAtPositionZero = _list[0];
double valueOne = (double) objectAtPositionZero;
double valueTwo = (double) _list[1];
```

The code creates a list and adds two decimal numbers. Everything in C# is an object, including numbers. All objects in C# inherit from the `object` class. An `ArrayList` stores objects. Here, numbers have been added but the `ArrayList` does not know they are numbers; to the `ArrayList` they are just objects. Objects are the only thing it knows. When the number is passed to `ArrayList.Add` it is converted to an `object` type and added to its collection of objects.

Every time an object is taken out of the list, it must be cast back from an object to its original type. All the casts are inefficient and they clutter the code making it harder to read, which makes non-generic code unpleasant to work with. Generics fix this problem. To understand how they fix the problem, you need to understand the difference between reference types and value types.

C# has two broad categories of type, reference types and value types. Value types are the basic types such as `int`, `float`, `double`, `bool`, `string`, etc. Reference types are the large data structures you define yourself using the `class` keyword such as `Player`, `Creature`, `Spaceship`, etc. You can also define custom value types using the `struct` keyword.

```
// An example reference type
public class SpaceShip
{
    string _name;
    int _thrust;
}
// An example value type
public struct Point
{
    int _x;
    int _y;
}
```

Value types store their data directly in memory. Reference types store their data indirectly in memory. In the memory address of a reference type is another memory address to where the data is actually stored. This can be confusing at first, but once you are familiar with the concepts it's quite simple. The differences in memory are shown in Figure 1.2.

If the computer's memory is thought of as a vast library full of bookshelves, then creating a value type is simply adding some books to the shelf. Creating a

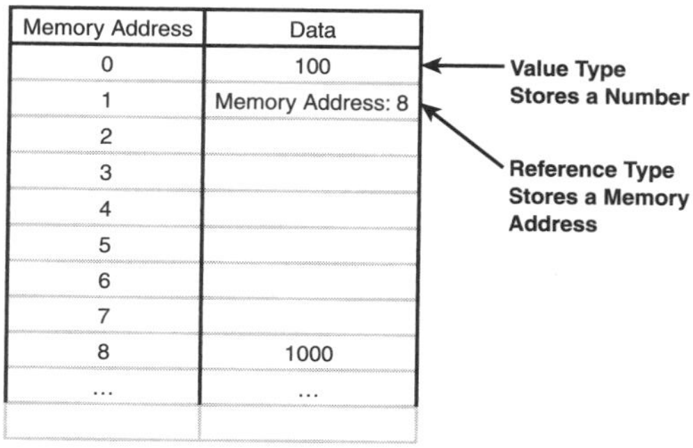

Figure 1.2
Value and reference types in memory.

reference type is more like adding a note to the shelf that gives directions to a different part of the library where the books are stored.

Here's an example of a value type.

```
int i = 100;
```

If we looked in memory to see where i was stored, we'd get the number 100. In our human-readable code we use the variable name i; in assembly code i is a memory address. This line of code, therefore, says put the value 100 in the next available memory address and call that memory address i.

```
int i = 100;
int j = i; // value type so copied into i
Console.WriteLine(i); // 100
Console.WriteLine(j); // 100
i = 30;
Console.WriteLine(i); // 30
Console.WriteLine(j); // 100
```

In this example, the value type i is assigned to j, which means its data is copied. Everything stored in memory address j is now the same as whatever was in i.

The next example is similar but it uses reference types. First, a reference type needs to be created by defining a new class. All this class will do is store a number, like our own version of the int type. Our type will be called Int using a capital I to differentiate it from C#'s built-in int type.

```
class Int()
{
```

```
   int _value;
   public Int (int value)
   {
     _value = value;
   }
   public void SetValue (int value)
   {
     _value = value;
   }
   public override string ToString ()
   {
     return _value.ToString ();
   }
}

Int i = new Int (100);
Int j = i; // reference type so reference copied into i
Console.WriteLine (i); // 100
Console.WriteLine (j); // 100
i.SetValue (30);
Console.WriteLine (i); // 30
Console.WriteLine (j); // 30 <- the shocking difference
```

Here when i changed so did j. This is because j did not have its own copy of the data; it just had the same reference to the data that i did. When the underlying data changes, it doesn't matter if that data is accessed with i or j, the same result will always be returned.

To use the library example again, you check the library index system and it returns two shelf locations for the book you want. The first position, i, doesn't have a book at all; it just has a small note, and when you check position j you find a similar note. Both of these notes points to a third location. If you follow either note, you will find the book you were searching for. There is only one book, but two references point to it.

Boxing is the process of taking a value type and converting it to a reference type. Unboxing is the process of converting the new reference type back to the original value type. In the first version of C#, lists of objects, even if they were all value types, had to be converted to reference types when they were added to the list. This all changed with the introduction of generics. Here's some example code using generic functionality; compare this with the earlier example using an ArrayList.

```
List<float> _list = new List<float>();
_list.Add(1);
_list.Add(5.6f);
float valueOne = _list[0];
float valueTwo = _list[1];
```

This example code creates a list of floats. Floats are value types. Unlike before, the floats don't have to boxed and unboxed by casting; instead it just works. The generic list knows the type it is storing so it doesn't need to cast everything to an object type. This makes the code far more efficient because it's not always swapping between types.

Generics are great for building reusable data structures like lists.

Anonymous Delegates

In C# a delegate is a way of passing a function as an argument to another function. This is really useful when you want to do a repetitive action to many different lists. You have one function that iterates through the list, calling a second function to operate on each list member. Here is an example.

```
void DoToList (List<Item> list, SomeDelegate action)
{
  foreach(Item item in list)
  {
    action(item);
  }
}
```

Anonymous delegates allow the function to be written straight into the DoToList function call. The function doesn't need to be declared or predefined. Because it's not predefined, it has no name, hence anonymous function.

```
// A quick way to destroy a list of items
DoToList (_itemList, delegate(Item item) { item.Destroy(); });
```

This example iterates through the list and applies the anonymous function to each member. The anonymous function in the example calls the Destroy method on each item. That could be pretty handy, right? But there's one more trick to anonymous functions. Have a look at the following code.

```
int SumArrayOfValues (int[] array)
{
  int sum = 0;
```

```
Array.ForEach(
  array,
  delegate(int value)
  {
    sum += value;
  }
);
return sum;
}
```

This is called a closure. A delegate is created for each loop iteration, and uses the same variable, sum. The variable sum can even go out of scope, but the anonymous delegates will continue to hold a reference to it. It will become a private variable only accessible to the functions that have *closed* it. Closures are used heavily in functional programming languages.

C# 3.0

The release of C# 3.0 introduced more than just a few incremental changes. The new features are extremely innovative and massively reduce the amount of boiler plate code needed. The biggest change was LINQ system.

LINQ

LINQ stands for Language-Integrated Query. It's a little like SQL (SQL, Structured Query Language, is the language used to manipulate and retrieve data from databases) for data structures. The best way to get a feel for it is to look at some examples.

```
Monster
{
  string _name;
  int _currentLevel = 1;
  int _currentExperience = 0;
  int _nextLevelExperience = 1000;

  public Monster(string name, int currentExperience)
  {
    _name = name;
    _currentExperience = currentExperience;
  }
  public string Name()
```

```
  {
    return _name;
  }

  public int CurrentExperience()
  {
    return _currentExperience;
  }

  public int NextLevelRequiredExperience()
  {
    return _nextLevelExperience;
  }

  public void LevelUp()
  {
    Console.WriteLine(_name + `` has levelled up!'');
    _currentLevel++;
    _currentExperience = 0;
    _nextLevelExperience = _currentLevel * 1000;
  }
}

List<Monster> _monsterList = new List<Monster>();
_monsterList.Add(new Monster(``Ogre'', 1001));
_monsterList.Add(new Monster(``Skeleton'', 999));
_monsterList.Add(new Monster(``Giant Bat'', 1004));
_monsterList.Add(new Monster(``Slime'', 0));

// Select monsters that are about to level up
IEnumerable<Monster> query = from m in _monsterList
                             where m.CurrentExperience() >
                               m.NextLevelRequiredExperience()
                             orderby m.Name() descending
                             select m;
foreach (Monster m in query)
{
  m.LevelUp();
}
```

When run, this query retrieves all the monsters that can gain a level, and then orders that list by name. LINQ isn't just used with collections; it can be used with

XML and databases too. LINQ works with another new addition to C# 3.0: lambda functions.

Lambda Functions

Remember anonymous delegates? Well, lambda functions are a much more convenient way to write anonymous delegates. Here's an example that destroys all items in a player's inventory.

```
_itemList.ForEach(delegate(Item x) { x.Destroy(); });
```

Using the lambda functions, it can be written more concisely as follows.

```
_itemList.ForEach(x => x.Destroy());
```

Less boilerplate code is required making it easier to read.

Object Initializers

Object initializers allow objects to be constructed in a more flexible manner, and constructors no longer need to be so verbose. Here's an example without object initializers.

```
Spaceship s = new Spaceship();
s.Health = 30;
```

This can now be written in a more concise way.

```
Spaceship s = new Spaceship { Health = 30 };
```

This is used in some LINQ queries. Object initializers can help prevent the need to write multiple constructors that only set a few fields.

Collection Initializers

Collection initializers let you initialize lists in a pleasing way. As before, the best way to demonstrate the improvement is to show the old way.

```
class Orc
{
  List<Item> _items = new List<Item>();

  public Orc()
  {
    _items.Add(new Item(''axe''));
```

```
    _items.Add(new Item(''pet_hamster''));
    _items.Add(new Item(''skull_helm''));
  }
}
```

Initializing lists in this way requires a certain amount of setup code that has to be put inside the constructor or in a separate initialization method. But by using collection initializers everything can be written in a much more concise way.

```
class Orc
{
  List<Item> _items = new List<Item>
  {
    new Item(''axe''),
    new Item(''pet_hamster''),
    new Item(''skull_helm'')
  };
}
```

In this example case, we don't use the constructor at all anymore; it's done automatically when an object is created.

Local Variable Type Inference and Anonymous Types

Using code with generics can get a little messy if there are several generic objects being initialized at the same time. Type inference can make things a little nicer.

```
List<List<Orc>> _orcSquads = new List<List<Orc>>();
```

In this code, there's a lot of repeated typing, which means more pieces of the code to edit when changes happen. Local variable type inference can be used to help out in the following way.

```
var _orcSquads = new List<List<Orc>>();
```

The var keyword is used when you would like the compiler to work out the correct type. This is useful in our example as it reduces the amount of code that needs to be maintained. The var keyword is also used for anonymous types. Anonymous types occur when a type is created without a predefined class or struct. The syntax is similar to the collection initializer syntax.

```
var fullName = new { FirstName = ''John'', LastName = ''Doe'' };
```

The fullName object can now be used like a reference type. It has two read-only fields, FirstName and LastName. This is useful when you have a function and you really want to return two values. Both values can be combined in an anonymous type and returned. The more common use for anonymous type is when storing the data returned from LINQ queries.

C# 4.0

C# 4.0 is the very latest release of C# and the major change is the addition of dynamic types. C# is a statically typed language. Static typing means that all the types of the various objects are known at compile time. Classes are defined with fields and methods; these fields and methods don't change during the course of the program. In dynamic typing, objects and classes are more fluid—functions and fields can be added and taken away. IronPython and IronRuby are both dynamic languages that run on the CLR.

Dynamic Objects

Dynamic objects get a new keyword: dynamic. Here's an example of how it's used. Imagine we had several unrelated classes that all implemented a method called GetName.

```
void PrintName(dynamic obj)
{
  System.Console.Writeline(obj.GetName());
}
PrintName(new User(''Bob'')) // Bob
PrintName(new Monster(''Axeface'')) // Axeface
```

If an object is dynamic when a function is called, that function is looked up at runtime. This is called duck typing. The look-up is done using reflection, or if the object implements the interface IDynamicObject, then it calls the method GetMetaObject and the object is left to deal with it internally. Duck typing is a little slower because it takes time to determine if the function is present or not. In traditional C#, a function or field's presence is determined once at compile time.

The following code will compile under C# 4.0.

```
public dynamic GetDynamicObject()
{
  return new object();
}
```

```
dynamic testObj = GetDynamicObject();
testObj.ICanCallAnyFunctionILike();
```

The method `ICanCallAnyFunctionILike` probably doesn't exist, so when the program runs and executes that section of code, it will throw an exception.

Calling any method or accessing any member of a dynamic object requires the object to do a runtime look-up to see if that member or method exists. That means if the programmer makes a typo, the error isn't caught during compiling, only when the code is run. In C# if a method or field on a dynamic object isn't found, the exception that's thrown is of type `RuntimeBinderException`.

The dynamic keyword is useful if you intend to do a lot of dynamic scripting in your game or if you want write a function that takes advantage of duck typing, as in the `PrintName` example. `PrintName` is slower because the `GetNames` method must be looked up each time it is called. It may be worth taking the speed hit in certain situations, but it's best to be aware of it.

Optional Parameters and Named Arguments

Until version 4.0, C# had no support for optional parameters in methods. This is a standard feature of C++. Here's how it works.

```
class Player
{
  // Knock the player backwards
  public void KnockBack(int knockBackDamage = 0)
  {
  // code
  }
}
Player p = new Player();
p.KnockBack(); // knocks the player back and by default deals no damage
p.KnockBack(10); // knocks the player back and gives 10 damage
```

Optional parameters allow the programmer to give default values to the method arguments. Named arguments allow multiple optional parameters to be used in an elegant way.

```
enum HairColor
{
  Blonde,
  Brunette,
```

```
    Red,
    Black
  }
  enum Sex
  {
    Male,
    Female
  }
  class Baby
  {
    public string Name { get; set; }
    public Sex Sex { get; set; }
    public HairColor HairColor { get; set; }
  }
  class Player
  {
    public Baby HaveBaby(string babyName, Sex sex = Sex.Female, HairColor
  hairColor = HairColor.Black)
    {
      return new Baby()
      {
        Name = babyName,
        Sex = sex,
        HairColor = hairColor
      };
    }
  }
  Player player = new Player();
  player.HaveBaby(``Bob'', Sex.Male);
  player.HaveBaby(``Alice'');
```

In this example, the player class has code that allows the player to give birth. The HaveBaby method takes in a name and some other optional arguments and then returns a new baby object. The HaveBaby method requires a name to be given but the sex and hairColor arguments are optional. The next example shows how to set the hair color argument but leave the sex as the default female value.

```
player.HaveBaby(``Jane'', hairColor: HairColor.Blonde)
```

Named arguments provide a way to only set the arguments we want to set.

Summary

C# is a modern, garbage-collected, objected-orientated language and it's come a long way since its debut at the July 2000 Microsoft Professional Developers Conference in Orlando. C# runs on a virtual machine called the Common Language Runtime or CLR for short. The CLR can be used to run many different languages in the same program.

C# is a living language; as time passes more functionality and features are added. There have been four major versions of C# and each has brought new and useful features. These features can often make programs easier to write and more efficient so it's important to keep up with the changes. C# 4.0, the latest version, was released in April 2010.

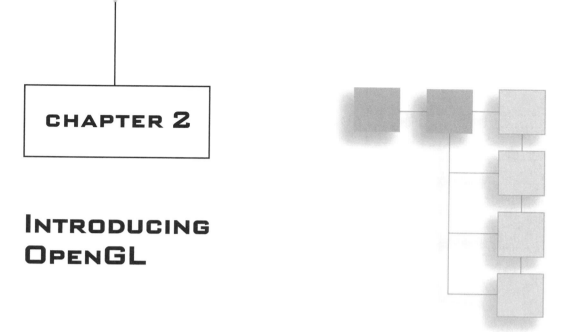

CHAPTER 2

INTRODUCING OPENGL

Every computer has special graphics hardware that controls what you see on the screen. OpenGL tells this hardware what to do. Figure 2.1 shows how OpenGL is used by a computer game, or any other piece of software, to issue commands to the graphics hardware using the device drivers supplied by the manufacturer.

The Open Graphics Library is one of the oldest, most popular graphics libraries game creators have. It was developed in 1992 by Silicon Graphics Inc. (SGI) but only really got interesting for game players when it was used for GLQuake in 1997. The GameCube, Wii, PlayStation 3, and the iPhone all base their graphics libraries on OpenGL.

The alternative to OpenGL is Microsoft's DirectX. DirectX encompasses a larger number of libraries, including sound and input. It is more accurate to compare OpenGL to the Direct3D library in DirectX. The latest version of DirectX is DirectX 11. The Xbox 360 uses a version of DirectX 9.0. DirectX 10 and 11 will only work on computers with the Windows Vista or Windows 7 operating systems installed.

The feature sets of Direct3D and OpenGL are pretty much equivalent. Modern game engines—for example, Unreal—usually build in a layer of abstraction that allows the user to switch between OpenGL and Direct3D as they desire, as shown in Figure 2.2. This abstraction is required when producing multiplatform games that will be released for both the PlayStation 3 and Xbox 360. The Xbox 360 must use Direct3D calls, whereas the PS3 uses OpenGL calls.

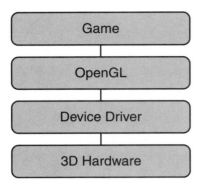

Figure 2.1
The typical use of OpenGL.

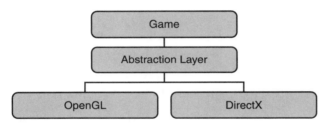

Figure 2.2
Using an abstraction layer.

DirectX and OpenGL are both excellent graphics libraries. DirectX works on Microsoft platforms, whereas OpenGL is available on a much wider range of platforms. DirectX tends to be updated more often, which means it has access to the very latest graphics features. OpenGL moves slower and the latest graphics features can only be accessed through a rather unfriendly extension mechanism. OpenGL's slow movement can be quite advantageous as the interface rarely changes and therefore code written years ago will still work with the latest OpenGL versions. Each new version of DirectX changes the interface, which breaks compatibility and requires older code to be tweaked and changed to be updated.

DirectX can be used with C# using the Managed DirectX libraries; unfortunately, these libraries are no longer officially supported or updated. Managed DirectX has been superseded by Microsoft's XNA game creation library. XNA uses DirectX, but it is a much higher level framework for quickly creating and prototyping games. SlimDX is an independent C# API for DirectX, which is a good alternative to Managed DirectX.

Architecture of OpenGL

OpenGL is a C-style graphics library. C style means there are no classes or objects; instead, OpenGL is a large collection of functions. Internally, OpenGL is a state machine. Function calls alter the internal state of OpenGL, which then affects how it behaves and how it renders polygons to the screen. The fact that it is a state machine can cause some issues; you may experience a bug in some far flung region of your code by accidentally setting a state in some other area. For this reason, it is very important to carefully note which states are being changed.

Vertices—The Building Blocks of 3D Graphics

The basic unit in OpenGL is the vertex. A vertex is, at its simplest, a point in space. Extra information can be attached to these points—how it maps to a texture, if it has a certain weight or color—but the most important piece of information is its position.

Games spend a lot of their time sending OpenGL vertices or telling OpenGL to move vertices in certain ways. The game may first tell OpenGL that all the vertices it's going to send are to be made into triangles. In this case, for every three vertices OpenGL receives, it will attach them together with lines to create a polygon, and it may then fill in the surface with a texture or color.

Modern graphics hardware is very good at processing vast sums of vertices, making polygons from them and rendering them to the screen. This process of going from vertex to screen is called the pipeline. The pipeline is responsible for positioning and lighting the vertices, as well as the projection transformation. This takes the 3D data and transforms it to 2D data so that it can be displayed on your screen. A projection transformation may sound a little complicated, but the world's painters and artists have been doing these transformations for centuries, painting and drawing the world around them on to a flat canvas.

Even modern 2D games are made using vertices. The 2D sprites are made up of two triangles to form a square. This is often referred to as a quad. The quad is given a texture and it becomes a sprite. Two-dimensional games use a special projection transformation that ignores all the 3D data in the vertices, as it's not required for a 2D game.

The Pipeline

The pipeline flow is shown in Figure 2.3. This pipeline is known as the fixed function pipeline. This means once the programmer has given the input to the pipeline, all the functionality is set and cannot be modified—for instance, adding a blue tint to the screen could easily be done at the pixel processing stage, but in the fixed function pipeline the programmer has no direct control over this stage.

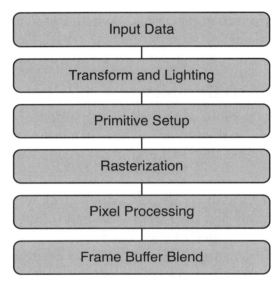

Figure 2.3
The basic fixed function pipeline.

There are six main stages in the fixed function pipeline. Nearly all these stages can be applied in parallel. Each vertex can pass through a particular stage at the same time, provided the hardware supports it. This is what makes graphics cards so much faster than CPU processing.

- **Input stage.** This input is given in the form of vertices, and all the vertices' properties including position, color, and texture data.

- **Transform and lighting.** The vertices are translated according to the current view. This involves changing the vertex positions from 3D space, also known as world space, to 2D space, also known as screen space. Some vertices can be discarded at this stage if they are not going to affect the final view. Lighting calculations may also be performed for each vertex.

- **Primitive setup.** This is the process of creating the polygons from the vertex information. This involves connecting the vertices together according to the OpenGL states. Games most commonly use triangles or triangle strips as their primitives.

- **Rasterization.** This is the process of converting the polygons to pixels (also called fragments).

- **Pixel processing.** Pixel processing may also be referred to as fragment processing. The pixels are tested to determine if they will be drawn to the frame buffer at this stage.

- **Frame buffer.** The frame buffer is a piece of memory that represents what will be displayed to the screen for this particular frame. Blend settings decide how the pixels will be blended with what has already been drawn.

In the last few years, the pipeline has become programmable. Programs can be uploaded to the graphics card and replace the default stages of the fixed function pipeline. You have probably heard of shaders; this is the name for the small programs that overwrite certain parts of the pipeline.

Figure 2.4 shows the stages of the programmable pipeline. Transform and lighting has been removed; instead, there are vertex and geometry shaders. The pixel processing stage has also become programmable, as a pixel shader. The vertex shader will be run on every vertex that passes through the pipeline. Vertex shaders cannot add vertices, but the properties such as position, color, and texture coordinates can be modified.

Geometry shaders were added a little more recently than pixel and vertex shaders. Geometry shaders take a whole primitive (such as a strip of lines, points, or triangles) as input and the vertex shader is run on every primitive. Geometry shaders can create new vertex information, points, lines, and even primitives. Geometry shaders are used to create point sprites and dynamic tessellation, among other effects. Point sprites are a way of quickly rendering a lot of sprites; it's a technique that is often used for particle systems to create effects like fire and smoke. Dynamic tessellation is a way to add more polygons to a piece of geometry. This can be used to increase the smoothness of low polygon game models or add more detail as the camera zooms in on the model.

Pixel shaders are applied to each pixel that is sent to the frame buffer. Pixel shaders are used to create bump mapping effects, specular highlights, and per-pixel lighting. Bump map effects is a method to give a surface some extra

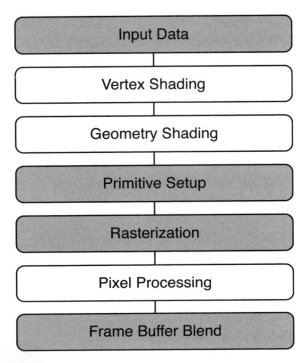

Figure 2.4
The basic programmable pipeline.

height information. Bump maps usually consist of an image where each pixel represents a normal vector that describes how the surface is to be perturbed. The pixel shader can use a bump map to give a model a more interesting texture that appears to have some depth. Per-pixel lighting is a replacement for OpenGL's default lighting equations that work out the light for each vertex and then give that vertex an appropriate color. Per-pixel uses a more accurate lighting model in which each pixel is lit independently. Specular highlights are areas on the model that are very shiny and reflect a lot of light.

OpenGL Is Changing

This is a great time to learn OpenGL. The current version of OpenGL is very friendly to learners of the library. There are many easy-to-use functions and a lot of the graphics work can be done for you. Think of it like the current version of OpenGL is a bike that comes with training wheels that can be used to help you learn and then be removed when no longer needed. The next version of OpenGL is more like a performance motorbike, everything superfluous has been removed and all that remains is raw power. This is excellent for an experienced OpenGL programmer but a little intimidating for the beginner.

The versions of OpenGL available depend on the graphics cards drivers installed on your system. Nearly every computer supports OpenGL 2.1 and a reasonably recent graphics card will support OpenGL 3.x.

OpenGL ES

OpenGL ES is a modern version of OpenGL for embedded systems. It is quite similar to recent versions of OpenGL but with a more restricted set of features. It is used on high-end mobile phones such as the Android, BlackBerry, and iPhone. It is also used in military hardware for heads-up displays on things like warplanes.

OpenGL ES supports the programmable pipeline and has support for shaders.

WebGL

WebGL is currently still in development, but it is a version of OpenGL specifically made for use over the web. Using it will require a browser that supports the HTML 5 canvas tag. It's hard to know at this stage if it is going to be something that will take off. 3D for the web has been tried before and failed. For instance, VRML (Virtual Reality Modeling Language) was similar to HTML but allowed users to create 3D worlds; it had some academic popularity but never gained traction with general users.

WebGL has some promising backers; a number of big name companies such as Google, Apple, and Mozilla are in the WebGL working group and there are some impressive demos. Currently the performance is very reasonable and it is likely to compete with Flash if it matures.

OpenGL and the Graphics Card

OpenGL is a library that allows the programmer to send instructions to the graphics card. The graphics card is a piece of specialized hardware to display 3D data. Graphics cards are made up of a number of standard components including the frame buffer, texture memory, and the GPU. The GPU, graphics processing unit, controls how the vertices are processed and displayed on screen.

The CPU sends instructions and data to the GPU, describing how each frame should appear on the screen. The texture memory is usually a large store of memory that is used for storing the vast amount of texture data that games require. The frame buffer is an area of memory that stores the image that will be displayed on the screen in the next frame. Modern cards may have more than one GPU, and on each GPU are many shader processing units for doing massively parallel shader operations. This has been exploited by distributed applications such as Folding@home, which runs protein folding simulations, and on hundreds of thousands of computers all over the world.

The first popular 3D graphics card was the 3dfx Voodoo 1. This was one of the very early graphics cards; it had 2 megabytes of texture memory and 2 megabytes for the frame buffer, and it used the PCI bus and a clock speed of 135MHz. It accelerated early games such as *Tomb Raider, Descent II, Quake,* and the demo of *Quake II,* allowing the games to run much smoother and with greater detail. The Voodoo 1 used a standard PCI bus that allows the CPU to send data to the graphics card at an upper limit of 533MB/s. Modern cards have moved on from the PCI bus to the AGP (Accelerated Graphics Port), which achieved a maximum of 2GB/s and then on again to the PCI Express. Current generations of the PCI Express card can send up to 8GB/s.

New graphics cards seem to come out monthly, each faster than the last. At the time of this writing, the fastest card is probably the ATI Radeon HD 5970. It has two GPUs and each GPU has 1,600 shader processors. It has a clock speed of 725MHz and a total computing performance of 4.64 teraflops.

Most modern cards have unique specialized hardware for new operations. This hardware is exposed to OpenGL through the use of extensions. OpenGL is capable of exposing new functionality present in the driver and graphics card when given a string identifying the new extension. For example, the ATI Radeon HD 5970 has two GPUs; this is rather unusual, and to make full use of both GPUs, there are some new extension methods such as AMD_gpu_association. This extension allows the user to split tasks between the two GPUs. If a number of vendors implement the same extension, then it has the letters "EXT" somewhere in the extension string. In some cases, it is possible that the architecture review board that controls the OpenGL specification will elevate an extension to official status. In that case, the extension gets the letters "ARB" included in the string and all vendors are required to support it.

Shaders—Programs on the Graphics Card

The term shader is a bit misleading. Initially, shader programs were primarily used to shade models by operating on the pixels that make up the surface of each polygon. Over time the abilities of shader programs have expanded; they can now change vertex properties, create new vertices, or even complete general operations.

Shaders operate differently from normal programs that run on the CPU. Shader programs are executed on a large number of elements all at the same time. This means that shader programs are massively parallel, whereas programs on the CPU are generally run serially and only one instance at a time. Shader programs are excellent for doing operations on the mass of pixels and vertices that are the building blocks of a 3D world.

Until recently there were three kinds of shaders—vertex, geometry, and pixel—and each could do only certain operations. Vertex shaders operated on vertices; pixel shaders on pixels; and geometry shaders on primitives. To reduce complexity and allow hardware makers to optimize more efficiently, all these types of shaders were replaced with one called the unified shader.

Shaders are programmed in special languages that run on the graphics card. At the moment, these languages are a lot lower level than C++ (never mind C#). OpenGL has a shading language called GLSL or Open GL Shading Language. It's a little like C with lots of special operations for dealing with vectors and matrices. DirectX also has its own shading language called HLSL or High Level Shading Language. Both these languages are quite similar. To add to the confusion, there is a third language called Cg, which was developed by Microsoft and Nvidia; it is quite similar to HLSL.

Shaders in games are excellent for creating computationally heavy special effects like lighting of parallax mapping. The current technology makes shader programs useful for little else. This book will concentrate on game programming; therefore, the programmable pipeline won't be covered as it's a rather large topic. If you are interested, check the recommended reading section for several excellent books.

Shaders are on the cusp of becoming used for general parallel programming tasks rather than just graphics. For instance, the Nvidia PhysX library allows physics calculations to be done on the GPU rather than the CPU, resulting in much better performance. PhysX is written using yet another shader language called CUDA, but CUDA is a little different. It is a language that is less concerned about pixels and vertices and more concerned with general purpose parallel programming. If in your game you were simulating a city and came up with a novel parallel algorithm to update all the residents of the city, then this could be performed much faster on the GPU, and free the CPU for other tasks. CUDA is often used for scientific research projects as it is a cheap way to harness massive computing power. Some of the applications using CUDA include quantum chemistry calculations, simulating heart muscles, and modeling black holes.

The Tao Framework

The Tao Framework is a way for C# to use the OpenGL library. Tao wraps up a number of C libraries (shown in Table 2.1) and makes them easy to use from C#. Tao has bindings to Mono, so there's support for Linux and Macs too.

Tao gives C# access not only to OpenGL but a selection of other useful libraries.

OpenAL is short for Open Audio Library, and is a powerful open source library. It was the sound library used in *BioShock, Quake 4, Doom III*, and the recent

Table 2.1 The Libraries in the Tao Framework

Library	Use
Tao.OpenAl	OpenAL is a powerful sound library.
Tao.OpenGl	OpenGL is the graphics library we'll be using.
Tao.Sdl	SDL (Simple DirectMedia Layer), a 2D library built on OpenGL.
Tao.Platform.Windows	Support for using OpenGL with Windows.Forms.
Tao.PhysFs	A wrapper for I/O, supports archives like .zips for game assets.
Tao.FreeGlut	OpenGL Utility Toolkit is a set of wrappers for setting up an OpenGL program as well as some draw routines.
Tao.Ode	Open Dynamics Engine is a real-time physics engine for games.
Tao.Glfw	OpenGL Framework is a lightweight multiplatform wrapper class.
Tao.Devil	DevIL is an excellent package for loading various image types into OpenGL (bmp, tif, gif, png, etc.).
Tao.Cg	Cg is a high-level shading language.
Tao.Lua	Lua is one of the most common scripting languages used in the game industry.
Tao.FreeType	A font package.
Tao.FFmpeg	Mainly used for playing video.

Unreal games. It is modeled on OpenGL and has the same state machine style design and extension methods.

SDL, Simple Direct Media Layer, is a cross-platform library that supports input, sound, and graphics. It's quite a popular library for game makers, especially for independent and open source games. One of the more famous open source games made with SDL is *FreeCiv,* a multiplayer *Civilization* clone. It's also used in most Linux game ports.

PhysFs initially might sound like some kind of physics library, but it's a small IO library. It allows all the game assets to be packaged in one big binary file or several small ones. Many commercial games have similar systems; for example, *Doom*'s wad system or *Quake*'s pak system. It allows games to be easily modified and updated once released.

FreeGLUT is a free version of the OpenGL Utility Toolkit. This is a library that has functions to get the user up and running with OpenGL right away. It has methods for receiving input from the keyboard and mouse. It also has methods for drawing various basic shapes, such as spheres, cubes, and even a teapot (this teapot is quite famous in computer graphics and was modeled by Martin Newell while at the University of Utah). The teapot is quite a complicated surface so it's useful when testing new graphical techniques. The *Toy Story* animated movie features the teapot model and DirectX even has its own teapot creation method; D3DXCreateTeapot()). It's often used when teaching OpenGL, but it is quite restrictive and rarely used for serious projects.

ODE, Open Dynamics Engine, is a multiplatform physics engine that does collision detection and rigid body simulation. It was used in the PC first-person shooter game, *S.T.A.L.K.E.R.* Glfw, is the third portable OpenGL wrapper that Tao provides access to. Glfw stands for OpenGL framework, and it looks to expand on the functionality provided by GLUT. If you don't want to use SDL but do want to use a framework to access OpenGL, this may be worth looking at.

DevIL, Developer's Image Library, is a library that loads textures from disk into OpenGL. It's similar to OpenGL in that it's a state machine and it has similar method names. It's cross-platform and supports a wide range of different image formats (43!). Cg is one of the shader languages mentioned earlier in the chapter. Using Tao.Cg, shader programs can be loaded from a text file or string, processed, and used in OpenGL.

Lua is probably the most popular scripting language for game development. It's a small, easily embedded language that's very expressive. Tao.Lua lets functions and data pass between the script and C# program. Tao.FreeType is a basic font package that will convert a free type font to a bitmap. It has a very simple, usable interface.

The final library Tao provides is FFmpeg. The name comes from MPEG, a video standard, and FF, which means Fast Forward. It provides a way to play video. If you wanted to have a cutscene in your game, then this would be a good first stop.

Everything in Tao is totally open source. Most libraries are free to use in a commercial project, but it's worth checking the license for the specifics. Tao is an excellent package for the budding game creator to get started with. It's not in the scope of this book to investigate all these libraries; instead, we'll just concentrate on the most important ones. The OpenGL and `Tao.Platform.Windows` libraries are used from Chapter 5 onwards. DevIL is covered in Chapter 6. Chapter 9 covers playing sound with OpenAL and handling gamepad input with SDL. All the libraries are useful so it's worth taking the time to investigate any of the ones that sound interesting.

Summary

OpenGL and DirectX3D are the two major industrial graphics libraries in use today. These graphics libraries are a standardized way to talk to the underlying graphics hardware. Graphics hardware is usually made from several standard pieces and is extremely efficient at transforming 3D vertex information to a 2D frame on the screen. This transformation from 3D vertices to a 2D frame is known as the graphics pipeline. There are two types of graphics pipeline; the fixed pipeline, which cannot be programmed, and the programmable pipeline, which allows certain stages of the pipeline to be programmed using shaders.

The Tao Framework is a collection of useful libraries including OpenGL. C# can make use of the Tao Framework to write games using OpenGL. The Tao Framework also includes several other libraries useful for game development. OpenAL, DevIL, and SDL will all be used in this book to develop a simple side-scrolling shooter game.

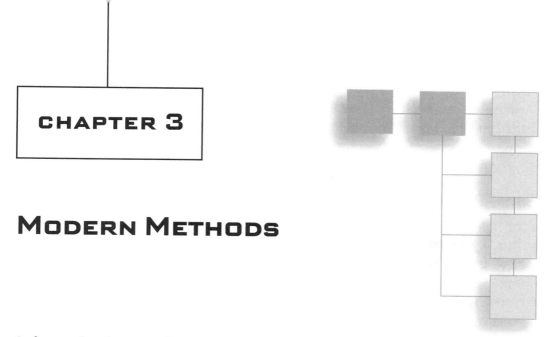

CHAPTER 3

MODERN METHODS

Software development has problems—buggy games, blue screens of death, random crashes, programs not responding; the problems are numerous. Architects and civil engineers do not have these problems. The pyramids are doing pretty well and they are nearly 3,000 years old. Once a building is put up it tends to stay up, but humans have been putting up buildings for a lot longer than they have been writing software.

In the last few years, lots of interestingly named new software development methodologies have started to appear. These methodologies are an attempt to improve the way software is created and the final quality of the product. In this section, we'll look at some of the more useful methodologies that you can put in your programmer's toolkit.

Pragmatic Programming

Pragmatic programming is the ability to finish a program satisfactorily within a desired timeframe. This works by first understanding what is expected of the final program, then a basic bare bones version of the program is written as quickly as possible. This barely functional version is changed until it reaches the original requirements. Changes may be drastic and require rewriting of entire sections of the program, but that's okay. The most important thing is that at all times the program is basically functional.

In the world of game development, it's always a good idea to have something working, because then if a deadline is moved forward or a demo is required, something can be ready immediately. If you're working alone, you have something to show people to get feedback. Feedback offers a much better idea about what will work and what won't.

Game Programming Traps

Many developers start out wanting to make a game but suddenly find that they're writing a framework or game engine instead, and it will be useful to make any sort of game. But the developer never does make his game and falls into the framework trap, redeveloping his framework over and over, adding the latest features but never actually getting on to the game creation part.

Pragmatic programming helps you avoid the framework trap. It expressly forbids you to start working on a framework; creating a functional game is first and most important.

Pragmatic programming has two major coding principles: KISS and DRY. These are two great development tools that will improve your coding ability.

KISS

KISS stands for "Keep It Simple Stupid." Don't needlessly complicate your game programming.

"Hmm ... my space invaders game will be much more efficient if all the enemies and bullets are in a quadtree. So I better start building that..."

This is the wrong way to think if you want to make a game. It's a great way to think if you want to learn about quadtrees. You have to decide which is more important to you and focus only on that. If you want to make a game, get the game functional as soon as possible, then decide if the extra complexity is needed.

DRY

DRY stands for "Don't Repeat Yourself."

If you start seeing snippets of code repeated all the over the place, then that code should be consolidated. The fewer places the code is repeated, the fewer places that need to be modified when making a change. Let's take the space invader example again.

```
class Invader
{
  ...
  int _health = 10;
  bool _dead = false;
  void OnShot ()
  {
      _health--;
      if (_health <= 0)
      {
          _dead = true;
      }
  }
  ...
}
class FlyingSaucer
{
  ...
  int _health = 10;
  void OnShot ()
  {
      _health--;
      if (_health <= 0)
      {
        _dead = true;
      }
  }  ...
}
class Player
{
  ...
  int _health = 10;
  void OnShot ()
  {
      _health--;
      if (_health <= 0)
      {
          _dead = true;
      }
  }
  ...
}
```

In the above example, repeated code is found in all the classes. That means three different areas that need to be modified in case of change. That is more work for you, the coder; it's also more code so it is less clear. The more code, the greater the chance for bugs to appear.

Now shields need to be added to the space invader creatures.

```
class Invader
{
  . . .
  int _health = 10;
  bool _dead = false;
  int _shieldPower = 2;
  void OnShot ()
  {
    if (_shieldPower > 0)
    {
      _shieldPower--;
      return;
    }
      _health--;
      if (_health <= 0)
      {
          _dead = true;
      }
  }
  . . .
}
class FlyingSaucer
{
  . . .
  int _health = 10;
  bool _dead = false;
  int _shieldPower = 2;
  void OnShot ()
  {
    if (_shieldPower > 0)
    {
      _shieldPower--;
      return;
    }
      _health--;
```

```
    if (_health <= 0)
    {
        _dead = true;
    }
  }  ...
}
class Player
{
  ...
  int _health = 10;
  bool _dead = false;
  int _shieldPower = 2;
  void OnShot ()
  {
    if (_shieldPower > 0)
    {
      _shieldPower--;
      return;
    }
    _health--;
    if (_health <= 0)
    {
        _dead = true;
    }
  }
  ...
}
```

The above code is becoming more difficult to maintain. It could be a lot cleaner if the repeated code was refactored into a parent class.

```
class Spacecraft
{
  int _health = 10;
  bool _dead = false;
  int _shieldPower = 2;
  void OnShot ()
  {
    if (_shieldPower > 0)
    {
      _shieldPower--;
      return;
    }
```

```
    _health--;
    if (_health <= 0)
    {
        _dead = true;
    }
  }
}
}
class Invader : Spacecraft
{
}
class FlyingSaucer : Spacecraft
{
}
class Player : Spacecraft
{
}
```

Now that the code is all in one place, it's much easier to change in the future.

C++

C++ does not follow the DRY principle from its very foundations. In C# there is one file that defines classes and methods: the .cs file. In C++, there is a header defining the class and all the method prototypes. A second file with a .cpp extension defines the functions again but this time with their bodies. So you have something like the following.

```
// Header File Player.h
class Player
{
    void TeleportTo(Vector position);
};
  // CPP File Player.cpp
void Player::TeleportTo(Vector position)
{
  // code
}
```

If we want to add a return value, to report if the teleport was successful, the code must be modified in two places. That's not DRY! In C++, the class implementation is defined in one file and the class interface in another; this code duplication is shown in the above code snippet. All but the smallest C++

programs use classes, and all classes require implementation duplication. Therefore, the DRY principle is violated by the very heart of how C++ functions. Both Java and C# were developed after C++ and both were heavily inspired by C++ (copying a large amount of the syntax and features), but they both decided to ditch header files.

You can be better than this; just remember the DRY principle.

If you'd like to know more about pragmatic programming, I recommend *The Pragmatic Programmer* by Andrew Hunt and David Thomas. The details are in Appendix A, "Recommended Reading."

Source Control

Source code is what you type into your editor when you're programming. When source code is compiled, machine code is produced. The source code is for you, the human, and machine code is for the computer. The computer uses the machine code to execute a program. Source control is a program that keeps track of all the changes you make to your source code. (See Figure 3.1.)

Knowing how your code has changed and developed is not just really cool; it's also useful. Source control gives you an unlimited numbers of "undos." You can keep going back to previous versions of the code if you make a mistake. This is particularly useful when developing a new feature and you somehow manage to break everything. Without source control, you'd be looking forward to a painful process of trying to remember what you'd changed. With source control, you can just compare your current version with the previous version and see immediately what's changed, as can be seen in Figure 3.2.

You can also revert to the previous working version of the code and lose all the broken code you added. Reverting is the process of replacing your current code files with an earlier version of those files. It's like time travel! In the kitchen you might decide you want to cut some carrots but accidentally remove your finger. If humans had source control this would be no problem. You would just revert to the version of yourself 15 minutes ago and your finger would be back.

Source control is also great for backup. It stores all your code in one place—the source repository. This might be a local directory on your machine (c:\source_control) or it could be a server anywhere in the world accessible over the internet. If your house burns down, your source code is still safe.

```
class Creature                          Version 1
{
    string _name;

    public string GetName()
    {
        return _name;
    }
}


class Creature                          Version 2
{
    string _name;
    int _health = 50;
    int _power = 10;

    public string GetName()
    {
        return _name;
    }

    public void Attack(Creature otherCreature)
    {
        // todo: Write code
    }
}


class Creature                          Version 3
{
    string _name;
    int _health = 50;
    int _power = 10;

    public string GetName()
    {
        return _name;
    }

    public void TakeDamage(int amount)
    {
        _health -= amount;
    }

    public void Attack(Creature otherCreature)
    {
        otherCreature.TakeDamage(_power);
    }
}
```

Figure 3.1
Changes to a piece of source code.

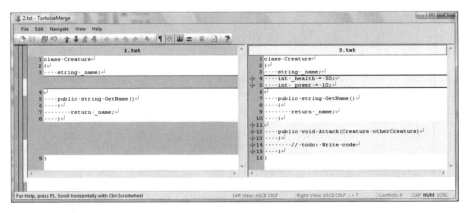

Figure 3.2
Comparing changes to a piece of source code.

Source control systems also let you create *branches*. This is a way to split programs into two separate versions. For instance, your chess game is going pretty well but you're pretty sure it would be better if it had a first-person shooter mode. Adding such a mode will require a lot of code changes, and it might fail. With source control there's no need to worry. You can create a branch. All the new code changes can be made in a new branch repository. Changes here won't affect the main repository, called the trunk. If you fail at making ChessFPS then you can switch back to the main trunk and forget all about your failed branch. If you succeed then you can merge the branch and the trunk together again.

Source control is extremely useful for the lone developer, but one of its primary uses is allowing a team of programmers to work on the same codebase at the same time. Source control lets any programmer edit the code, and any other programmer can update and see those changes. To make a game with a group of friends, source control should certainly be used!

Using Source Control

Hopefully, by now I've convinced you that source control is great and you need to use it. The code in this book uses a source control system called Subversion, but it's a good idea to know a little about the many different source control systems.

- **CVS**—This is used primarily on older projects. It's best to avoid, as Subversion has all its functionality and more.

- **Visual Source Safe**—Try not to use this. It is made by Microsoft, but not even Microsoft uses it internally. It has some stability issues.

- **Subversion**—Great free open source control with good Windows integration. My choice.

- **Perforce**—Used by many game companies, very good merge tools, good at handling large amounts of binary data (like images and models). Not free, or cheap.

- **Git**—Git is quite new and is used as source control for the Linux kernel. It's not dependent on a central server, and it's fast and scalable. Mostly command line based at the moment, though there are some GUI tools.

- **Mercurial**—A bit of a newcomer and mainly command line based, but once again there are a few GUI tools. Its goals are stated as high performance and scalability, decentralized, fully distributed collaborative development. Git and Mercurial have similar aims.

If you really want to be at the cutting edge of revision control, then look into Git or Mercurial. If you want simple and easy to use, my recommendation is Subversion.

Unit Testing

When a programmer writes some new functionality, he'll usually write a snippet of code to test it. Unit testing is just a clever way of gathering these little snippets of code together. Then they can be run each time the code is compiled. If suddenly a previously working test fails, it is obvious that something is broken. As the word "snippets" suggests, unit tests should be very small pieces of code that test one thing and one thing only.

In the unit-testing world, it's very common to write the tests first and then code. This might be best illustrated with an example. Let's say we are creating a game and a class is needed to represent the player. Players should have a health status, and when you create a player, he should have greater than zero health. Let's write that in code form

```
class PlayerTests
{
  bool TestPlayerIsAliveWhenBorn()
  {
    Player p = new Player();
    if (p.Health > 0)
    {
        return true; // pass the test
    }
    return false; // fail the text
  }
}
```

This code won't compile yet as we haven't even created a player class. But I think the test is pretty self-explanatory. If you create a player, he should have greater than zero health; otherwise, this test fails. Now that the test is written, let's create the player.

```
class Player
{
    public int Health { get; set; }
}
```

Now all the tests can be run using the unit-testing software. The test will fail because by default, integers are initialized to zero. To pass the test, the code must be altered.

```
class Player
{
    public int Health { get; set; }
    Player()
  {
    Health = 10;
  }
}
```

Running the unit-testing software again, the test will pass. We now know this code is working under the tested condition. Let's add two more tests.

```
class PlayerTests
{
  bool TestPlayerIsHurtWhenHit()
  {
      Player p = new Player();
      int oldHealth = p.Health;
      p.OnHit();
      if (p.Health < oldHealth)
      {
        return true;
      }
      return false;
  }
  bool TestPlayerIsDeadWhenHasNoHealth()
  {
      Player p = new Player();
      p.Health = 0;
      if ( p.IsDead() )
      {
          return true;
      }
```

```
        return false;
    }
}
```

Two more tests have been added—each requiring a new player function.

```
class Player
{
  public int Health { get; set; }
  public bool IsDead()
  {
      return false;
  }
  public void OnHit()
  {
  }
  public Player()
  {
    Health = 10;
  }
}
```

The general method of unit testing is to write the test, update the code, run the test, and if it fails, modify the code until it passes the test. If the new tests are run on the updated code, they will both fail. Let's fix that.

```
class Player
{
  public int Health { get; set; }
  public bool IsDead()
  {
      return Health == 0;
  }
  public void OnHit()
  {
      Health--;
  }
  public Player()
  {
      Health = 10;
  }
}
```

Don't worry if you've noticed a bug; it's there on purpose, I promise! Run the tests and they should all pass. The code is verified, but the tests don't exhaustively cover all the code. For instance, there is a `TestPlayerIsDead-WhenHasNoHealth` but not a "test the player is **not** dead when health is greater than 0". I'll leave this one as a reader exercise.

Let's say we keep on developing in this way and get to the stage where we have a full working game. Then during testing something strange occurs; sometimes, when the player *should* die, he doesn't, and after that he's invincible. This isn't how the game is supposed to work. All the tests are passing, so that means the bug isn't being tested for. Doing some clever debugging, it's discovered that the bug occurs when the player has low life, perhaps two or less units of health, and is then hit a lot of times by a number of enemies.

In unit testing, the first task is to write a test that reproduces the bug. Once this test is written, the code can be fixed and the test can confirm it. Here's a test that covers the bug.

```
class PlayerTests
{
  bool TestPlayerShouldBeDead()
  {
    Player p = new Player();
    p.Health = 2; // give him low health
    // Now hit him a lot, to reproduce the bug description
    p.OnHit();
    p.OnHit();
    p.OnHit();
    p.OnHit();
    p.OnHit();
    if ( p.IsDead() )
    {
        return true;
    }
    return false;
  }
}
```

This test is run, and it fails. Now we've got a unit test that reproduces the bug. The code must now be changed to pass this test. The death function seems a good place to fix the bug.

```
class Player
{
  bool IsDead()
  {
     return Health <= 0;
  }
  ...
}
```

If the player has zero health or less, then he is dead. This causes all the unit tests to pass, and we're now sure that this bug won't crop back up without us knowing about it.

Test Driven Development

The method of writing tests, then skeleton code, and then making that code pass the test is called *Test Driven Development*. Developing code this way reduces bugs and you can have faith in what your code actually does. This is very important if you're developing a big project. It also encourages classes to be quite modular and self-contained. This is because unit tests need to be small; therefore, you want to avoid having to make 50 classes and setting them all up just to run one simple test. For this reason, lots of needless coupling between classes is avoided.

The other big win on unit testing is refactoring. For instance, if the inventory system in your game needs to be massively redesigned, then with unit testing you have all the tests required to confirm you've replaced the system correctly.

With unit testing, you can confidently say your code is bulletproof. Unfortunately, not everything can be tested; graphics are very hard to test and you just have to assume the libraries such as OpenGL will work correctly.

Unit Testing in C#

The best unit-testing software for C# is called NUnit (Figure 3.3). It's free and easy to use.

In the following chapters, we'll download NUnit and walk through the setup. All the code in the book is unit tested, but for the sake of brevity, most unit-test code is left out of the code examples.

Summary

Writing high quality software can be difficult; it's hard to write bug-free software and it's hard to finish projects on time or even finish them at all. Modern

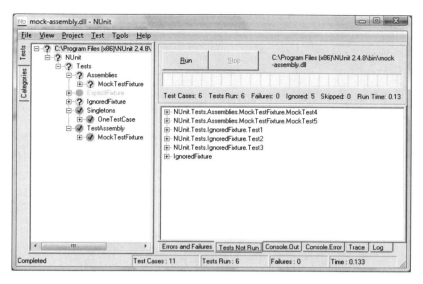

Figure 3.3
Running tests in NUnit.

programming methodologies and practices try to improve the software development process.

Pragmatic programming is the ability to finish a program satisfactorily within a desired timeframe. It is a development method that emphasizes creating a minimal version of the program as quickly as possible and then iteratively developing this program until it starts to resemble the original vision. Pragmatic programming has two main guidelines known as DRY and KISS. DRY stands for "Don't Repeat Yourself," and KISS stands for "Keep It Simple Stupid"; together these mean you should avoid duplicating code or functionality and you should avoid the temptation to over-complicate your programs.

Source control is used to keep your code safe and allow multiple developers to work on the same project at the same time. Unit testing is the practice of writing small tests that confirm your code is working as expected. These small tests help document how the code base should be used and are also used to catch any bugs that might be introduced when making large changes to the code. These tools and guidelines help to make software creation easier and help to make the final product more elegant and robust.

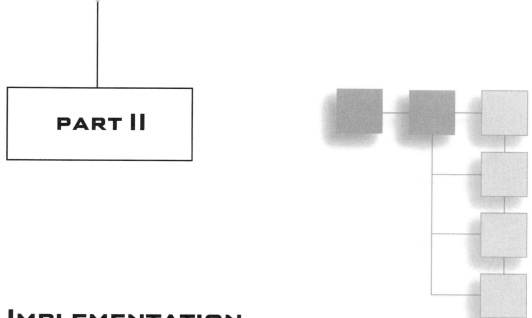

PART II

IMPLEMENTATION

CHAPTER 4

Setup

This chapter covers getting started with all the necessary tools and libraries to start making games. All the tools are free, and you'll quickly get set up with a fully functional C# IDE, source control to keep your files safe with a record of all your program changes, and a way to unit test your code. All the tools covered here have installers in the App directory of the CD.

Introducing Visual Studio Express—A Free IDE for C#

Visual Studio Express is a free IDE for C# from Microsoft. Visual Studio makes writing C# very easy; with a single button press it compiles and runs the code. There are other ways of making C# programs; for example, all programming could be written in Notepad and run through the complier via the command line. There are also a number of alternative IDEs that can edit C#, but the very best free tool for editing C# is Visual Studio Express!

Visual Studio Express can be downloaded from the Microsoft site (http://www. microsoft.com/express/vcsharp/). It's also available on the CD.

Follow the installation wizard, as shown in Figure 4.1. The wizard will ask if it should install the Silverlight runtime (Silverlight will not be used in this book, so you do not need to install it). Once the wizard finishes and after rebooting, Visual Studio Express will be installed. Now we can start some C# programming!

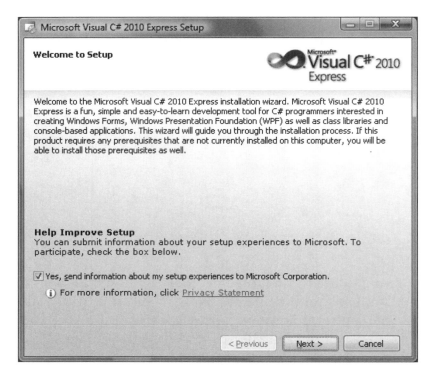

Figure 4.1
The installation wizard for Visual Studio Express.

A Quick Hello World

Creating a quick "Hello World" program will demonstrate the features of Visual Studio Express. It should now be installed in the start menu so you can launch it from there.

In Visual Studio Express, there are solutions and projects. Solutions may contain any number of projects. Each project is a collection of code files and one project can use the code from another. New projects can be started by opening the File menu and selecting New Project. A dialog box will pop up like the one pictured in Figure 4.2.

There are a number of project choices here. Windows Forms Application is a project that will make use of the forms library. A form is a .NET term for nearly all Windows GUI programs. Windows Console Application is for text-based projects. Class Library is code that's written to be used by other projects, but it cannot be executed alone.

Figure 4.2
Starting a new project.

Hello World programs are traditionally text based so Windows Console Application is most suitable. There's also a prompt to give the project a name; by default, this will be ConsoleApplication1. A more descriptive name, such as HelloWorld makes the purpose of the project clearer. Clicking the OK button will create the project.

Figure 4.3 shows the new project. The majority of the application is taken up by Program.cs; this is the only code file in the project. On the left is a subwindow with the title Solution Explorer. In the solution explorer is a tree of all the projects in the solution. The top level of the tree shows the HelloWorld solution we've just made. The only child of this tree is a project also called HelloWorld. Solutions and projects may have the same name.

At the very top of the Visual Studio Express window is a toolbar. In the toolbar is a small green arrow. Pressing this compiles the project and executes the code. Press it now!

A console window should pop up and then briefly disappear. This happens because the program has no code at the moment. The C# program starts its

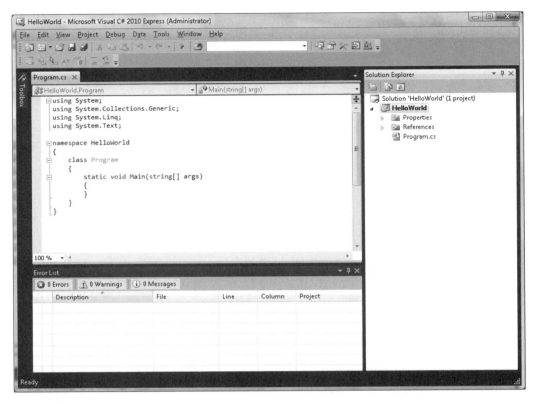

Figure 4.3
The start of a brand new project.

execution by calling the static `Main` method in the `Program` class. This is the place to have the program output Hello World.

```
namespace HelloWorld
{
  class Program
  {
    static void Main(string[] args)
    {
      System.Console.WriteLine("Hello World");
      System.Console.ReadKey();
    }
  }
}
```

The first line is a function call that prints `Hello World` to the system console. The second line waits for a keypress on the system console. If the second line wasn't there, the program would run, display `Hello World`, see there's nothing else to do, and shut down the program.

Press the green arrow and bask in the Hello World example glory (see Figure 4.4).

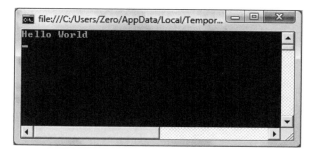

Figure 4.4
The Hello World program.

The results demonstrate that everything is working as expected. It is important to save this code so it can be preserved for the ages. Go to the File menu and choose Save All. This will pop up a dialog asking you where to save the file. By default, this will be in the My Documents folder under Visual Studio 2010; this is fine.

Visual Studio Express Tips

If you typed the Hello World program, you may have noticed that Visual Studio helps you out with autocomplete and drop-down boxes showing the name-spaces, classes, and appropriate variables. This is some of the more obvious help Visual Studio will give. There are also some less obvious features that are worth highlighting.

Automatic Refactoring and Code Generation

Refactoring is a software development term; it means rearranging or rewriting parts of a current program to make it clearer, smaller, or more efficient, but not changing its functionality. Code generation allows Visual Studio to write some code for you. Visual Studio has a number of tools to help you; it splits them into two headings: Refactor for changing the code and Generate for automatically adding new code. There are a large number of automatic refactorings, but the following three are the ones I use most commonly.

Renaming

Namespace, class, member, field, and variable names should all be descriptive and useful. Here's some example code that has a poor naming style.

```
class GameThing
{
  int _health = 10;
  int _var2 = 1;

  public void HealthUpdate (int v)
  {
      _health = _health - Math.Max (0, v - _var2);
  }
}
```

GameThing is a poor name unless every single thing in your game is going to have a health value. It would be better to name it GameCreature. Imagine if you were halfway through development of a large game. The GameThing class is repeated hundreds of times across many different files. If you wanted to rename the GameThing class manually, you could either hand edit all those hundreds of files or carefully use Visual Studio's Find and Replace tool (this codebase also has many entirely unrelated classes using similar names such as GameThingMa- nager, which the Find and Replace tool could accidentally change). Visual Studio's refactor function can rename the GameThing class safely with only two clicks of the mouse.

Right-click GameThing. This will bring up a context menu, as shown in Figure 4.5. Choose the Refactor menu and click Rename.

A new dialog box will appear, and the new name can be entered, as shown in Figure 4.6.

This will now rename the class everywhere it appears in code. There are options to also rename this class in comments and strings. The same process can be done for the function and variable names, resulting in something like this.

```
class GameCreature
{
  int _health = 10;
```

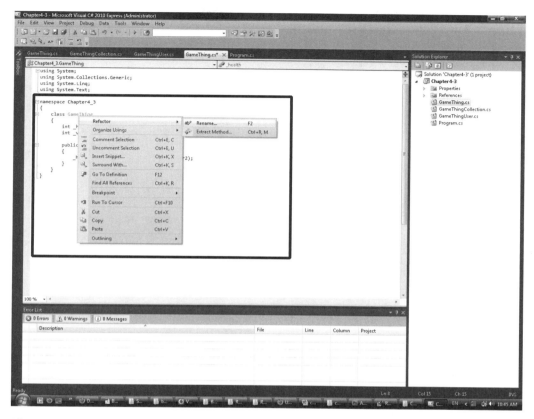

Figure 4.5
The Refactor > Rename menu.

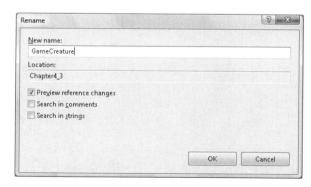

Figure 4.6
Entering a new more descriptive name.

```
int _armor = 1;

public void TakeDamage(int damage)
{
  _health = _health - Math.Max(0, damage - _armor);
}
}
```

Far more understandable!

Creating Functions

Often when writing a section of code, a function that's not been written yet is needed. The generate tools in Visual Studio let you write your code as if the function did exist, and then automatically create it. As an example, let's take an update loop for a player class.

```
class Player
{
  public void Update(float timeSinceLastFrame)
  {

  }
}
```

In the update loop, the player animation needs to be updated. It's best to do this in a separate function, and that new function would look something like this.

```
class Player
{
  public void Update(float timeSinceLastFrame)
  {
    UpdateAnimation(timeSinceLastFrame);
  }
}
```

This function doesn't exist yet. Instead of writing it all out manually, the generate functions can do it (see Figure 4.7).

Right-click the function name and choose Generate > Method Stub. The following code will be created in the `Player` class.

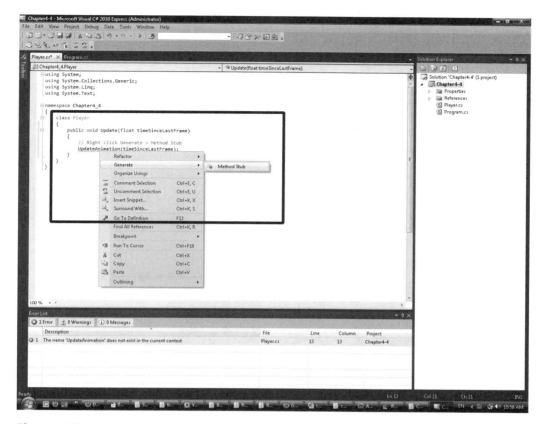

Figure 4.7
Refactor menu for creating a function.

```
private void UpdateAnimation(float timeSinceLastFrame)
{
  throw new NotImplementedException();
}
```

All of this was created automatically without any manual typing. The function has an exception saying no code has been written yet. Calling this function in a program will cause the exception to be thrown. After writing code for the function, that exception can simply be deleted.

Separating Chunks of Code

It's quite common in large programming projects for one area to get bloated. An update loop for a common object such as the player may become hundreds of lines long. If this happens, it's a good idea to break out some of that code into separate functions. Let's consider the game world's update loop.

```
class World
{
  bool _playerHasWonGame = false;
  public void Update()
  {
    Entity player = FindEntity("Player");

    UpdateGameCreatures();
    UpdatePlayer(player);
    UpdateEnvironment();
    UpdateEffects();

    Entity goldenEagle = FindEntity("GoldenEagle");

    if (player.Inventory.Contains(goldenEagle))
    {
      _playerHasWonGame = true;
      ChangeGameState("PlayerWinState");
    }
  }

  // additional code
}
```

This loop isn't that bad, but the last piece of code looks a little untidy; it could be moved into a separate function. To do this automatically, select the code as if about to copy and paste it. Start the selection from the line `Entity golden-Eagle...` to the closing brace of the if-statement. Now right-click.

The context menu will come up as in Figure 4.8; select Refactor, and then choose Extract Method. You will be prompted to name the method. I chose `Check-ForGameOver`. The selected code will then be removed and placed in a new function; any variables that it uses will be passed in as arguments to the newly created function. After the refactor, the code will look like the following:

```
bool _playerHasWonGame = false;
public void Update()
{
  Entity player = FindEntity("Player");
```

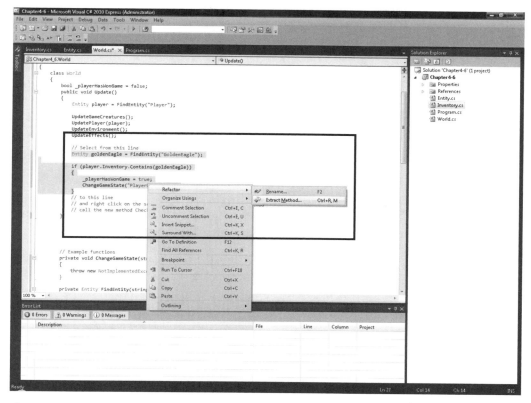

Figure 4.8
Refactor menu for extracting a function.

```
  UpdateGameCreatures();
  UpdatePlayer(player);
  UpdateEnvironment();
  UpdateEffects();

  CheckForGameOver(player);
}

private void CheckForGameOver(Entity player)
{
  Entity goldenEagle = FindEntity("GoldenEagle");

  if (player.Inventory.Contains(goldenEagle))
```

```
{
  _playerHasWonGame = true;
  ChangeGameState("PlayerWinState");
}
}
```

The world update function is now shorter and more readable.

It's worth investigating and becoming familiar with the refactor functions as they can be excellent time savers.

Shortcuts

Visual Studio and Visual Studio Express have many useful shortcut keys; Table 4.1 shows some of the most useful. A few of the shortcuts are general to most text editors.

Subversion, an Easy Source Control Solution

Subversion is the source control system we'll use to keep our source code safe. Subversion is often abbreviated to SVN. The easiest way to install SVN on Windows is to use TortoiseSVN. TortoiseSVN integrates itself into the Windows context menu, making it very simple to manage source control operations.

Where to Get It

The official website for TortoiseSVN is http://tortoisesvn.net/, and the latest build should be available to download from http://tortoisesvn.net/downloads/. It's also available on the CD. There are two versions x86 and x64; these are for 32-bit machines and 64-bit machines, respectively.

Installation

Installation is simple, just double-click the icon and accept all the default options. This will install the program to your program files directory. After installation has finished, you will be prompted to restart.

Once your system has restarted, right-click on your desktop. You should have three extra items in your context menu, as can be seen in Figure 4.9. These menu items will be used to manage your source code.

Creating the Repository

A source control repository is the place where all the code and data will be stored. We'll make our repository on the hard disk. It's a good idea to choose a location

Table 4.1 Visual Studio Shortcuts

Key Combination	Function
Ctrl+A	Select all
Ctrl+Space	Force the autocomplete box to open.
Shift+Home	Select to the start of the line.
Shift+End	Select to the end of the line.
Shift+Left	Arrow Key Select next left-most character.
Shift+Right	Arrow Key Select next right-most character.
Ctrl+Closing Curly Brace	If the cursor is next to a curly brace character, this will find the associated closing or opening brace.
Ctrl+K then Ctrl+F	This will correctly indent all the selected text. Very useful if you've copied some code from an online example and all the formatting is messed up.
Tab	If you have some code selected and then press Tab, all this code will be tabbed in.
Shift+Tab	If you have some code selected and press Shift+Tab, all this code will be tabbed backwards.
Ctrl+U	Any text selected will be changed to lowercase.
Ctrl+Shift+U	Any text selected will be changed to uppercase.
Alt+LeftMouseButton and drag	This will allow you to select text vertically. Character columns instead of character rows.
F5	Build and execute the project.
F12	If the cursor is over some method or class name, it will jump the cursor to the definition.
Ctrl+Shift+B	Build the current project.
Ctrl+K, Ctrl+C	Comment out the current selection.
Ctrl+K, Ctrl+U	Uncomment the current selection.
Ctrl+F	Brings up the Find dialog.
Ctrl+Shift+F	Brings up the Find dialog, but this time it will search through all the projects instead of the current code file.

that will be easy to backup. Somewhere like My Documents is a good place. Think of the repository like a safe that's going to look after all the code written from now on.

Once you've decided where you want the repository to be, create a new directory. All the source control files will go in here. You can name the directory whatever

Figure 4.9
SVN context menu.

you want. I named mine, "MyCode". Open the folder and right-click. The context menu will appear; choose the menu item labeled Tortoise SVN. This will give some more options, as shown in Figure 4.10; choose Create Repository here.

Some new files will appear in the directory, as shown in Figure 4.11.

Congratulations! You've just made your first source code repository. Let's have a look inside! Go up to the parent directory. Now right-click on the directory containing your repository. This time choose SVN Repo-browser. This brings up a dialog, but it's empty. That's because there is nothing in the repository—not yet anyway. In time, you'll fill this up with all your great coding ideas and projects.

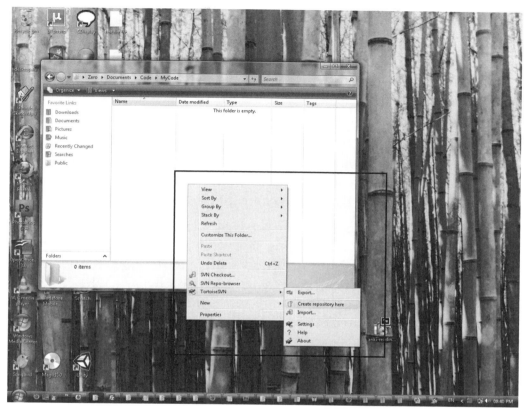

Figure 4.10
Using the context menu to create a repository.

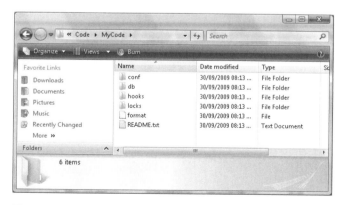

Figure 4.11
Files in the repository.

Adding to the Repository

Remember the Hello World project? That's some pretty important code and should be put under source control so that it can be kept safe. If you saved the project to the default directory, it will be in C:\Users\YourUserName\Documents\Visual Studio 2010\Projects\ on Windows 7 and Vista and C:\Documents and Settings\YourUserName\My Documents\Visual Studio 2010\Projects for XP.

Now, go to the directory with your source control repository and explore the repository as before. Right-click on the right-most window and a context menu will appear. Choose Create Folder and name it HelloWorld.

In the projects directory, right-click on the HelloWorld folder and choose SVN Checkout. This will bring up a dialog box with a text box labeled URL of Repository; this should have your repository path in it. If it doesn't, click on the folder icon, browse to your repository folder, and select it. Click OK. The dialog box will change and show a single directory called HelloWorld. Select that directory. The check out directory text box should read something like C:\Users\YourUserName\Documents\Visual Studio 2010\Projects\HelloWorld for Windows 7 and Vista and C:\Documents and Settings\YourUserName\My Documents\Visual Studio 2010\Projects\HelloWorld for XP.

At the moment, the repository is empty; all it has in it is the empty Hello World directory that was just created. The next step is checking out this empty directory into the same place as the Hello World project. In the checkout window, click OK. This will check out the repository in the same place that the code currently is. Figure 4.12 shows inside the Hello World directory, and the changes that have occurred.

All the files now have small question mark icons. These indicate that the files have not been added to the source control repository but they're in the checked out directory. There's also a hidden folder called .svn. This hidden folder contains the information that SVN uses to manage itself.

The next step is to add all the important code files into the HelloWorld repository. HelloWorld.sln is important; it's the file that says how the solution is set up and what projects are included.

Right-click on HelloWorld.sln, click TortoiseSVN > Add (shown in Figure 4.13), refresh the directory, and a plus sign will appear next to HelloWorld.sln, as

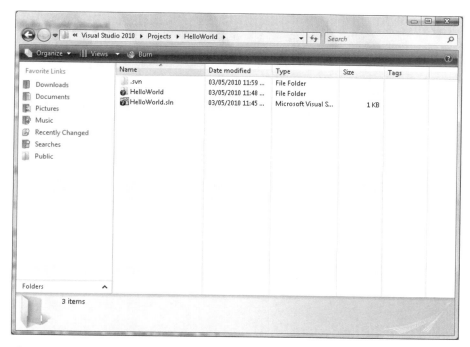

Figure 4.12
The checked out HelloWorld project.

shown in Figure 4.14. HelloWorld.sln has been added to the repository. First, let's add the rest of the files. There's a directory called HelloWorld; this is the project directory. Right-click on it and choose Add, the same way we did for HelloWorld.sln.

This will bring up a list of all the files in the directory. Unselect all the files and type the following.

```
HelloWorld/
HelloWorld/HelloWorld.csproj
HelloWorld/Program.cs
HelloWorld/Properties
HelloWorld/Properties/AssemblyInfo.cs
```

These are the files we'll be editing. The other files are automatically generated so there's no need to add them to source control. Once the files are selected, they're ready to commit. Committing copies the new files from your local check out and adds them to the source repository.

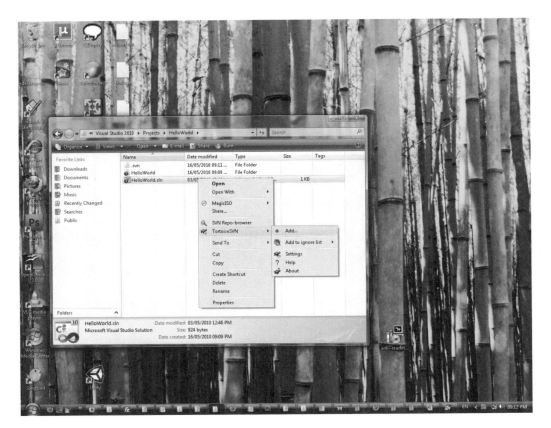

Figure 4.13
Adding to the repository.

The easiest way to do a check in is to open your projects folder, right-click on the HelloWorld folder and choose SVN Commit.

This brings up a dialog listing all the files to commit. There is also a comment box for the commit. It's good practice to always add a comment about what changes have been made. In this case, we're adding a new project, so it's fine to list the comment as "First commit of hello world project." Press commit and the code is committed.

The code is now safe in the repository. Let's test it! Delete the HelloWorld folder, or if you're a little less trusting, rename it to HelloWorld. Now right-click and select SVN Checkout. The HelloWorld project should be selected; click OK. You'll notice a new directory has appeared titled HelloWorld. Enter the directory and double-click the brand new HelloWorld.sln icon. This will launch Visual

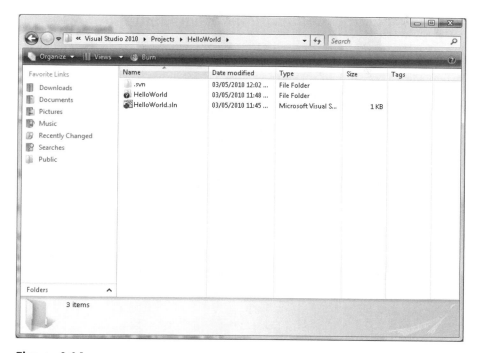

Figure 4.14
Plus sign to indicate files are to be added to source control.

Studio; pressing the green arrow will cause the Hello World program to compile and run perfectly.

When working with a team, everyone can check out the project and all start working on it.

History

One of the nice things about source control is that it allows you to look back on the project and see how it's evolved. Right-clicking on the Hello World project directory and selecting SVN Show Log will pop up the history dialog. This shows all commits with your high-quality descriptive comments (see Figure 4.16).

So far, the history view shows only two commits. The first is the creation of the project, and then the second when the files were added. Play around with the history options. The statistics button gives graphs and information about the commits. It also reports who committed what. This is very useful when working in a team.

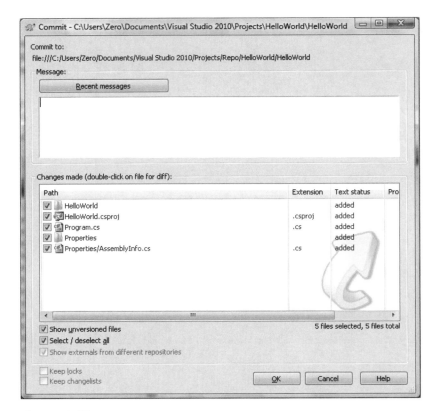

Figure 4.15
Committing source code.

Extending Hello World

Open up Visual Studio and edit the Hello World program to look like the following.

```
public static void Main(string[] args)
{
  System.Console.WriteLine("Let's make some games.'');
  System.Console.ReadKey();
}
```

The program is developing nicely. We don't want to lose these changes so we had better do one more commit. Return to the Hello World project directory and select SVN Commit again. Program.cs will come up as modified. Add a useful comment such as "Changed hello world text" and click OK. Now the code and source control are both up to date.

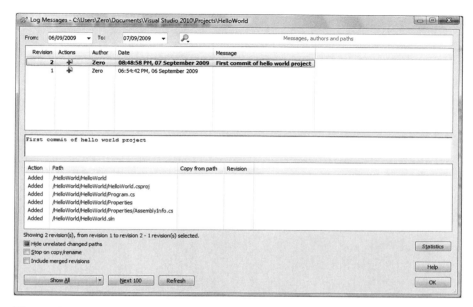

Figure 4.16
Viewing the history.

With that commit, another feature of SVN can be introduced. Open the history window again by going to SVN Show Log. Click on the most recent commit, revision number three. In the third dialog window, you'll see the modified /HelloWorld/HelloWorld/Program.cs file. Right-click on this and choose Show Changes, as shown in Figure 4.17.

This will bring up a new program called TortoiseMerge. TortoiseMerge will display two files at once: the current commit and the previous commit, as is shown in Figure 4.18. In the previous commit, Hello World is crossed out and highlighted in red; this means it's the area of code that's changed and the text has been removed. In the current commit, we can see that it has changed to "Let's make some games."

This merge tool is very useful for seeing how code has changed.

Tao

Tao allows C# to access OpenGL's functionality. It's very simple to install and add to a game project. The installer is available from sourceforge (http://source-forge.net/projects/taoframework/), and it is also included on the CD. As new features are added to OpenGL, Tao is updated to include them.

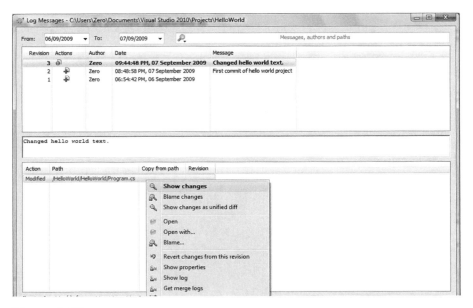

Figure 4.17
How to compare changes.

Figure 4.18
Using the merge tool to compare.

Once the installer finishes running, nothing else needs to be done. The Tao libraries are now accessible to C#.

The Tao framework is a coding project like any other and so it uses source control. In fact, it also uses SVN. If you want the latest, bleeding-edge version of the Tao framework, browse the repository, right-click any folder or the desktop, and choose SVN Repo-browser. Enter https://taoframework.svn.sourceforge.net/svnroot/taoframework/trunk at the prompt. After a short wait, the latest code of the Tao framework will appear, as shown in Figure 4.19. To check out the latest copy, follow the same steps, but select SVN Checkout instead of SVN Repo-browser.

NUnit

NUnit is one of the most popular unit testing tools available for C#. The installer is available on the CD, and the latest version is available at http://www.nunit.com/. Run the installer and choose a typical installation when prompted.

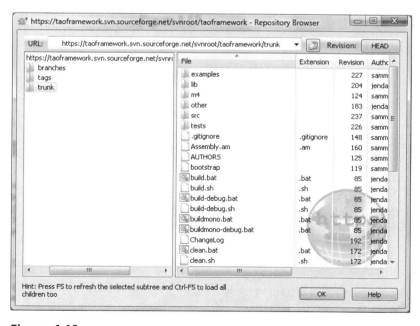

Figure 4.19
Using SVN to browse the Tao framework.

Using NUnit with a Project

NUnit is very simple to use, but before writing tests, a project is needed. In Visual Studio, start a new project by selecting File > New Project as shown in Figure 4.20. Once again, choose a Console Application project and call it PlayerTest.

This will create a default project with one file named Program.cs. Right-click on the project and select Add > Class, as shown in Figure 4.20. This will be the player class.

This brings up a dialog box with a number of preset class types from which to choose, shown in Figure 4.21. The one needed here is simply a class, so choose that and name it Player.cs. A separate class will also be needed for the tests; add another class the same way, but call it TestPlayer.cs.

Figure 4.20
Adding a class in Visual Studio.

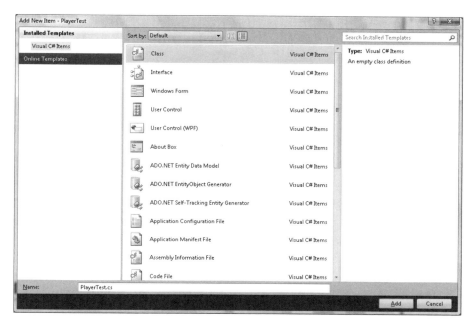

Figure 4.21
Naming a class in Visual Studio.

To use NUnit, it needs to be added to the project as a reference. In the Solution Explorer, right-click on the References node and select Add Reference, as shown in Figure 4.22.

This will bring up a very large list of references. The reference that needs to be added is NUnit.Framework. Once the reference has been added, it can be used by adding a `using` statement. In TestPlayer at the top of the file, there are a number of statements starting with "using...". To use NUnit, an extra line must be added `using NUnit.Framework;`. Then a simple test can be added.

```
using System;
using System.Collections.Generic;
using System.Linq;
using System.Text;
using NUnit.Framework;

namespace PlayerTest
{
  [TestFixture]
  public class TestPlayer
```

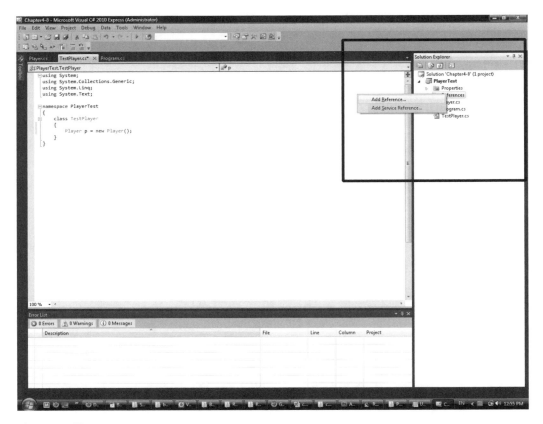

Figure 4.22
Adding a reference.

```
{
  [Test]
  public void BasicTest()
  {
    Assert.That(true);
  }
}
}
```

The first things to notice in this code snippet are the attributes. In C#, an attribute is a bit of metadata—some descriptive information about a class, function, or variable that can be accessed programmatically. Attributes are surrounded by square brackets. Here the class has an attribute of type TestFixture. In NUnit terminology, a test fixture is a group of related unit tests. The TestFixture attribute is used to tell NUnit that the class `TestPlayer` will have a number of tests in it.

The second attribute is on the function `BasicTest`. This is a test attribute, which means the function `BasicTest` is a test that needs to be run. As the `Player` code is written, more of these small test functions will be added to the `TestPlayer` class.

Make sure the code compiles by pressing the green arrow or by pressing F5. A console window will flash briefly, and then quickly disappear again. This behavior is fine for now.

Running Tests

NUnit has a special GUI program for running tests. NUnit GUI is found in the Start menu. Once run, it looks like Figure 4.23.

NUnit works on compiled code. Visual Studio compiles the code every time the green arrow or F5 is pressed. The compiled code is stored in the project directory (normally, \Projects\PlayerTest\PlayerTest\bin\(Debug/Release)\). The default

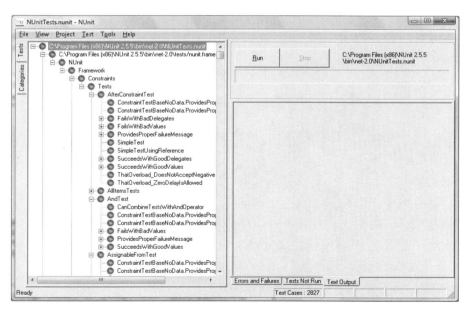

Figure 4.23
NUnit GUI on startup.

location for the projects directory is in the MyDocuments directory under Visual Studio 2010.

In here, you will find an exe file. This is the compiled version of the code. There is also an nunit.framework.dll file; this is the NUnit reference that was included earlier. The exe file won't be able to run without this dll.

To run the tests, select File > Open Project in the NUnit GUI. Navigate to the compiled code in the release directory. Click on the PlayerTest.exe file. This will load the test we wrote earlier in NUnit, as shown in Figure 4.24.

Click the Run button; the project tree should turn green and a tick will appear next to `BasicTest`. This means the test ran successfully. If the code is changed so that the test fails, the little green circles will turn red. Try changing the code to fail then running the tests again.

An Example Project

The player class in the game must represent the concept that if the player eats a mushroom, he gets bigger. It's assumed all players begin life small. That will be the first test.

```
namespace PlayerTest
{
  [TestFixture]
  public class TestPlayer
  {
    [Test]
```

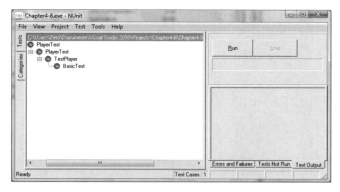

Figure 4.24
NUnit GUI loading the project.

```
    public void BasicTest()
    {
      Assert.That(true);
    }


    [Test]
    public void StartsLifeSmall()
    {
      Player player = new Player();
      Assert.False(player.IsEnlarged());
    }
  }
}
```

The `Assert` class is part of NUnit and is the workhorse of writing the unit tests. The function `IsEnlarged` does not exist yet. Using the refactor tools, Visual Studio can automatically create this function. This will result in the following code in the `Player` class.

```
class Player
{
  internal bool IsEnlarged()
  {
    throw new NotImplementedException();
  }
}
```

Running the unit test in NUnit now will result in a failure with the following error message

```
PlayerTest.TestPlayer.StartsLifeSmall:
System.NotImplementedException : The method or operation is not
implemented.
```

The test fails because one of the methods in the `Player` class hasn't been implemented yet. That can be solved by adding the functionality.

```
class Player
{
    bool _enlarged = false;
    internal bool IsEnlarged()
```

```
    {
        return _enlarged;
    }
}
```

It will now pass the test. Build the project, run NUnit again, and a green circle will appear next to the project. The next test is for eating a mushroom. Here's the test.

```
namespace PlayerTest
{
  [TestFixture]
  public class TestPlayer
  {
    [Test]
    public void BasicTest()
    {
        Assert.That(true);
    }

    [Test]
    public void StartsLifeSmall()
    {
      Player player = new Player();
      Assert.False(player.IsEnlarged());
    }

    [Test]
    public void MushroomEnlargesPlayer()
    {
      Player player = new Player();
      player.Eat("mushroom");
      Assert.True(player.IsEnlarged());
    }
  }
}
```

This new test has a pleasing symmetry with the previous test. As tests are built up, they form living documentation for the project. Someone new to the code can read all the tests associated with a certain function and get a very good idea about what it's supposed to do.

Like the previous test, additional functionality has been added. The player does not yet have an `Eat` method. Like the previous example, Visual Studio's refactor tools can quickly generate the required method.

```
class Player
{
  bool _enlarged = false;
  internal bool IsEnlarged()
  {
    return _enlarged;
  }

  internal void Eat(string p)
  {
    throw new NotImplementedException();
  }
}
```

The new test will now fail if NUnit is run. The test can be made to pass with the following code.

```
class Player
{
  bool _enlarged = false;
  internal bool IsEnlarged()
  {
    return _enlarged;
  }

  internal void Eat(string thingToEat)
  {
    if (thingToEat == "mushroom")
    {
      _enlarged = true;
    }
  }
}
```

All the tests pass, proving this code is correct and working as desired. That's basically it for unit testing. It's not a very complicated technique, but it does give the writer faith in the code and the ability to change it without breaking functionality.

Summary

Visual Studio Express is one of the best ways to develop C# programs; it's free and has many features. It's a full IDE with support for writing, compiling, and debugging C# programs. There are many helpful functions for refactoring existing code and generating new code. It also has many shortcut keys to make writing code faster. Source control is a way of recording all the changes to the code and keeping the source in one place. SVN is a great source control program with an easy to use Windows wrapper called TortoiseSVN.

Unit tests are small pieces of code that verify a small piece of your program is working correctly. NUnit is a unit testing program for C# that provides interface to write tests for your code. Once the tests are written, NUnit has a program that will visually display and run all the tests, putting a green tick next to passing tests and a red cross next to failing tests. These three programs are an excellent starting point for C# development.

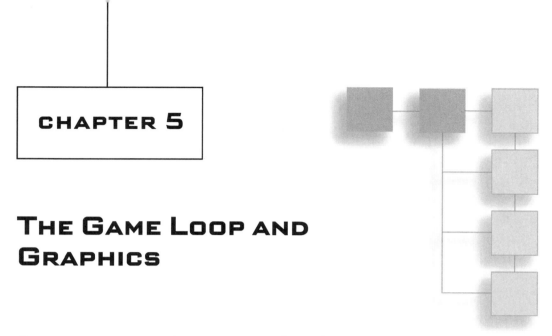

CHAPTER 5

THE GAME LOOP AND GRAPHICS

Computer games come in many genres, from abstract puzzle games like *Tetris* to turn-based strategy games like *Civilization* to fast-paced first-person shooters like *Half-Life*. All these games, and all computer games, are programmed in a similar way.

How Do Games Work?

The most important way a game communicates with the player is via the TV screen or computer monitor. It's quite common to hear about *frame-rate* in games. A good frame-rate is from 30 frames per second to 60 frames per second. But what does frame-rate actually mean when programming a game?

A single frame is the time between screen updates. The computer program is responsible for updating the screen with new information at least 30 times a second. Computers are very fast; it's no problem for a computer to update the screen this quickly.

How much time does the computer have to update each frame? If the minimum requirement is 30 frames per second, that is 33 milliseconds per frame. The computer has 33 milliseconds to "think" about what should happen in the next frame. A computer can do a vast amount of calculation in 33 milliseconds; more than most humans could do in a week.

All game code has a central loop called the game loop. While the game is running, the central loop is called repeatedly and as often as possible. The game loop has three main stages: it first gets the state of any input (such as gamepad or the keyboard), updates the state of the game world, and finally updates all the pixels on the screen.

A Closer Look at the Game Loop

Game code is not just responsible for updating the graphics on the screen; it has two other very important tasks to do. It must take input from the user such as "If the user is pressing button B, then make the character jump," and it must update the game world, "If the player has just killed the end boss, then go to the credits."

All game loops follow a similar pattern.

```
while (true)
{
  // Find out what state keyboard and joypads are in
  UpdateInput();
  // Handle input, update the game world, move characters etc
  Process();
  // Draw the current state of the game to the screen
  Render();
}
```

These are the three main stages of the loop: update the player input, update the game world, and then tell the graphics card what to render.

Implementing a Fast Game Loop in C#

Open Visual Studio. Visual Studio assumes by default you will be making a software application that's event-driven rather than one that's executing code continuously, such as a game. Event-driven programs execute code in response to events coming from the operating system or from user input. It's easier to write games with a main loop that can be used to continually update the state of the game world. The default code needs to change a little to get a fast game loop implemented. It's important that the loop runs as often as possible, so this C# code uses some C functions to ensure it's the fastest possible game loop.

Create a new Windows Form Application and call the project GameLoop. A Program.cs file will automatically be generated with the following code:

```
namespace GameLoop
{
  static class Program
```

```
    {
      /// <summary>
      /// The main entry point for the application.
      /// </summary>
      [STAThread]
      static void Main ()
      {
        Application.EnableVisualStyles();
        Application.SetCompatibleTextRenderingDefault(false);
        Application.Run(new Form1());
      }
    }
}
```

If this code is run, it will just show a standard Windows form. At the moment, this is an event-driven application. If it was executing continuously then it might look like this.

```
namespace GameLoop
{
  static class Program
  {
    /// <summary>
    /// The main entry point for the application.
    /// </summary>
    [STAThread]
    static void Main ()
    {
      Application.EnableVisualStyles();
      Application.SetCompatibleTextRenderingDefault(false);
      Application.Run(new Form1());
    }
    static void GameLoop ()
    {
      // GameCode goes here
      // GetInput
      // Process
      // Render
    }
  }
}
```

The GameLoop function should be called each frame. To do this, a new class needs to be created. Right-click the GameLoop project in the solution explorer tab and choose Add > Class. This will prompt you for a class name; name the class FastLoop. The FastLoop class is going to be used by the Program class. It will force the function GameLoop to be called each frame. Before GameLoop is written, let's consider how it might be used.

```
static class Program
{
  static FastLoop _fastLoop = new FastLoop (GameLoop);
  /// <summary>
  /// The main entry point for the application.
  /// </summary>
  [STAThread]
  static void Main()
  {
    Application.EnableVisualStyles();
    Application.SetCompatibleTextRenderingDefault(false);
    Application.Run(new Form1());
  }
  static void GameLoop()
  {
    // GameCode goes here
    // Get Input
    // Process
    // Render
  }
}
```

The FastLoop class will take only one argument. That argument will be the function GameLoop. That's all that will be needed to convert a project so that it continually executes.

Open FastLoop.cs. In the Program class, the FastLoop constructor call takes in a reference to the function GameLoop. Therefore the FastLoop class must define its constructor to have a function passed into it as a parameter.

```
public class FastLoop
{
  public delegate void LoopCallback();
  public FastLoop(LoopCallback callback)
```

```
    {
    }
}
```

In C#, functions can be stored as variables by using a delegate that defines the function signature—what the function returns and what parameters it takes in. In this case, a delegate is used to define a function type with no return value or parameters; it's named `LoopCallback`. `FastLoop` has one constructor that takes in the callback. The callback will be called every frame to allow the game to update itself.

All C# form programs have a static class called `Application`. This class represents the program and its settings. It can also be used to modify a program so that it can be used in real-time.

A program can have a large number of events to handle; the user might be maximizing the form or Windows may be shutting down. The `Application` is the part of the code that handles all these events. When it has no events to handle, it calls a callback `Application.Idle`. This means it's about to enter idle time. This idle time, when the application is not busy, is when the game logic needs to be updated. To use the `Application` code, `using System.Windows. Forms` needs to be added near the top of the file.

```
using System.Windows.Forms;
namespace GameLoop
{
  public class FastLoop
  {
    public delegate void LoopCallback();
    LoopCallback _callback;

    public FastLoop(LoopCallback callback)
    {
      _callback = callback;
      Application.Idle += new EventHandler(OnApplicationEnterIdle);
    }
    void OnApplicationEnterIdle(object sender, EventArgs e)
    {
    }
  }
}
```

Here the game loop callback has been stored in a member variable, `_callback`, for later use. The `Application.Idle` event has been given a handler, `OnApplicationEnterIdle`. This will be called when the application begins to idle. The next part is a bit trickier. The code needs to know if the application is still in the idle state, and if it is then it needs to continually call the loop callback. Read this code to see how the callback will be called.

```
void OnApplicationEnterIdle(object sender, EventArgs e)
{
  while (IsAppStillIdle())
  {
    _callback();
  }
}
private bool IsAppStillIdle()
{
  Message msg;
  return !PeekMessage(out msg, IntPtr.Zero, 0, 0, 0);
}
```

The code calls the callback continuously unless `IsAppStillIdle` returns false. `IsAppStillIdle` uses a new `PeekMessage` function to check if the application has any important events that need to be dealt with. If there are important messages for the application then these need to be handled before returning to the game loop.

To check if the application is idle, we need to have a look at the Windows message queue. Windows has a big queue of events. If a window is moved, an event is added to the event queue; if it's minimized, an event is added to the queue; if a user presses a key on the keyboard, an event is added—many different actions generate events. All forms need to handle their own events. If our application has some events in its queue, then it needs to stop idling and deal with them.

The easiest way to check the event queue is by using some Windows C functions. In C#, this is called InterOp, short for InterOperation. Using some C functions in a C# program is actually very easy to do. To see what's in the event queue, we're going to use a C function called `PeekMessage`. We just want to have a peek at the queue and see if anything's there. This is the C definition.

```
BOOL PeekMessage(
  LPMSG lpMsg,
```

```
  HWND hWnd,
  UINT wMsgFilterMin,
  UINT wMsgFilterMax,
  UINT wRemoveMsg
);
```

According to the documentation

- If a message is available, the return value is nonzero.

- If no messages are available, the return value is zero.

This is the perfect function to decide if there are events waiting for our particular application.

It's not very important to understand all the details of this C function. The important thing is how the function is called from C#. To call it from C#, the function arguments need changing from C types to the equivalent C# types.

The first argument, lpMsg is a message type. This type isn't available in C#; it needs to be imported. The second type is a Windows handle; this is just a reference to our form. The last three arguments are all unsigned integers, which are a standard C# type. Here's the C message structure, which is the first argument.

```
typedef struct {
  HWND hwnd;
  UINT message;
  WPARAM wParam;
  LPARAM lParam;
  DWORD time;
  POINT pt;
} MSG, *PMSG;
```

The structure members aren't that important; here's how to import this C type into C#. First, include the using statement using System.Runtime.InteropServices; at the top of the FastLoop.cs with the other using statements. This library has useful functions for importing C types and structures.

```
using System.Runtime.InteropServices;
using System.Windows.Forms;
namespace GameLoop
{
  [StructLayout(LayoutKind.Sequential)]
```

```
public struct Message
{
  public IntPtr hWnd;
  public Int32 msg;
  public IntPtr wParam;
  public IntPtr lParam;
  public uint time;
  public System.Drawing.Point p;
}
```

Adding this C struct is just a case of correctly matching the C types to the C# types. The attribute [StructLayout(LayoutKind.Sequential)] tells C# to lay out the structure in memory exactly the way it's written. Without this attribute, C# might try to be clever and make the structure more memory-efficient by rearranging it. C expects the structure to be laid out in memory the exact way it's written.

Now the message type is imported; all that remains is to import the PeekMessage function.

```
public class FastLoop
{
  [System.Security.SuppressUnmanagedCodeSecurity]
  [DllImport("User32.dll", CharSet = CharSet.Auto)]
  public static extern bool PeekMessage(
    out Message msg,
    IntPtr hWnd,
    uint messageFilterMin,
    uint messageFilterMax,
    uint flags);
```

The first attribute, [System.Security.SuppressUnmanagedCode Security], just says, "We are calling C, an unmanaged language, so don't do any managed security checks." The second attribute, [DllImport("User32. dll", CharSet = CharSet.Auto)], references the DLL file that the C function is to be imported from. User32.dll is one of the major files for interacting with the Windows operating system using C. The PeekMessage function fills out the Message structure, so it needs to be able to write to it. That's why the out keyword is used on the first argument. The remaining arguments can all be ignored and no useful information will be passed into them.

With `PeekMessage` defined, it can now be used to determine if there are any messages waiting in the application's event queue.

```
private bool IsAppStillIdle()
{
  Message msg;
  return !PeekMessage(out msg, IntPtr.Zero, 0, 0, 0);
}
```

That's it. With `IsAppStillIdle` defined correctly, the program now has an extremely fast game loop. This `FastLoop` class can be reused for any game project you make in the future.

Now to test that the game loop really works, go to Project.cs and add the following line of code.

```
static void GameLoop()
{
  // GameCode goes here
  // GetInput
  // Process
  // Render
  System.Console.WriteLine("loop");
}
```

Every time the game loop is called, it will output the word "loop" to the console. To see the console, go to Debug > Windows > Output; this will bring up another window. Run the application and in the output window, the word "loop" will keep scrolling down the screen.

Adding High-Precision Timing

To animate things smoothly, it's important to know how much time has elapsed between frames. This time can then be used to keep animation independent of the frame-rate. Games should run the same speed on all computers; a game character shouldn't suddenly be able to run faster if the computer is faster!

Timing in computer games is very important. The time between frames must be accurate and of a high resolution or the game will appear to be jerky. To get the best timing functions, some C code needs to be used. This is less daunting as we've already used InterOp to peek at Windows messages. The time between frames is often called `elapsedTime` or the delta time, sometimes `dt` for short, and it's measured in fractions of a second.

Create a new class called `PreciseTimer`. It's not a big class, so here's the code all in one go. Have a look through it and try to work out what it's doing.

```
using System.Runtime.InteropServices;
namespace GameLoop
{
  public class PreciseTimer
  {
    [System.Security.SuppressUnmanagedCodeSecurity]
    [DllImport("kernel32")]
    private static extern bool QueryPerformanceFrequency(ref long
PerformanceFrequency);
    [System.Security.SuppressUnmanagedCodeSecurity]
    [DllImport("kernel32")]
    private static extern bool QueryPerformanceCounter(ref long
PerformanceCount);
    long _ticksPerSecond = 0;
    long _previousElapsedTime = 0;
    public PreciseTimer()
    {
      QueryPerformanceFrequency(ref _ticksPerSecond);
  GetElapsedTime(); // Get rid of first rubbish result
    }
    public double GetElapsedTime()
    {
      long time = 0;
      QueryPerformanceCounter(ref time);
      double elapsedTime = (double)(time - _previousElapsedTime) /
(double)_ticksPerSecond;
      _previousElapsedTime = time;
      return elapsedTime;
    }
  }
}
```

The `QueryPerformanceFrequency` function retrieves the frequency of the high-resolution performance counter. Most modern hardware has a high-resolution timer; this function is used to get the frequency at which the timer increments. The `QueryPerformanceCounter` function retrieves the current value of the high-resolution performance counter. These can be used together to time how long the last frame took.

`GetElapsedTime` should be called once per frame and this will keep track of the time. The elapsed time is so important that it should be incorporated into the game loop. Open the Program.cs file and change the game loop so it takes one argument.

```
static void GameLoop(double elapsedTime)
{
  // GameCode goes here
  // GetInput
  // Process
  // Render
  System.Console.WriteLine("loop");
}
```

FastLoop.cs needs to be changed as well; the delegate must take an elapsed time value and the `PreciseTimer` needs to be added as a member.

```
public class FastLoop
{
  PreciseTimer _timer = new PreciseTimer();
  public delegate void LoopCallback(double elapsedTime);
```

The timer is then called once per frame and elapsed time is passed on to `FastLoop`'s callback.

```
void OnApplicationEnterIdle(object sender, EventArgs e)
{
  while (IsAppStillIdle())
  {
    _callback(_timer.GetElapsedTime());
  }
}
```

The game loop can now be used to smoothly animate any game! By the end of this chapter, the game loop will be used to smoothly rotate a 3D triangle—the "Hello World" application of OpenGL programming.

Graphics

Now that the game loop is working, the next step is to get something to display on screen. You can either continue the current project with FastLoop.cs and Game-Loop.cs or you can make a new project and modify it so it has a fast game loop.

To display graphics, the Tao libraries must be included in the project. If you've not installed the Tao framework yet, now is a good time to do it.

In Visual Studio, find the solution explorer window. The solution explorer will contain only one project. Expand the project and you will see an icon labeled References. Right-click this icon and choose Add Reference.

This will bring up the reference dialog box. Click the Browse tab and navigate to the Tao framework install directory. On Windows 7 and Vista this path will be C:\Program Files (x86)\TaoFramework\bin. For XP it will be C:\Program Files \TaoFramework\bin. Once you navigate to the correct directory, you will see something similar to Figure 5.1. Choose Tao.OpenGL.dll and Tao.Platform. Windows.dll, then click OK. The Tao framework comes with a control, called `SimpleOpenGLControl`, that allows OpenGL to render in a Windows form. To enable the control, double-click the form in the solution explorer. This will bring up the form designer, as shown in Figure 5.2.

Right-click the toolbar pane and select Choose Items; this will bring up the dialog box shown in Figure 5.3.

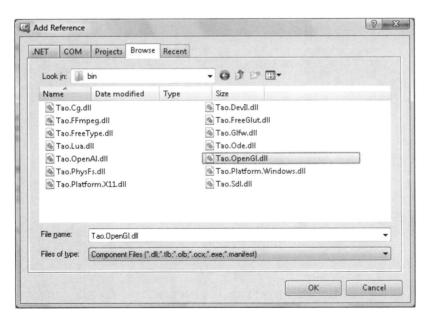

Figure 5.1
A list of references.

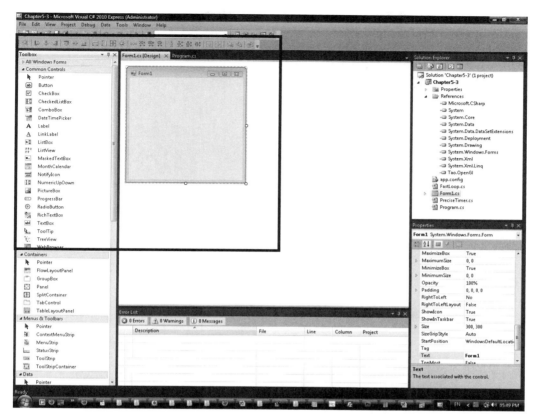

Figure 5.2
The form designer.

One of the options in the dialog should be `SimpleOpenGLControl`. This was installed by the Tao installer. If the `SimpleOpenGLControl` isn't there, then click the Browse button, navigate to the Tao framework binary directory (the same directory used for adding the references), and select the Tao.Platform.Windows.dll file. Check the box shown in Figure 5.3 and click OK. A new control, `SimpleOpenGLControl`, has now been added to the Toolbox. Drag this new control from the Toolbox on to the form in the form designer. Your form will look like Figure 5.4.

The little black window on the form is where all OpenGL rendering will take place. It's a little small at the moment. To make it the same size as the form, right-click the control and click Properties. This will bring up the Properties window. Find the property called `Dock` and set it to `Fill`. This will make the `OpenGLControl` fill all the space on the control.

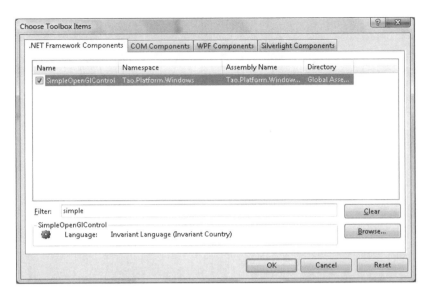

Figure 5.3
Choose Toolbox Items dialog.

If you press the green play button now an error will appear that says "No device or rendering context available." This is because the OpenGL control hasn't been initialized yet.

Open the form in code view and add the following line.

```
public Form1()
{
  InitializeComponent();
  simpleOpenGlControl1.InitializeContexts();
}
```

Run the program and a form will be created with a black screen. That's OpenGL working with C#—congratulations! The variable _openGLControl reads better than simpleOpenGlControl1; the refactor tools can be used to rename it.

Full Screen Mode

Most games allow the player to play the game full screen. This is an easy option to add. Here's the code.

```
bool _fullscreen = true;
public Form1()
```

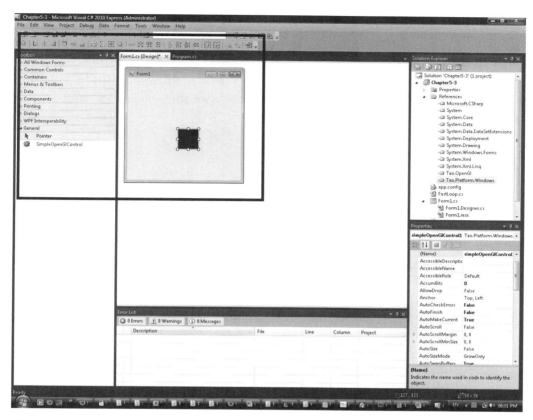

Figure 5.4
Adding `SimpleOpenGLControl`.

```
{
  InitializeComponent();
  _openGLControl.InitializeContexts();
  if (_fullscreen)
  {
    FormBorderStyle = FormBorderStyle.None;
    WindowState = FormWindowState.Maximized;
  }
}
```

The border style is the bits on the outside of the window, the menu bar, and the border. With these parts of the form removed, the size of the form will directly reflect the size of the OpenGL control. Forms have three possible Window-States: Normal, Minimized, and Maximized. Maximized gives the full-screen mode needed. Full-screen mode is good for playing games, but while developing a game, windowed mode is better. If the program is in a window, the debugger can be used while the game is running. For that reason, it's probably best to set _fullscreen to false.

Rendering

To make games, we need to learn how to get OpenGL to start drawing to the screen. When learning a new program like OpenGL, it's important to have fun, be curious, and play around with the API. Don't be afraid to experiment or break things. All OpenGL functions are documented on the OpenGL website at http://www.opengl.org/sdk/docs/man/. This is a good site to start exploring the library.

Clearing the Background

Rendering graphics using OpenGL first requires a game loop. Previously, a game was created in the Program.cs class; this time the game loop will be created in Form.cs so that it has access to the openGLControl.

```
using Tao.OpenGl;
namespace StartingGraphics
{
  public partial class Form1 : Form
  {
    FastLoop   _fastLoop;
    bool      _fullscreen = false;
    public Form1()
    {
      _fastLoop = new FastLoop(GameLoop);
      InitializeComponent();
      _openGLControl.InitializeContexts();
      if (_fullscreen)
      {
        FormBorderStyle = FormBorderStyle.None;
        WindowState = FormWindowState.Maximized;
      }
    }
```

```
    void GameLoop(double elapsedTime)
    {
      _openGLControl.Refresh();
    }
  }
}
```

This game loop code is very similar to the code written before. Remember to add the using Tao.OpenGl; statement or it won't have access to the OpenGL libraries.

GameLoop is called every frame. At the moment, it just refreshes the OpenGL control. The refresh call tells the OpenGL control to update its graphics. Running the program will give a boring black screen, but with the game loop set up, that screen can now be changed.

```
void GameLoop(double elapsedTime)
{
  Gl.glClearColor(1.0f, 0.0f, 0.0f, 1.0f);
  Gl.glClear(Gl.GL_COLOR_BUFFER_BIT);
  Gl.glFinish();
  _openGLControl.Refresh();
}
```

Three new lines have been added to the game loop. The first line tells OpenGL what color to use to clear the screen. OpenGL represents colors as four values: red, green, blue, and alpha. Alpha determines the transparency of the color: 1 is fully opaque, and 0 is fully transparent. Each value ranges from 0 to 1. In this case, red has been set to 1, green and blue to zero, and alpha to 1 as well. This will result in a bright red color. For the clear color, the alpha value is ignored. The clear color only needs to be set once, but to keep all the new code together, it's currently being set every frame.

The second line issues the clear command. This function uses the clear color we set in the previous line to clear the screen. The final line, glFinish, tells OpenGL that we've finished for this frame and to make sure all commands are carried out.

Running the program will now give the window a new bright red background. It's important to play with the library and get comfortable with it. Try switching up the commands or changing the color. For example, review this code and try to guess what will happen before running it.

```
Random r = new Random();
Gl.glClearColor((float)r.NextDouble(), (float)r.NextDouble(), (float)
r.NextDouble(), 1.0f);
```

Vertices

Vertices are the building blocks that make up virtual worlds. At their most basic they are position information; x and y for a two-dimensional world; x, y, and z for a three-dimensional world.

It's easy to introduce vertices in OpenGL using immediate mode. Immediate mode is a way of telling the graphics card what to draw. These commands need to be sent every frame, even if nothing has changed. It's not the fastest way to do OpenGL programming, but it is the easiest way to learn.

Let's begin by drawing a point.

```
void GameLoop(double elapsedTime)
{
  Gl.glClearColor(0.0f, 0.0f, 0.0f, 1.0f);
  Gl.glClear(Gl.GL_COLOR_BUFFER_BIT);
  Gl.glBegin(Gl.GL_POINTS);
  {
    Gl.glVertex3d(0, 0, 0);
  }
  Gl.glEnd();
  Gl.glFinish();
  _openGLControl.Refresh();
}
```

There are three new OpenGL commands here. glBegin tells the graphics card that you will be drawing something. glBegin takes one argument; this describes what you will be drawing. The value passed in is GL_POINTS; this tells OpenGL to render any vertices as points (as opposed to triangles or quads).

glBegin must be followed by glEnd. Immediately after glBegin, there is an opening brace. This isn't strictly necessary; it just provides indentation so that it's clear where the glEnd should go. In between the parentheses is a glVertex command; the command ends in 3d. The 3 means it will use three dimensions—an x, y, and z—to make up the position. The d means the positions are expected to be doubles.

You may draw as many vertices as you want between the begin and end calls. The current vertex is being drawn at 0,0,0, which will be right in the center of the screen. The scene is currently set up according to OpenGL's default settings. Figure 5.5 is a drawing of a cube that describes the default setup of the OpenGL scene. A point can be rendered anywhere in this cube, but if any of the coordinate numbers are lower than minus one or greater than one, then the point will be outside the scene and therefore won't be visible. The camera viewing this scene can be considered to be at 0, 0, 1 facing −1 on the Z axis.

The position 0,0,0 is often referred to as the origin of the scene. After the vertex is drawn, the closing brace is written, followed by the end call. Run the program and you should see a white pixel in the middle of the screen. This is the point being drawn. It's quite small, but the point drawing size is easy to adjust in OpenGL. Add `Gl.glPointSize(5.0f);` just before the `glBegin` statement. The point should be much easier to see now.

Triangles

OpenGL supports a number of primitive types that can be made from vertices. The majority of games use triangle strips to represent everything. The 3D

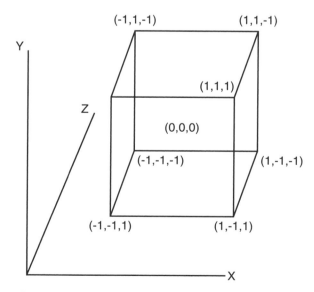

Figure 5.5
Default OpenGL scene.

characters in your favorite FPS or fighting game are just a list of vertices that can be joined up to make a list of triangles.

```
Gl.glBegin(Gl.GL_POINTS);
{
  Gl.glVertex3d(-0.5, 0, 0);
  Gl.glVertex3d(0.5, 0, 0);
  Gl.glVertex3d(0, 0.5, 0);
}
Gl.glEnd();
```

Run the above code snippet. It will draw three vertices as points in a triangle shape. To actually draw a full triangle, the argument passed into glBegin needs to change from GL_POINTS to GL_TRIANGLES. Run the program after making this change and you'll see a white triangle like in Figure 5.6.

GL_TRIANGLES reads three vertices and then draws a triangle using those vertices. When loading meshes, it's more common to use GL_TRIANGLE_STRIP. GL_TRIANGLE requires three vertices to draw a triangle. GL_TRIANGLE_STRIP is similar; the first triangle requires three vertices, but then each additional triangle only requires one more vertex. The difference is shown in Figure 5.7.

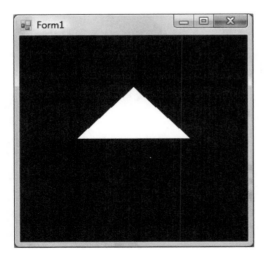

Figure 5.6
A rendered triangle.

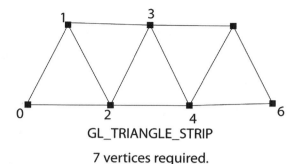

GL_TRIANGLE_STRIP

7 vertices required.

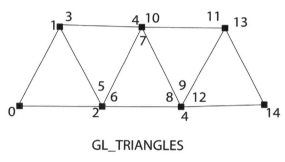

GL_TRIANGLES

15 vertices required for the same figure.

Figure 5.7
GL_TRIANGLES and GL_TRIANGLE_STRIP.

Coloring and Spinning the Triangle

The Hello World program of the 3D programming world is a spinning triangle with each vertex colored for red, green, and blue. This demonstrates all the basic graphics functionality is working, and an experienced graphics programmer can easily build from this.

Vertices can store lots of different information. At the moment, the three vertices here only have position data. Color data can be added in immediate mode by setting the color information before each vertex call.

```
Gl.glBegin(Gl.GL_TRIANGLE_STRIP);
{
  Gl.glColor3d(1.0, 0.0, 0.0);
  Gl.glVertex3d(-0.5, 0, 0);
  Gl.glColor3d(0.0, 1.0, 0.0);
  Gl.glVertex3d(0.5, 0, 0);
```

```
Gl.glColor3d(0.0, 0.0, 1.0);
  Gl.glVertex3d(0, 0.5, 0);
}
Gl.glEnd();
```

Running this code will produce a triangle with a red, green, and blue corner. Along the surface of the triangle, the colors mix and fade into each other. By default, OpenGL will interpolate colors between vertices. In practice, this means if you give each vertex of a triangle a different color, then each pixel of the rendered triangle will be colored according to the distance from each of the vertices. Basic lighting systems get the lighting information for each vertex and then use this interpolation to decide how the surface should be shaded.

All that remains now is to spin the triangle. There are two ways to spin the triangle: move all the vertices or move the entire scene. It's simpler to move the entire scene as OpenGL has a helpful function for rotation.

```
Gl.glRotated(10 * elapsedTime, 0, 1, 0);
Gl.glBegin(Gl.GL_TRIANGLE_STRIP);
{
  Gl.glColor4d(1.0, 0.0, 0.0, 0.5);
  Gl.glVertex3d(-0.5, 0, 0);
  Gl.glColor3d(0.0, 1.0, 0.0);
  Gl.glVertex3d(0.5, 0, 0);
  Gl.glColor3d(0.0, 0.0, 1.0);
  Gl.glVertex3d(0, 0.5, 0);
}
Gl.glEnd();
```

There are a few subtle points to touch on here. glRotate takes four arguments. The first argument is the angle to rotate in degrees and the last three are the axis to rotate around. The rotation is cumulative, which means if glRotated was called twice, those rotations will both be applied—rotating the object twice as much. In our case, the update call is being called as often as possible so the degree of rotation continually increases, which appears to make the triangle rotate. The rotate function automatically wraps at 360 so a rotation of 361 is equivalent to a rotation to 1.

The next three arguments describe the axis. These three arguments are actually a normalized vector. Vectors will be described later in the book. For now, just think of a vector as a line that is one unit of length long. The line described here is 1 on the Y axis, so it's a straight line along the Y axis. Imagine this line pushed through the center of the triangle, passing from the point at the top through the middle of its wide base. Rotating the line then rotates the entire triangle. Try to visualize how the triangle would rotate with the arguments (1, 0, 0) and (0, 0, 1), then amend the program to check if you were correct.

The first argument, the angle in degrees, is being multiplied by the elapsed time. This is to ensure time-independent movement and should make the animation smoother. If the program is playing at 60 frames per second, that means each elapsed frame time will be around 0.1 seconds. This means to move the triangle 10 degrees will take 1 second. If someone else runs your program on a slower computer, and it can only go, say, 30 frames per second, then each frame will take about 0.2 seconds to complete. There are fewer frames per second but the triangle will take the same amount of time to rotate on both machines. If the degrees were not multiplied by the elapsed time, then the program would run twice as fast on the machine that runs at 60 frames per second.

Summary

Most games have a central loop that checks the player input, updates the game world, and then updates the screen. By default, C# does not have a central loop so some C functions need to be used to create a fast game loop useful for creating games. Additional C functions are used to get access to timing information so each frame can be timed. This time can be used to ensure the game runs smoothly, even on computers that run at different speeds.

The Tao framework library has a control called `SimpleOpenGLControl`. This control allows OpenGL to be used easily within a Windows Form. A spinning triangle is often used as the "Hello World" program for OpenGL. The triangle is made up of three vertices and each can be assigned a different color. If the vertices of a triangle are different colors, the triangle's pixels will be colored according to the distance from each vertex. OpenGL has a function called `glRotated`, which takes care of the final task of rotating the triangle.

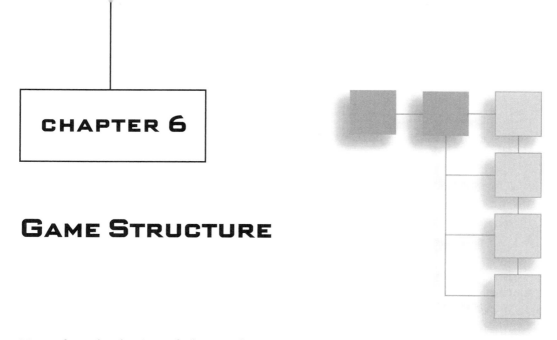

CHAPTER 6

GAME STRUCTURE

Now that the basics of the rendering are working, it's time to revisit game architecture. Even small games (*Pong*, for example) usually require a large amount of code. *Pong* is a pretty simple game; the player moves a paddle left or right and attempts to hit a ball past an opponent's paddle. It was one of the first popular computer games released in 1987 so there have been numerous reimplementations since then. SourceForge (www.sourceforge.net) is a website that hosts hundreds of thousands of open source projects. There are quite a few open source *Pong* clones, and even the simplest ones are over 1,000 lines of code. As a game programmer, it's important to have strategies to manage that complexity.

Big games are orders of magnitude more complex than *Pong*. Kelly Brock revealed that there was a single function over 32,000 lines long in the *Sims* computer game. This was posted in a discussion on the Software Development for Games mailing list (a great list to join for any aspiring game programmer; you can register to join on this website http://lists.midnightryder.com/listinfo.cgi/ sweng-gamedev-midnightryder.com). Games with strict deadlines and lots of pressure can cause the code to become large and unmanageable. Being familiar with some basic architecture techniques can help make code clearer and its function more separated and defined.

The Basic Pattern of a Game Object

The majority of game objects need at least two functions: an update function where the object can handle its animation or anything that changes over time, and a render function where the object can draw itself on screen. This can easily be described in C# using an interface.

```csharp
public interface IGameObject
{
    void Update(double elapsedTime);
    void Render();
}
```

Now anything you want to create in the game can inherit from this interface. The I in IGameObject is used to identify the interface as an interface in the code. When designing the game structure, the code can refer to IGameObjects in general without having to worry about the specifics of what any game object actually is. We can start using game objects right away to describe game state.

Handling Game State

Games are usually broken up into lots of different states. At the top level there's perhaps a company splash screen followed by a title menu, there are submenus for options such as sounds, an option to start the game, and perhaps several others. Here's a naïve way to program that kind of game state.

```csharp
enum GameState
{
  CompanySplash,
  TitleMenu,
  PlayingGame,
  SettingsMenu,
}

GameState _currentState = GameState.CompanySplash;

public void Update(double elapsedTime)
{
  switch (_currentState)
  {
  case GameState.CompanySplash:
      {
          // Update the starting splash screen
      } break;
```

```
    case GameState.SettingsMenu:
      {
          // Update the settings menu
      } break;
    case GameState.PlayingGame:
      {
          // Update the game
      } break;
    case GameState.TitleMenu:
      {
          // Update title menu
      } break;
    default:
      {
          // Error invalid state
      } break;
    }
}
```

There are a few things to notice here. The code is very long and prone to become complicated and hard to follow. It also breaks the DRY principle. To add a new state, let's say a credits screen, a new entry must be added to the game state enum and then added to the switch statement. When extending the code, the fewer places that require change the better.

This big switch statement can be replaced with a much better system using the IGameObject interface, where every game state is a game object.

It's probably best to start a new project with a game loop to follow this example. Once this is done, it's time to create a new class implementing the IGameObject interface for each game state.

```
namespace GameStructure
{
    class SplashScreenState : IGameObject
    {
    }
}
```

Here a splash screen class has been created that inherits from the IGameObject interface. The above code is invalid because it doesn't implement any of the IGameObject methods. Instead of typing the methods out by hand, one of the refactoring shortcuts can be used to create them automatically. Right-click the `IGameObject` text and a context menu will appear, as shown in Figure 6.1.

There are two options. Implement Interface Explicitly will do the same as Implement Interface but instead of creating the method `Render()`, it will create the method `IGameObject.Render();`, explicitly describing where the method comes from. Here is the code once the refactoring tools have implemented the `IGameObject` interface.

```
class SplashScreenState : IGameObject
{
  #region IGameObject Members

  public void Update(double elapsedTime)
  {
      throw new NotImplementedException();
  }
```

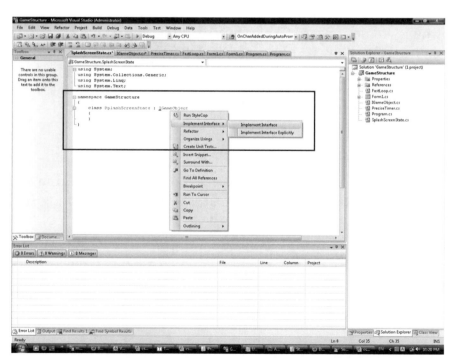

Figure 6.1
Implementing an interface.

```
public void Render()
{
    throw new NotImplementedException();
}


#endregion
}
```

We're not implementing the splash screen functionality at the moment; therefore, the exceptions can be removed to make testing the code easier. Something like the following will be easier to work with.

```
public void Update(double elapsedTime)
{
    System.Console.WriteLine("Updating Splash");
}

public void Render()
{
    System.Console.WriteLine("Rendering Splash");
}
```

That's one state—the rest can be created in much the same way. Create a few of the states for practice.

Once the states are made, the code to handle these states is quite simple. To follow the rest of the code, you should create the `TitleMenuState`. It doesn't need any functionality. If it just prints out its name in the render and update functions, then that's great. If you're still not sure how to create it then you can check the code on the CD.

Here's an example of how the states might be used in the Form.cs file.

```
StateSystem _system = new StateSystem();
public Form1()
{
    // Add all the states that will be used.
    _system.AddState("splash", new SplashScreenState(_system));
    _system.AddState("title_menu", new TitleMenuState());
    // Select the start state
    _system.ChangeState("splash");
```

States are created and added to a state system with a name to identify them. States can then be selected by calling `ChangeState` and passing in a state name. The state system will manage the update and render of the current active state. Sometimes a state will want to change the active state. For example, a splash screen usually displays an image or animation and then changes state to the title screen. For a splash screen state to change state it must have a reference to the state system.

```
class SplashScreenState : IGameObject
{
  StateSystem _system;
  public SplashScreenState(StateSystem system)
  {
     _system = system;
  }

  #region IGameObject Members

  public void Update(double elapsedTime)
  {
     // Wait so many seconds then call _system.ChangeState("title_menu")
     System.Console.WriteLine("Updating Splash");
  }

  public void Render()
  {
     System.Console.WriteLine("Rendering Splash");
  }

  #endregion
}
```

Then when creating the state, the `StateSystem` can be passed into the constructor.

```
  _system.AddState("splash", new SplashScreenState(_system));
class StateSystem
{
   Dictionary<string, IGameObject> _stateStore = new Dictionary<string,
IGameObject>();
  IGameObject _currentState = null;
```

```
public void Update(double elapsedTime)
{
if (_currentState == null)
{
    return; // nothing to update
}
_currentState.Update(elapsedTime);
}

public void Render()
{
    if (_currentState == null)
{
    return; // nothing to render
}
_currentState.Render();
}

public void AddState(string stateId, IGameObject state)
{
    System.Diagnostics.Debug.Assert( Exists(stateId) == false );
    _stateStore.Add(stateId, state);
}

public void ChangeState(string stateId)
{
    System.Diagnostics.Debug.Assert(Exists(stateId));
    _currentState = _stateStore[stateId];
}

public bool Exists(string stateId)
{
    return _stateStore.ContainsKey(stateId);
}
}
```

The StateSystem class is a good class for unit testing—try writing some tests in NUnit. The tests should be short snippets of code that check just one area; here's an example:

```
[TestFixture]
public class Test_StateSystem
```

```
{
  [Test]
  public void TestAddedStateExists()
  {
    StateSystem stateSystem = new StateSystem();
    stateSystem.AddState("splash", new SplashScreenState
    (stateSystem));

    // Does the added function now exist?
    Assert.IsTrue(stateSystem.Exists("splash"));
  }
```

The rest of the tests can be found on the CD at Code\Chapter 6\Chapter6-2\
Test_StateSystem.cs. Try to write your own and then compare them with the
code on the CD.

Game State Demo

Now that the StateSystem has been created, a simple demo can show it in
action. We can start with implementing the splash screen state. As we can only
draw spinning triangles, it's not going to be that impressive, but it's good enough
for a demo. Let's begin by implementing the title splash screen.

```
class SplashScreenState : IGameObject
{
    StateSystem _system;
    double _delayInSeconds = 3;

  public SplashScreenState(StateSystem system)
  {
    _system = system;
  }

  #region IGameObject Members

  public void Update(double elapsedTime)
  {
    _delayInSeconds -= elapsedTime;
    if (_delayInSeconds <= 0)
  {
    _delayInSeconds = 3;
    _system.ChangeState("title_menu");
```

```
    }
  }

  public void Render()
  {
    Gl.glClearColor(1, 1, 1, 1);
    Gl.glClear(Gl.GL_COLOR_BUFFER_BIT);
    Gl.glFinish();
  }

  #endregion
}
```

This code has the state wait three seconds and then it changes the state to the title menu. The splash screen state will render the screen white while it's active. We'll have to cover 2D rendering and sprites before something interesting can be shown.

```
class TitleMenuState : IGameObject
{
    double _currentRotation = 0;
    #region IGameObject Members

  public void Update(double elapsedTime)
  {

    _currentRotation = 10 * elapsedTime;
  }

  public void Render()
  {
    Gl.glClearColor(0.0f, 0.0f, 0.0f, 1.0f);
    Gl.glClear(Gl.GL_COLOR_BUFFER_BIT);
    Gl.glPointSize(5.0f);

    Gl.glRotated(_currentRotation, 0, 1, 0);
    Gl.glBegin(Gl.GL_TRIANGLE_STRIP);
  {
    Gl.glColor4d(1.0, 0.0, 0.0, 0.5);
    Gl.glVertex3d(-0.5, 0, 0);
    Gl.glColor3d(0.0, 1.0, 0.0);
    Gl.glVertex3d(0.5, 0, 0);
```

```
    Gl.glColor3d(0.0, 0.0, 1.0);
    Gl.glVertex3d(0, 0.5, 0);
  }
  Gl.glEnd();
  Gl.glFinish();
  }


  #endregion
}
```

It's the spinning triangle from before. These states have already been loaded in to the state system in the earlier examples. The only remaining task is to call the `Update` and `Render` functions in the Form.cs.

```
private void GameLoop(double elapsedTime)
{
  _system.Update(elapsedTime);
  _system.Render();
  _openGLControl.Refresh();
}
```

That's it. Run the code now and a white screen will appear for three seconds, followed by a spinning triangle. That proves the state system works quite well and we can now use this to break up the code. Next, it's time to leave the high-level concepts of architecture and return to the details of rendering.

Setting the Scene with Projections

Up until now the OpenGL scene has not been explicitly setup; the default settings have been used. By setting up the scene manually, much more control is given to how a game appears.

Form Size and OpenGL Viewport Size

The size of the form is currently rather arbitrary; it's been left at the default size that Visual Studio made it. Real games need to specify how large their window is going to be. With the current settings, try enabling full-screen mode. The result is shown in Figure 6.2.

The program has successfully gone full-screen, but the triangle is being rendered in the bottom-left corner. This issue arises from there being two different sizes with which to be concerned. One is the size of the form. This is what's changed

Figure 6.2
Problems with full-screen mode.

when in full-screen mode. The second size is the OpenGL viewport; this hasn't changed at all, and that's why it's still rendering the triangle the same small size.

To fix this we must know when the form changes size and inform OpenGL about the change. The form's size can be accessed in a number of ways. Figure 6.3 shows the difference between the form `Size` and `ClientSize` values. Size includes things like the frame and title bar. We're only interested in the size of the form where the OpenGL graphics are drawn. This can be obtained by querying the `ClientSize` value of the form.

In the form you'll see an overridable method call, `OnClientSizeChanged`; this is the perfect place to update the OpenGL viewport size. In Form.cs, add this method.

```
protected override void OnClientSizeChanged(EventArgs e)
{
  base.OnClientSizeChanged(e);
  Gl.glViewport(0, 0, this.ClientSize.Width, this.ClientSize.Height);
}
```

Now any time the client size is changed, such as going to full-screen, the OpenGL viewport will be changed to match it. This also allows the form to be resized at

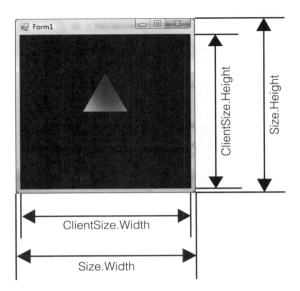

Figure 6.3
`Size` and `ClientSize` of the form.

runtime without problem. Check full-screen again and the triangle will be full-sized.

The initial size of the form can be set by setting the `ClientSize` property.

```
ClientSize = new Size(800, 600);
```

This will set the form's client area to 800 pixels by 600 pixels.

Aspect Ratio

Humans, as you are no doubt aware, have two eyes. The eyes are set in the face horizontally, and this gives us a wider horizontal viewing range than vertical. Widescreen TVs and monitors are more natural for us to use than square or vertically tall ones. The relationship between the width and height of a viewing area is called the aspect ratio. Certain aspect ratios are more comfortable than others. It's easy in code to provide a range of different aspect ratios.

If the `ClientSize` is set to 800 by 600, its aspect ratio is 1.33—the width is 1.33 times longer than the height. This ratio is also referred to as 4:3. 4:3 is a minimum; as widescreens become more popular, aspect ratios of 16:9 become more popular. PlayStation 3 has a default resolution of 1280 by 720; the width is

1.73 times greater than the height, and this is commonly referred to as a 16:9 aspect ratio.

```
if (_fullscreen)
{
  FormBorderStyle = FormBorderStyle.None;
  WindowState = FormWindowState.Maximized;
}
else
{
  ClientSize = new Size(1280, 720);
}
```

Play around with different aspect ratios to decide what you like. Bear in mind that if you wish to release your game to a large number of people, they may not be able to support resolutions as high as you can. It may be worth trying to support a number of different aspects and resolutions.

When playing around with resolutions, you may observe that in certain resolutions the triangle seems a little squashed or distorted. OpenGL's viewport is now set correctly, but OpenGL's default aspect is 1:1, a square. It's not going to map to 4:3 or 16:9 very gracefully. OpenGL aspect is 1:1 because that is how the aspect is set up by default. In order to change it, the projection matrix must be altered.

The Projection Matrix

Computer monitors and televisions display 2D pictures while OpenGL deals with 3D data. A projection matrix transforms the 3D data to the 2D screen. There are two types of projection matrix that we're concerned with, orthographic and perspective. Simply, orthographic is used for 2D graphics like hud elements, 2D games, and text. Perspective is used for 3D games like an FPS game.

The orthographic matrix ignores the depth information; it doesn't matter how far away an item is from the user, it remains the same size. With a perspective projection, things that are farther away are smaller. Those are the main differences.

2D Graphics

Even 3D games need to be able to render 2D graphics.

A new function should be made in Form.cs named Setup2DGraphics.

```
private void Setup2DGraphics (double width, double height)
{
  double halfWidth = width / 2;
  double halfHeight = height / 2;
  Gl.glMatrixMode (Gl.GL_PROJECTION) ;
  Gl.glLoadIdentity () ;
  Gl.glOrtho (-halfWidth, halfWidth, -halfHeight, halfHeight, -100, 100) ;
  Gl.glMatrixMode (Gl.GL_MODELVIEW) ;
  Gl.glLoadIdentity () ;
}
```

This code has a lot of new OpenGL functions, but they're all straightforward. OpenGL has a number of matrix modes. The value `GL_PROJECTION` changes the OpenGL state. Once the state is changed, all OpenGL commands will affect the projection matrix. This matrix can now be altered to set up an orthographic projection matrix.

`glLoadIdentity` clears the current projection information. The next command `glOrtho`, sets up an orthographic projection matrix. There are six arguments for this function.

```
void glOrtho (GLdouble  left,
   GLdouble  right,
   GLdouble  bottom,
   GLdouble  top,
   GLdouble  nearVal,
   GLdouble  farVal) ;
```

The first four arguments describe how big you want the view of the world to be. Figure 6.4 shows the orthographic projection and how the six arguments affect it. At the moment, the origin is right in the center of the screen. I've decided to keep that. To make the origin the top-left corner, you could write the following.

```
Gl.glOrtho (0, width, -height, 0, -100, 100) ;
```

The final two values are the near and far planes. If the z position of a vertex is greater than the far plane, the vertex isn't rendered. If it's lower than the near plane, then it also isn't rendered. Generally, 2D graphics have the z position all set to 0 so the near and far planes don't really matter. They're much more important for rendering 3D graphics.

The setup function can be called in the Form.cs constructor.

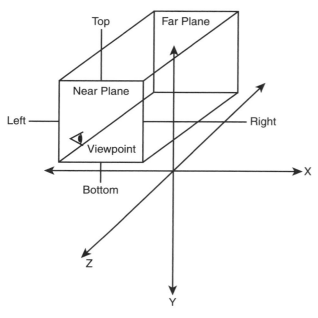

Figure 6.4
Orthographic projections.

```
public Form1()
{
  // Add all the states that will be used.
  _system.AddState("splash", new SplashScreenState(_system));
  _system.AddState("title_menu", new TitleMenuState());

  // Select the start state
  _system.ChangeState("splash");

  InitializeComponent();
  _openGLControl.InitializeContexts();

  if (_fullscreen)
  {
      FormBorderStyle = FormBorderStyle.None;
      WindowState = FormWindowState.Maximized;
  }
  else
  {
      ClientSize = new Size(1280, 720);
  }
```

```
    Setup2DGraphics(ClientSize.Width, ClientSize.Height);
    _fastLoop = new FastLoop(GameLoop);
}
```

The projection matrix will need re-creating anytime the form changes size. Therefore, a call to `Setup2DGraphics` should also be added to the `On-ClientSizeChanged` callback.

```
protected override void OnClientSizeChanged(EventArgs e)
{
    base.OnClientSizeChanged(e);
    Gl.glViewport(0, 0, this.ClientSize.Width, this.ClientSize.Height);
    Setup2DGraphics(ClientSize.Width, ClientSize.Height);
}
```

The title state renders a triangle, but the triangle's maximum width is only 1 OpenGL unit. The previous projection matrix had a width and height of 2 so the triangle appeared a good size. The width and height of this new projection matrix is 1280 and 720 so the triangle barely takes up a pixel and therefore cannot be seen!

An easy way to fix this is to make the triangle bigger. Find the triangle drawing code and make the width and height 50 instead of 1.

```
Gl.glColor4d(1.0, 0.0, 0.0, 0.5);
Gl.glVertex3d(-50, 0, 0);
Gl.glColor3d(0.0, 1.0, 0.0);
Gl.glVertex3d(50, 0, 0);
Gl.glColor3d(0.0, 0.0, 1.0);
Gl.glVertex3d(0, 50, 0);
```

This will make the triangle visible once again. Most 2D graphics use two triangles to make a quad. This quad then has a texture applied to it and forms the basis of a 2D game or heads-up display.

Sprites

The first step of creating a sprite is to create a quad. A triangle is made of three vertices; a quad is made of four. See Figure 6.5. A sprite is a pretty basic game element, and it's a good idea to make it into its own class. There will also be a class responsible for drawing the sprites. This class will be called the `Renderer`. Before implementing the `Renderer` and `Sprite` classes, it's useful to first

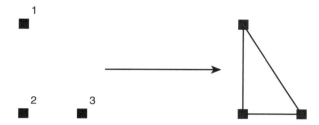

A triangle is made from three vertices, using GL_TRIANGLES.

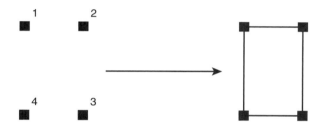

A quad can be made from four vertices using GL_QUADS.

Figure 6.5
Sprite layout.

consider how they will be used. Here is some pseudo code of how sprites might be used.

```
Renderer renderer = new Renderer();
Sprite spaceship = new Sprite();
spaceship.SetPosition(0, 0);
spaceship.SetTexture(_textureManager.Get("spaceship"));
renderer.DrawSprite(spaceship);
```

A quad is made from four vertices, but it's common practice to use six vertices and draw two triangles to make up the quad. Graphics cards work very well with triangles, so many engines have all their assets broken up into triangles or triangle strips. The quad is broken up as shown in Figure 6.6.

Coding as you read helps you understand the material. There's no need to start a new project; the GameStructure project can be reused. Create a new class that inherits from IGameObject, called DrawSpriteState.

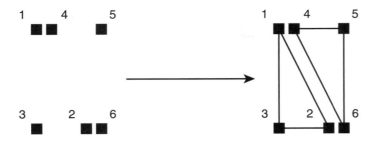

A quad can be made of six vertices using GL_TRIANGLES.
If vertices 1,4 and 2,6 have exactly the same position a quad is created.

Figure 6.6
A quad made from two triangles.

```
class DrawSpriteState : IGameObject
{
  #region IGameObject Members

  public void Update(double elapsedTime)
  {
  }

  public void Render()
  {
  }

  #endregion
}
```

Remember to include the statement using Tao.OpenGl; at the top of the file so OpenGL commands can be used. This game state will be used to test the sprite drawing code. It needs to be the state that's loaded as soon as the program starts; modify the code in Form.cs as follows.

```
public Form1()
{
  // Add all the states that will be used.
  _system.AddState("splash", new SplashScreenState(_system));
  _system.AddState("title_menu", new TitleMenuState());
  _system.AddState("sprite_test", new DrawSpriteState());

  // Select the start state
  _system.ChangeState("sprite_test");
```

This will load the currently empty sprite drawing state. Running the code will display a blank window. A quad is made from two triangles arranged to form a square shape. OpenGL draws triangles clockwise.

```
public void Render()
{
  Gl.glClearColor(0.0f, 0.0f, 0.0f, 1.0f);
  Gl.glClear(Gl.GL_COLOR_BUFFER_BIT);
  Gl.glBegin(Gl.GL_TRIANGLES);
  {
      Gl.glVertex3d(-100, 100, 0); // top left
      Gl.glVertex3d(100, 100, 0); // top right
      Gl.glVertex3d(-100, -100, 0); // bottom left
  }
  Gl.glEnd();
}
```

This code will draw the top half of the quad. Running the code will produce an image similar to Figure 6.7.

Drawing the second half is easy. In clockwise order, the top-right vertex needs to be drawn, then the bottom right, and finally the bottom left. The code to do this should be written just after the first half of the quad.

Figure 6.7
The first part of the quad.

```
Gl.glVertex3d( 100, 100, 0); // top right
Gl.glVertex3d( 100, -100, 0); // bottom right
Gl.glVertex3d(-100, -100, 0); // bottom left
```

These two triangles make a full square. Not all game sprites will be perfect squares. Therefore, it's important to be able to specify the width and height. The current quad is 200 by 200. OpenGL doesn't have explicit dimensions; the 200 can be whatever unit you like—feet, meters, etc. The screen has been set up so that 200 OpenGL units map up to 200 pixels, but that isn't always guaranteed. Currently the width, height, and position of the sprite are all hard coded. These magic numbers need to be replaced with variables.

```
double height   = 200;
double width   = 200;
double halfHeight   = height / 2;
double halfWidth   = width / 2;


Gl.glBegin(Gl.GL_TRIANGLES);
{
  Gl.glVertex3d(-halfWidth, halfHeight, 0); // top left
  Gl.glVertex3d( halfWidth, halfHeight, 0); // top right
  Gl.glVertex3d(-halfWidth, -halfHeight, 0); // bottom left

  Gl.glVertex3d( halfWidth, halfHeight, 0); // top right
  Gl.glVertex3d( halfWidth, -halfHeight, 0); // bottom right
  Gl.glVertex3d(-halfWidth, -halfHeight, 0); // bottom left
}
```

The values are exactly the same as before, but now the height and width are stored as variables following the DRY principle. The height and width can now be altered easily to form any number of interestingly shaped rectangles.

Positioning the Sprite

The sprite's size is now easy to modify, but there's no way to modify the position. Changing the position is what will be added next.

```
double x = 0;
double y = 0;
double z = 0;
```

```
Gl.glBegin(Gl.GL_TRIANGLES);
{
  Gl.glVertex3d( x - halfWidth, y + halfHeight, z); // top left
  Gl.glVertex3d( x + halfWidth, y + halfHeight, z); // top right
  Gl.glVertex3d( x - halfWidth, y - halfHeight, z); // bottom left

  Gl.glVertex3d(x + halfWidth, y + halfHeight, z); // top right
  Gl.glVertex3d(x + halfWidth, y - halfHeight, z); // bottom right
  Gl.glVertex3d(x - halfWidth, y - halfHeight, z); // bottom left
}
Gl.glEnd();
```

This is equivalent to the previous code, but now the x, y, and z positions can be altered. The position represents the center of the quad. Try changing the x, y, and z values and move the quad about.

Managing Textures with DevIl

Textures are very easy to apply to the quad we have. The tricky part of textures is loading them from the hard disk into memory. A texture class needs to be created to represent the textures in memory, as well as a `TextureManager` class to store the textures. Internally, OpenGL references textures by an integer id; the texture struct will just store that id and the width and height of the texture.

```
public struct Texture
{
  public int Id { get; set; }
  public int Width { get; set; }
  public int Height { get; set; }

  public Texture(int id, int width, int height) : this()
  {
    Id = id;
    Width = width;
    Height = height;
  }
}
```

The texture class is quite straightforward. Its constructor calls the `this` constructor because it's a struct type and needs to have the members initialized for the autogenerated assessor methods to use.

Next, the `TextureManager` loads the texture data from the disk and associates it with an id provided by OpenGL. The texture is also associated with a human readable name so that it's easy to work with. The code to load the texture requires an additional reference, `Tao.DevIl`, to be added to the project. Add it the same way you added `Tao.OpenGL`. DevIl is short for Developer's Image Library. It can load most image formats so that OpenGL can use them.

The DevIL library also requires a number of DLL files to run; these must be in the same directory as your binary file. This directory will probably be `bin\debug`. Find the Tao Framework directory; it will most likely be in your C:\Program File (x86) (or the C:\Program Files directory on Windows XP). Navigate to \TaoFramework\lib and copy DevIl.dll, ILU.dll, and ILUT.dll into your bin \debug directory. When you do a release build, you will need to copy all relevant dlls to bin\release, too. Once this is done you can start using DevIl.

The DevIl library has to be initialized and told to work with OpenGL. Form.cs is a good place to initialize DevIl. Make sure you add the `using` statement, as shown below, to the top of the Form.cs file.

```
using Tao.DevIl;
```

Then in the form's constructor, add the following code.

```
// Init DevIl
Il.ilInit();
Ilu.iluInit();
Ilut.ilutInit();
Ilut.ilutRenderer(Ilut.ILUT_OPENGL);
```

Create a new class called `TextureManger`. At the top, add the `using` statements for DevIl and OpenGL.

Here's the basic `TextureManager` code

```
class TextureManager : IDisposable
{
  Dictionary<string, Texture> _textureDatabase = new Dictionary<string,
Texture>();

  public Texture Get(string textureId)
  {
     return _textureDatabase[textureId];
  }
```

```
#region IDisposable Members

public void Dispose()
{
    foreach (Texture t in _textureDatabase.Values)
    {
        Gl.glDeleteTextures(1, new int[] { t.Id });
    }
}

#endregion
}
```

The class implements `IDisposable`; it ensures that if the class is destroyed, it will release the textures from memory. The only other function is `Get`; this takes a name of a texture and returns the associated texture data. If the data doesn't exist, it will throw an exception.

The `TextureManager` class has one obvious omission: there is no function to load the texture from the hard disk.

```
public void LoadTexture(string textureId, string path)
{
    int devilId = 0;
    Il.ilGenImages(1, out devilId);
    Il.ilBindImage(devilId); // set as the active texture.

    if (!Il.ilLoadImage(path))
    {
        System.Diagnostics.Debug.Assert(false,
          "Could not open file, [" + path + "].");
    }
    // The files we'll be using need to be flipped before passing to OpenGL
    Ilu.iluFlipImage();
    int width   = Il.ilGetInteger(Il.IL_IMAGE_WIDTH);
    int height  = Il.ilGetInteger(Il.IL_IMAGE_HEIGHT);
    int openGLId = Ilut.ilutGLBindTexImage();

    System.Diagnostics.Debug.Assert(openGLId != 0);
    Il.ilDeleteImages(1, ref devilId);

    _textureDatabase.Add(textureId, new Texture(openGLId, width,
height));
}
```

The DevIL library was written to complement OpenGL so it has a very similar interface. An image is generated and then bound. Binding an image means all subsequent operations will affect that image. `ilLoadImage` is called, which loads the texture data into memory. `iluFlipImage` is called on the image, and this flips it on the Y axis; most of the common image formats need to be flipped to work correctly with OpenGL. The image is then queried for width and height information. Finally, the DevIl utility library is used to bind the texture to an OpenGL id. The id, width, and height are all wrapped in the texture class, which is then returned. DevIl still has the texture data in memory; this is freed using `ilDeleteImages`, as the data has now been moved from DevIl to OpenGL.

Testing the `TextureManager` requires a texture. A TIF image file, called face. tif, can be found on the CD in the Asset directory. Copy it into your project directory. Then in Visual Studio, right-click the project and choose Add > Existing Item. We're going to add the TIF file to the project. This brings up a dialog box. To see the image you will probably have to change the filter from C# Files to All Files. Select face.tif. The final step is to select the face.tif file in the solution explorer, right-click, and select Properties, as shown in Figure 6.8.

A number of fields are displayed describing the properties of the image file. Change the field Copy To Output Directory to Copy If Newer. This will copy the image file over to the bin directory, and once you run the program, the file will always be in the correct place. Adding the image file to the project isn't necessary, but it's a simple way to keep track of the assets and to make sure they are put in the right places.

The `TextureManager` object can be created in the Form.cs file and then passed into any state that requires it.

```
TextureManager _textureManager = new TextureManager();

public Form1()
{
  InitializeComponent();
  _openGLControl.InitializeContexts();

  // Init DevIl
  Il.ilInit();
  Ilu.iluInit();
  Ilut.ilutInit();
```

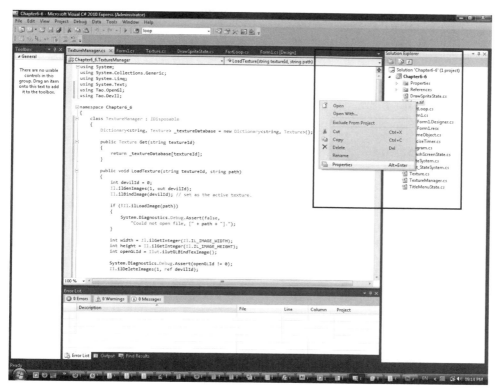

Figure 6.8
Viewing the properties of a file.

```
Ilut.ilutRenderer(Ilut.ILUT_OPENGL);

// Load textures
_textureManager.LoadTexture("face", "face.tif");


// Add all the states that will be used.
_system.AddState("splash", new SplashScreenState(_system));
_system.AddState("title_menu", new TitleMenuState());
_system.AddState("sprite_test", new DrawSpriteState());

// Select the start state
_system.ChangeState("sprite_test");
```

This setup code in the Form.cs creates the `TextureManager`, initializes the DevIL library, and then attempts to load a texture called face.tif. Run the program. If it works, that's great; you can now load textures from the disk. If it fails to run then there are a couple of things that may have gone wrong.

If you get an exception of the form `Unable to load DLL 'xx.dll': The specified module could not be found`, then xx.dll is not being found by your binary file. It should be in the bin\debug directory. Check if it's there. If it's not there then look in the Tao framework and copy it across.

If you get the exception `BadImageFormatException`, this has nothing to do with the texture you're trying to load. Instead, it's having trouble loading the DevIl libraries. The most likely reason for this is that you are developing with Visual Studio 2008 on a 64-bit system, but the libraries have been compiled for 32 bit. The easiest way to fix this is to go to the solution explorer. Right-click the project and select Properties. Click the Build tab on the left, as shown in Figure 6.9.

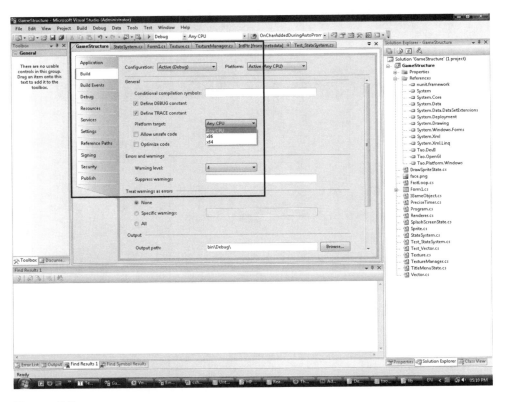

Figure 6.9
Viewing the project properties.

There is a drop-down box next to Platform Target. Choose x86; this will make the program build for 32-bit systems.

Finally, if you get an `Assertion Failed` message with the text `Could not open file, [face.tif]`, then face.tif is not in the binary directory; either copy the file into the correct location or make sure you added it to the solution correctly.

Textured Sprites

Once textures are being loaded, it's time to start using them. Texture maps are indexed from 0 to 1 on both axes. 0,0 is the top-left corner and 1,1 is the bottom right. For textures, the axes aren't called X and Y; instead, they're called U and V.

Figure 6.10 shows how the 2D U,V coordinates for each vertex are mapped on to the 3D vertex positions. It will be easier to play with the U,V mapping once texturing is working with the quad example.

Return to the `DrawSpriteState` class. A constructor that takes in a `TextureManager` needs to be created.

```
class DrawSpriteState : IGameObject
{
  TextureManager _textureManager;

  public DrawSpriteState(TextureManager textureManager)
```

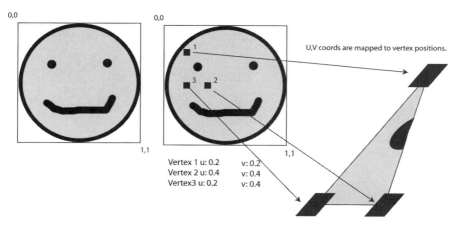

Figure 6.10
U,V mapping.

```
{
    _textureManager = textureManager;
}
```

In Form.cs, that `TextureManager` will now need to be passed in to the `Draw-SpriteState` constructor. The textures are easily accessible in the game state.

To use the texture, OpenGL needs to be told to start the texture mode, then the texture is bound as the active texture. All vertices will use the currently bound texture for their texture information. Finally, each vertex needs to have some 2D texture positions associated with it. Here it's just mapping from 0,0 to 1,1 so the full texture is used.

This code sets the texture information for the first triangle of the quad. The result can be seen in Figure 6.11.

Figure 6.11
Texture mapping half the quad.

```
Texture texture = _textureManager.Get("face");
Gl.glEnable(Gl.GL_TEXTURE_2D);
Gl.glBindTexture(Gl.GL_TEXTURE_2D, texture.Id);

Gl.glBegin(Gl.GL_TRIANGLES);
{
  Gl.glTexCoord2d(0, 0);
  Gl.glVertex3d(x - halfWidth, y + halfHeight, z); // top left
  Gl.glTexCoord2d(1, 0);
  Gl.glVertex3d(x + halfWidth, y + halfHeight, z); // top right
  Gl.glTexCoord2d(0, 1);
  Gl.glVertex3d(x - halfWidth, y - halfHeight, z); // bottom left
```

The second triangle's vertices are set in the same way.

```
Gl.glTexCoord2d(1, 0);
Gl.glVertex3d(x + halfWidth, y + halfHeight, z); // top right
Gl.glTexCoord2d(1, 1);
Gl.glVertex3d(x + halfWidth, y - halfHeight, z); // bottom right
Gl.glTexCoord2d(0, 1);
Gl.glVertex3d(x - halfWidth, y - halfHeight, z); // bottom left
```

This will now map the texture to a quad entirely. Try changing the size of the quad to see what happens.

The texture has been applied using a lot of magic numbers and these should be moved to variables according to the DRY principle. The U,V mapping for the quad can be described by two coordinates, the top-left U,V positions and the bottom-right U,V positions.

```
float topUV = 0;
float bottomUV = 1;
float leftUV = 0;
float rightUV = 1;

Gl.glBegin(Gl.GL_TRIANGLES);
{
  Gl.glTexCoord2d(leftUV, topUV);
  Gl.glVertex3d(x - halfWidth, y + halfHeight, z); // top left
  Gl.glTexCoord2d(rightUV, topUV);
  Gl.glVertex3d(x + halfWidth, y + halfHeight, z); // top right
  Gl.glTexCoord2d(leftUV, bottomUV);
```

```
    Gl.glVertex3d( x - halfWidth, y - halfHeight, z); // bottom left

    Gl.glTexCoord2d(rightUV, topUV);
    Gl.glVertex3d(x + halfWidth, y + halfHeight, z); // top right
    Gl.glTexCoord2d(rightUV, bottomUV);
    Gl.glVertex3d(x + halfWidth, y - halfHeight, z); // bottom right
    Gl.glTexCoord2d(leftUV, bottomUV);
    Gl.glVertex3d(x - halfWidth, y - halfHeight, z); // bottom left
}
Gl.glEnd();
```

It is now easy to change around the UV coordinates. Set the top left to 0,0 and the bottom right to 2,2. Then change the bottom right to −1, −1. Play around with different position for the top-left and bottom-right coordinates to see what happens.

Alpha Blending Sprites

It is very common to want to make part of a sprite transparent. There is a second sprite called face_alpha.tif available on the CD in the Assets folder. This image file has four channels, red, green, blue, and alpha. The alpha channel removes the white border around the smiley face. The face_alpha file should be added to the project in the same way as the previous texture. It then needs to be loaded into the TextureManager.

```
// Load textures
_textureManager.LoadTexture("face", "face.tif");
_textureManager.LoadTexture("face_alpha", "face_alpha.tif");
```

In the Render call of DrawSpriteState, change the line

```
Texture texture = _textureManager.Get("face");
```

to

```
Texture texture = _textureManager.Get("face_alpha");
```

Running the code now will produce exactly the same image as before. This is because OpenGL hasn't been told to deal with transparency yet. Transparency in OpenGL is achieved by blending. OpenGL blends the pixels that have already been drawn to the frame buffer with whatever pixels are about to be drawn to the frame buffer.

```
Gl.glEnable(Gl.GL_TEXTURE_2D);
Gl.glBindTexture(Gl.GL_TEXTURE_2D, texture.Id);
Gl.glEnable(Gl.GL_BLEND);
Gl.glBlendFunc(Gl.GL_SRC_ALPHA, Gl.GL_ONE_MINUS_SRC_ALPHA);
```

Blending needs to first be enabled. This can be done just underneath where the 2D texture mode was enabled. Then the `blend` function must be set. The `blend` function takes two arguments. The first argument modifies the value of the pixel to be drawn onto the frame buffer, and the second argument modifies the value of the frame buffer pixel that will be drawn over. The incoming pixel to be drawn onto the frame buffer is known also known as the "source". `GL_SRC_ALPHA` is an instruction to use the alpha of the incoming pixel. `GL_ONE_MINUS_SRC_ALPHA` is an instruction to take the alpha of the incoming pixel from one. These two instructions blend the incoming pixel onto the frame buffer using its alpha value. The `glBlendFunc` modifies the R,G,B values of the source and frame buffer pixels, after which the sum of these values is written to the frame buffer.

In all the examples given so far, the initial color of the frame buffer is black. Every pixel is of the RGBA form 0,0,0,1. The smiley face being rendered has lots of different types of pixels. The pixels in the corner areas are white but with an alpha of zero. The RGBA values are generally 1,1,1,0.

When the pixels in the corner areas of the smiley face texture are rendered, they will have an alpha value of zero. The value of one minus the source alpha is $(1 - 0)$, so, 1. The new frame buffer colors are calculated by multiplying the incoming pixels by the source alpha and then multiplying the current frame pixels by one minus the source alpha and then adding the two results together.

incomingRed * 0 + frameBufferRed * 1

incomingGreen * 0 + frameBufferGreen * 1

incomingBlue * 0 + frameBufferBlue * 1

As you can see, using this blend the incoming pixels are ignored, making the corners of the face appear transparent. The general equation is

(incomingRGB * incomingAlpha) + (framebufferRGB * (1 − incomingAlpha))

Try working through this as if the incoming alpha was 1 or 0.5. This is how OpenGL performs its blending.

Running the program will produce a face with the white backing removed.

Color Modulating Sprites

The current sprite code is quite comprehensive. It's easy to set the sprite texture, U, V mapping, position, width, and height. The final operation that is quite common with sprites is to alter the color. In many games, text can change color and images may flash yellow to attract the attention of the user. This is normally done through color modulation.

The basics of this technique have already been covered when the spinning triangle was created. Each vertex is given a color. It's easier if the sprite has one single color and then all vertices share it.

The color only needs to be set once, and then all the vertices will be set that color.

```
float red = 1;
float green = 0;
float blue = 0;
float alpha = 1;

Gl.glBegin(Gl.GL_TRIANGLES);
{
  Gl.glColor4f(red, green, blue, alpha);
```

This code will turn the sprite red. Altering the alpha will affect the entire sprite's transparency. Using this code, it's very easy to imagine how to fade something in by changing the alpha from 0 to 1 over time.

In certain cases it may be desirable to give a sprite a gradient rather than a solid color. This can be achieved by setting the bottom vertices one color and the top vertices a second color. The color will be interpolated by OpenGL and will create a gradient automatically.

A Sprite and Renderer Class

The basics of a sprite have been demonstrated, but it's all quite untidy at the moment, and very hard to reuse. All the code needs to be wrapped up into classes. The color, position, and U,V point data all need to be separated into their own classes. It would be ideal to use pre-existing C# classes for these data structures, but it's better to make our own as they will need to be tailored to work correctly with OpenGL.

The `sprite` class will contain the sprite data, but a separate `renderer` class will be responsible for rendering the sprites. Separating the functionality in this way allows the rendering code to be optimized later.

Here are the three structures.

```
[StructLayout(LayoutKind.Sequential)]
public struct Vector
{
  public double X { get; set; }
  public double Y { get; set; }
  public double Z { get; set; }

  public Vector(double x, double y, double z) : this()
  {
      X = x;
      Y = y;
      Z = z;
  }

}

[StructLayout(LayoutKind.Sequential)]
public struct Point
{
  public float X { get; set; }
  public float Y { get; set; }

  public Point(float x, float y)
   : this()
   {
   X = x;
   Y = y;
   }
}

[StructLayout(LayoutKind.Sequential)]
public struct Color
{
  public float Red { get; set; }
  public float Green { get; set; }
  public float Blue { get; set; }
```

```
public float Alpha { get; set; }

public Color(float r, float g, float b, float a)
    : this()
{
    Red   = r;
    Green = g;
    Blue  = b;
    Alpha = a;
}
}
```

Vectors are a common tool in game programming. Conceptually they are different than positions in 3D space, but they have the same X,Y,Z values. Generally vectors are used to represent positions as this makes the code simpler. The vector here doesn't have any methods; it will be fleshed out when we investigate what vectors are used for, later on.

The vector structure, and all the other structure, have metadata attached `[StructLayout(LayoutKind.Sequential)]`. This requires an additional `using` statement.

```
using System.Runtime.InteropServices;
```

This metadata informs the complier that it should layout the structures in memory the same as the C programming language would. This makes it easier to interact with OpenGL, which is written in C.

The `Point` structure will be used to describe the U,V coordinates. Double precision isn't need for the texture coordinates so a floating number is used instead. The `Color` is used to describe the colors of the vertices.

Here is the `renderer` class.

```
using Tao.OpenGl;
using System.Runtime.InteropServices;

namespace GameStructure
{
  public class Renderer
  {
    public Renderer()
```

```
    {
        Gl.glEnable(Gl.GL_TEXTURE_2D);
        Gl.glEnable(Gl.GL_BLEND);
        Gl.glBlendFunc(Gl.GL_SRC_ALPHA, Gl.GL_ONE_MINUS_SRC_ALPHA);
    }


    public void DrawImmediateModeVertex(Vector position, Color color,
Point uvs)
    {
        Gl.glColor4f(color.Red, color.Green, color.Blue, color.Alpha);
        Gl.glTexCoord2f(uvs.X, uvs.Y);
        Gl.glVertex3d(position.X, position.Y, position.Z);
    }


    public void DrawSprite(Sprite sprite)
    {
        Gl.glBegin(Gl.GL_TRIANGLES);
    {
        for (int i = 0; i < Sprite.VertexAmount; i++)
        {
            Gl.glBindTexture(Gl.GL_TEXTURE_2D, sprite.Texture.Id);
            DrawImmediateModeVertex(
                sprite.VertexPositions[i],
                sprite.VertexColors[i],
                sprite.VertexUVs[i]);
        }
    }
        Gl.glEnd();
    }
  }
}
```

In the constructor, the Renderer sets up the relevant texture and blend modes. These operations are now done once on start up rather than every frame as before. The DrawSprite function is responsible for taking a sprite and rendering it. All the OpenGL calls are the same as before; there is one to set the texture and then one for the color, texture, U,Vs, and position.

This leaves the sprite class itself. A lot of the functions can be inferred from its use in the renderer. Games generally have a lot of sprites so it's important to make the class as lightweight as possible and only include the most essential members.

```csharp
public class Sprite
{
  internal const int VertexAmount = 6;
  Vector[]  _vertexPositions  = new Vector[VertexAmount];
  Color[]   _vertexColors   = new Color[VertexAmount];
  Point[]   _vertexUVs  = new Point[VertexAmount];
  Texture _texture = new Texture();

  public Sprite()
  {
     InitVertexPositions(new Vector(0,0,0), 1, 1);
     SetColor(new Color(1,1,1,1));
     SetUVs(new Point(0, 0), new Point(1, 1));
  }

  public Texture Texture
  {
     get { return _texture; }
     set
     {
       _texture = value;
       // By default the width and height is set
       // to that of the texture
       InitVertexPositions(GetCenter(), _texture.Width, _texture.
Height);
     }
  }

  public Vector[] VertexPositions
  {
     get { return _vertexPositions; }
  }

  public Color[] VertexColors
  {
     get { return _vertexColors; }
  }
  public Point[] VertexUVs
  {
  get { return _vertexUVs; }
  }
```

```
  private Vector GetCenter()
  {
    double halfWidth  = GetWidth() / 2;
    double halfHeight   = GetHeight() / 2;


  return new Vector(
    _vertexPositions[0].X + halfWidth,
    _vertexPositions[0].Y - halfHeight,
    _vertexPositions[0].Z);
  }

  private void InitVertexPositions(Vector position, double width, double
height)
  {
    double halfWidth  = width / 2;
    double halfHeight   = height / 2;
    // Clockwise creation of two triangles to make a quad.

    // TopLeft, TopRight, BottomLeft
    _vertexPositions[0] = new Vector(position.X - halfWidth, position.Y +
halfHeight, position.Z);
    _vertexPositions[1] = new Vector(position.X + halfWidth, position.Y +
halfHeight, position.Z);
    _vertexPositions[2] = new Vector(position.X - halfWidth, position.Y -
halfHeight, position.Z);

    // TopRight, BottomRight, BottomLeft
    _vertexPositions[3] = new Vector(position.X + halfWidth, position.Y +
halfHeight, position.Z);
    _vertexPositions[4] = new Vector(position.X + halfWidth, position.Y -
halfHeight, position.Z);
    _vertexPositions[5] = new Vector(position.X - halfWidth, position.Y -
halfHeight, position.Z);
  }

  public double GetWidth()
  {
    // topright - topleft
    return _vertexPositions[1].X - _vertexPositions[0].X;
  }
```

```
public double GetHeight()
{
  // topleft - bottomleft
  return _vertexPositions[0].Y - _vertexPositions[2].Y;
}

public void SetWidth(float width)
{
  InitVertexPositions(GetCenter(), width, GetHeight());
}

public void SetHeight(float height)
{
  InitVertexPositions(GetCenter(), GetWidth(), height);
}

public void SetPosition(double x, double y)
{
SetPosition(new Vector(x, y, 0));
}

public void SetPosition(Vector position)
{
  InitVertexPositions(position, GetWidth(), GetHeight());
}

public void SetColor(Color color)
{
  for (int i = 0; i < Sprite.VertexAmount; i++)
{
  _vertexColors[i] = color;
}
}

public void SetUVs(Point topLeft, Point bottomRight)
{
  // TopLeft, TopRight, BottomLeft
  _vertexUVs[0] = topLeft;
  _vertexUVs[1] = new Point(bottomRight.X, topLeft.Y);
  _vertexUVs[2] = new Point(topLeft.X, bottomRight.Y);

  // TopRight, BottomRight, BottomLeft
```

```
  _vertexUVs[3] = new Point(bottomRight.X, topLeft.Y);
  _vertexUVs[4] = bottomRight;
  _vertexUVs[5] = new Point(topLeft.X, bottomRight.Y);


  }
}
```

The `sprite` class is quite large, mainly due to accessor functions and some overloaded functions. The sprite has a default constructor; it creates a sprite of size 1 by 1 with an empty texture. Once a texture is set, the width and height of the sprite is automatically set to the texture values. Once the sprite is created, the position, dimension, textures, and U,Vs can all be changed as needed.

Using the Sprite Class

With sprite code packaged into a class, it's now time to demonstrate how to use it. Create a new game state called `TestSpriteClassState`, load it into the state system, and make it the default state to run when the program executes. `TestSpriteClassState` will need to take the `TextureManager` in to its constructor like the `DrawSpriteState` did.

```
Renderer _renderer = new Renderer();
TextureManager _textureManager;
Sprite _testSprite = new Sprite();
Sprite _testSprite2 = new Sprite();

public TestSpriteClassState(TextureManager textureManager)
{
  _textureManager = textureManager;
  _testSprite.Texture = _textureManager.Get("face_alpha");
  _testSprite.SetHeight(256*0.5f);

  _testSprite2.Texture = _textureManager.Get("face_alpha");
  _testSprite2.SetPosition(-256, -256);
  _testSprite2.SetColor(new Color(1, 0, 0, 1));

}
public void Render()
{
  Gl.glClearColor(0.0f, 0.0f, 0.0f, 1.0f);
  Gl.glClear(Gl.GL_COLOR_BUFFER_BIT);
  _renderer.DrawSprite(_testSprite);
```

```
  _renderer.DrawSprite(_testSprite2);
  Gl.glFinish();
}
```

This state renders two different sprites: one is squashed; the other is offset from the center of the screen and colored red. The code is very straightforward and easy to use. All the heavy lifting has been done in the `Sprite` and `Renderer` classes. These classes are only written once but used everywhere, so it's worth making them as friendly and easy to use as possible.

It's very easy to animate these sprites by changing the U,Vs or changing the texture as time passes. The positions can also be easily changed with time. This should be done in the update loop. Feel free to dive in right now and see what you can make. If you're a little unsure where to start, then keep reading and the concepts will become apparent as you're guided through the creation of a game.

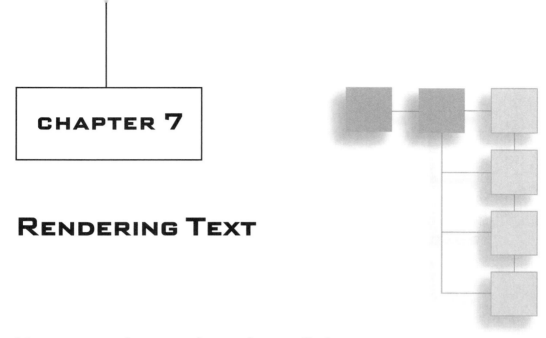

CHAPTER 7

RENDERING TEXT

Most games need text—at the very least to display a score or menu.

Text rendering is also very useful for rendering out variable values as the game is running. A basic font system can be made very simply; each letter and number is represented as a sprite. Then a string of text is translated into a list of sprites. This method is easy to extend to any language, though Asian languages such as Chinese will need a larger number of textures to account for all the different glyphs.

Font Textures

Figure 7.1 is a texture with the entire Roman alphabet, numbers, and some punctuation marks. This is a great base to use to draw text. Such textures are easy to create if the correct tools are used. An excellent tool for bitmap fonts is Andreas Jönsson's Bitmap Font Generator, which is freely available on the internet and is also included on the CD in Apps folder. It can take a True Type font and generate a bitmap suitable for efficient rendering in a game. This is how the texture shown in Figure 7.1 was created. The font texture can be found on the CD in the Assets folder along with a data file that describes the U,V coordinates of the glyphs in the texture.

To display this font, I've created a new project with a new game state called `TextTestState`. I've added the font texture to the project as font.tga (you can find this on the CD in the Assets folder); this has also been loaded into the

Figure 7.1
A font texture.

texture manager using the id `font`. Create a new sprite, set the new `font` texture as the texture, and render the font in the render loop.

```
class TextTestState : IGameObject
{
  Sprite _text = new Sprite();
  Renderer _renderer = new Renderer();
  public TextTestState(TextureManager textureManager)
  {
    _text.Texture = textureManager.Get("font");
  }
  public void Render()
  {
    Gl.glClearColor(0.0f, 0.0f, 0.0f, 1.0f);
    Gl.glClear(Gl.GL_COLOR_BUFFER_BIT);
    _renderer.DrawSprite(_text);
  }
  public void Update(double elapsedTime)
  {
  }
}
```

This displays the entire font in white on black. Change the clear color to confirm that the transparency is working correctly. Then uncomment the line with SetColor in it. This will turn the font black. It's easy to change the font color using the sprite code.

To render a single character, the sprite must have its UV settings altered. Try entering the following UV information.

```
_text.Texture = textureManager.Get("font");
_text.SetUVs(new Point(0.113f, 0), new Point(0.171f, 0.101f));
```

This will display a giant dollar sign. It will be very large because the sprite size is still set to 256 by 256. The natural resolution of the dollar sign is 15 by 26 pixels. Change the height and width and something like Figure 7.2 will appear.

```
_text.SetUVs(new Point(0.113f, 0), new Point(0.171f, 0.101f));
_text.SetWidth(15);
_text.SetHeight(26);
```

This UV data forms a small box around the dollar sign and allows it to be clearly cut out, as shown in Figure 7.3. The information about the location of each character in the texture map was generated by the Bitmap Font Program when the texture was generated. This information can be used to get the correct UVs.

Figure 7.2
A single character.

Figure 7.3
The UV information of a single character.

Font Data

The font data is a simple text file that is used to identify all the characters in the texture. It is supplied on the CD and should be added to the font project in the same way the texture was added. Remember to set its properties to ensure it's copied to the build directory. Here are the first few lines of the data file.

```
info face="Courier New" size=-32 bold=1 italic=0 charset="" unicode=1
stretchH=100 smooth=1 aa=1 padding=0,0,0,0 spacing=1,1 outline=0
common lineHeight=36 base=26 scaleW=256 scaleH=256 pages=1 packed=0
alphaChnl=0 redChnl=0 greenChnl=0 blueChnl=0
page id=0 file="font_0.tga"
chars count=95
char id=32  x=253  y=21  width=1  height=1   xoffset=0  yoffset=26
xadvance=19  page=0 chnl=15
char id=33  x=247  y=21  width=5  height=20  xoffset=7  yoffset=6
xadvance=19  page=0 chnl=15
char id=34  x=136  y=101 width=9  height=9   xoffset=4
```

The first three lines are header information and can be ignored. They contain information describing the font—that its size is 32 and its type is Courier New. This is all information our font system doesn't need to know.

The fourth line is how many characters are contained in the font file; in this case there are 95 characters. After this line you see information about every character, its pixel position in the texture, and its pixel width and height.

xoffset and yoffset are used to align the characters when rendered one after another in a word. The "y" character has a larger yoffset than an "l" character. The `xadvance` parameter represents the amount to advance on the x axis once the current character has been rendered. The `page` value is an index to a texture that contains the current character. We'll only be using fonts that have a single texture so the `page` value can be safely ignored. The channel information can also be ignored; it is sometimes used for a compression technique where different characters are written into the different color channels.

The characters need to be read into a suitable class.

```
public class CharacterData
{
  public int Id { get; set; }
  public int X { get; set; }
  public int Y { get; set; }
  public int Width { get; set; }
  public int Height { get; set; }
  public int XOffset { get; set; }
  public int YOffset { get; set; }
  public int XAdvance { get; set; }
}
```

This `CharacterData` class is a simple collection of parameters that we're interested in. One of these objects will be made per character in the data file.

Parsing the Font Data

The `CharacterData` class will be stored in a dictionary. The key to the dictionary will be the character they represent, as the following code shows.

```
CharacterData aData = _characterDictionary['a'];
```

Given a string, it's easy to iterate through all the characters and get the relevant character data for each one. To fill this dictionary from the data file, a parser is needed. Here's the code for a simple parser; when given a path to a font data file, it will return a dictionary filled with character data.

```
public class FontParser
{
  static int HeaderSize = 4;
  // Gets the value after an equal sign and converts it
```

```csharp
  // from a string to an integer
  private static int GetValue(string s)
  {
    string value = s.Substring(s.IndexOf('=') + 1);
    return int.Parse(value);
  }
  public static Dictionary<char, CharacterData> Parse(string filePath)
  {
    Dictionary<char, CharacterData> charDictionary = new
Dictionary<char, CharacterData>();
    string[] lines = File.ReadAllLines(filePath);
    for(int i = HeaderSize; i < lines.Length; i+=1)
    {
      string firstLine = lines[i];
      string[] typesAndValues = firstLine.Split(" ".ToCharArray(),
        StringSplitOptions.RemoveEmptyEntries);
      // All the data comes in a certain order,
      // used to make the parser shorter
      CharacterData charData = new CharacterData
      {
        Id = GetValue(typesAndValues[1]),
        X = GetValue(typesAndValues[2]),
        Y = GetValue(typesAndValues[3]),
        Width = GetValue(typesAndValues[4]),
        Height = GetValue(typesAndValues[5]),
        XOffset = GetValue(typesAndValues[6]),
        YOffset = GetValue(typesAndValues[7]),
        XAdvance = GetValue(typesAndValues[8])
      };
      charDictionary.Add((char)charData.Id, charData);
    }
    return charDictionary;
  }
}
```

This parser is very simple and doesn't do any error checking or validation. It requires the using System.IO statement to allow text files to be read from the disk. Each CharacterData structure is filled up and then its Id is cast to a character to use as the index. The Id is the ASCII number representing the character; casting the number to C#'s char type will convert it to the correct character.

Using the CharacterData

Here is a high-level look at how the text system will work. A new state has been created that shows the font system in action.

```
class TextRenderState : IGameObject
{
  TextureManager _textureManager;
  Font _font;
  Text _helloWorld;
  Renderer _renderer = new Renderer();
  public TextRenderState(TextureManager textureManager)
  {
    _textureManager = textureManager;
    _font = new Font(textureManager.Get("font"),
      FontParser.Parse("font.fnt"));
    _helloWorld = new Text("Hello", _font);
  }
  public void Render()
  {
    Gl.glClearColor(0.0f, 0.0f, 0.0f, 1.0f);
    Gl.glClear(Gl.GL_COLOR_BUFFER_BIT);
    _renderer.DrawText(_helloWorld);
  }
  public void Update(double elapsedTime)
  {
  }
}
```

There are two new classes in use here. First is a `Font` class, which determines what font will be used. The `Font` class contains a reference to the font texture and the character data. The second class is the `Text` class that is used to render text. Several different fonts could be loaded in and it would be very easy to swap between them.

The `Renderer` has been given an extra method called `DrawText`. `DrawText` takes a text object and uses it to render text. The text class will just be a collection of sprites so the renderer can reuse its `DrawSprite` code.

There is another class that isn't in the example; it's a class to represent the individual characters in the bitmap text string. It's called the `CharacterSprite` class and has only two members: one is the sprite representing the letter and one is a `CharacterData` class that has information about the character and how the sprite will be used.

```
public class CharacterSprite
{
  public Sprite Sprite {get; set;}
  public CharacterData Data { get; set; }
  public CharacterSprite(Sprite sprite, CharacterData data)
  {
    Data = data;
    Sprite = sprite;
  }
}
```

The `Text` class is a list of `CharacterSprites`. It is also responsible for ordering the letters. Given a simple text string, it creates a `CharacterSprite` for each character and orders them one after the other. It also handles the correct offsets. Here is the code.

```
public class Text
{
  Font _font;
  List<CharacterSprite> _bitmapText = new List<CharacterSprite>();
  string _text;
  public List<CharacterSprite> CharacterSprites
  {
    get { return _bitmapText; }
  }
  public Text(string text, Font font)
  {
    _text = text;
    _font = font;
    CreateText(0, 0);
  }
  private void CreateText(double x, double y)
  {
    _bitmapText.Clear();
    double currentX = x;
    double currentY = y;
    foreach (char c in _text)
    {
      CharacterSprite sprite = _font.CreateSprite(c);
```

```
        float xOffset = ((float)sprite.Data.XOffset) / 2;
        float yOffset = ((float)sprite.Data.YOffset) / 2;
        sprite.Sprite.SetPosition(currentX + xOffset, currentY - yOffset);
        currentX += sprite.Data.XAdvance;
        _bitmapText.Add(sprite);
      }
    }
}
```

The class is quite straightforward. The CreateText function is the heart of the class; it positions the character sprites correctly. For each sprite, the CharacterData is checked and the x position is advanced by the amount specified. Each character sprite also has an offset. All sprites are positioned around their center, but the offset values are taken from the top left. To convert this offset to a central position, the offset values are halved. As the offsets are integers, they need to be converted to floating point numbers before being divided. If the numbers aren't cast to floats, then the floating point information is thrown away and the text letters won't be aligned correctly.

The final class to consider is the Font class. The Font class holds the dictionary that translates a character into a CharacterData object. Given a word or sentence, all the letters can be used to index the dictionary and a set CharacterData will be returned, ready to be used to create text sprites.

```
public class Font
{
  Texture _texture;
  Dictionary<char, CharacterData> _characterData;
  public Font(Texture texture, Dictionary<char, CharacterData>
characterData)
  {
    _texture = texture;
    _characterData = characterData;
  }
  public CharacterSprite CreateSprite(char c)
  {
    CharacterData charData = _characterData[c];
    Sprite sprite = new Sprite();
    sprite.Texture = _texture;
    // Setup UVs
    Point topLeft = new Point((float)charData.X / (float)_texture.Width,
```

```
                    (float)charData.Y / (float)_texture.Height);
   Point bottomRight = new Point( topLeft.X + ((float)charData.Width /
(float)_texture.Width),
                                topLeft.Y +((float)charData.Height /
(float)_texture.Height));
   sprite.SetUVs(topLeft, bottomRight);
   sprite.SetWidth(charData.Width);
   sprite.SetHeight(charData.Height);
   sprite.SetColor(new Color(1, 1, 1, 1));

   return new CharacterSprite(sprite, charData);
   }
}
```

The U,V coordinates are provided in pixels, but OpenGL textures are indexed from 0 to 1. Pixels values are converted to OpenGL coordinates by dividing the x and y pixel coordinates by the width and height of the texture. The `CharacterData` numbers are all stored as integers and need to be cast to floats to get a result with decimal places when dividing. The height and width of the sprite is set using the `CharacterData` information, and the color is set to white as a default. Once the sprite is created, it is made into a `CharacterSprite` and returned.

Rendering Text

The font code is now usable. An immediate use for text is an fps, frames per second, display. The fps will indicate how fast the game code is running. Frames per second is a measure of how often the game loop is executed per second. Modern games aim for a frame-rate of 30 or 60 frames per second. The number of frames per second is not the only factor contributing to smooth graphics; the consistency of the frame-rate is also important. A game that hovers around 60 fps but sometimes drops to 30 fps will appear more choppy than one that runs consistently at 30 fps.

Create and add a new game state to the project. I've chosen `FPSTestState` but the name doesn't really matter. Make sure it's added to the `StateSystem` and is the first state loaded by default. The state requires the `TextureManager` to be passed in to the constructor to create the font object. Here is the code to render some text:

```
class FPSTestState : IGameObject
{
```

```
TextureManager _textureManager;
Font _font;
Text _fpsText;
Renderer _renderer = new Renderer();
public FPSTestState(TextureManager textureManager)
{
  _textureManager = textureManager;
  _font = new Font(textureManager.Get("font"),
    FontParser.Parse("font.fnt"));
  _fpsText = new Text("FPS:", _font);
}
#region IGameObject Members
public void Render()
{
  Gl.glClearColor(0.0f, 0.0f, 0.0f, 1.0f);
  Gl.glClear(Gl.GL_COLOR_BUFFER_BIT);
  _renderer.DrawText(_fpsText);
}
public void Update(double elapsedTime)
{
}
#endregion
}
```

Before the code can be tested, the DrawText call for the Renderer needs to be written. This will draw the text to the middle of the screen, which is fine for now. The DrawText method goes through the text and draws each sprite.

```
public void DrawText(Text text)
{
  foreach (CharacterSprite c in text.CharacterSprites)
  {
    DrawSprite(c.Sprite);
  }
}
```

Once this is added to the renderer, running the code will render the text "FPS:" to the screen, as can be seen in Figure 7.4.

Calculating the FPS

The frames per second is simple to calculate. The number of frames in a second need to be counted; then this number needs to be displayed to the screen. The

Figure 7.4
The text FPS being rendered.

higher the frame count, the faster your game is running. FPS is a useful statistic to have on screen because as you develop your game it's easy to notice if, after adding a feature, the fps has suddenly dropped. Silly mistakes can be caught early and avoided.

To count the number of frames each time the game loops, a _numberOf-Frames variable can be increased by one. The elapsedTime in the update loop tells us how long each frame took; if all these elapsedTime values are summed, how much time has passed can be measured. Once a second has passed, then the _numberOfFrames is the number of frames that were rendered during that second. This can easily be wrapped up in a class, as shown here.

```
public class FramesPerSecond
{
    int _numberOfFrames = 0;
    double _timePassed = 0;
    public double CurrentFPS { get; set; }
    public void Process(double timeElapsed)
    {
        _numberOfFrames++;
        _timePassed = _timePassed + timeElapsed;
        if (_timePassed > 1)
```

```
    {
      CurrentFPS = (double)_numberOfFrames / _timePassed;
      _timePassed = 0;
      _numberOfFrames = 0;
    }
  }
}
```

This class calculates the frames per second. Its process method must be called every frame. Add `FramesPerSecond` to the `FPSTestState` so we can render this value to the screen using the `Text` class.

```
class FPSTestState : IGameObject
{
  TextureManager _textureManager;
  Font _font;
  Text _fpsText;
  Renderer _renderer = new Renderer();
  FramesPerSecond _fps = new FramesPerSecond();
  // Constructor and Render have been ommitted.
  public void Update(double elapsedTime)
  {
    _fps.Process(elapsedTime);
  }
}
```

When the state is run, the fps is now recorded. Generally, the `FramesPerSecond` class would not exist in a game state; instead, it probably would be in the `Form` class. In this case, it's easier to test in the `FPSTestState`.

```
public void Render()
{
  Gl.glClearColor(0.0f, 0.0f, 0.0f, 1.0f);
  Gl.glClear(Gl.GL_COLOR_BUFFER_BIT);
  _fpsText = new Text("FPS: " + _fps.CurrentFPS.ToString("00.0"), _font);
  _renderer.DrawText(_fpsText);
}
```

The render loop renders the text "FPS:" followed by the fps value converted to a string. The `ToString` method is given some formatting information. This causes the double that represents the fps to only have one decimal place when in string form and to have two or more digits before the decimal point.

Run the program and see what your frame-rate is. Frame-rates differ wildly from computer to computer. There's not very much going on in the program, so the frame-rate is going be quite high. Figure 7.5 shows the output when running the program.

Initially the frame-rate displayed on my computer was about 60 frames per second. This was because I had V-Sync turned on under my display settings. Turning V-Sync off will give a better indication of the frames per second.

V-Sync and Frame-Rate

V-Sync is short for vertical synchronization. The computer screen refreshes a certain number of times a second. V-Sync is an option that ensures that the frame buffer is filled only as fast as the screen can read it. This prevents artifacts like tearing, where the frame buffer changes as the data is being written to the screen causing a visual tearing effect.

On some cards, V-Sync is turned on by default. V-Sync is the refresh rate of the monitor (how often the monitor updates its display). If your monitor refreshes at 60Hz and V-Sync is on, then your fps counter will never exceed 60fps. This is fine most of time, but when developing a game and profiling the frame-rate, it's important to not have the frame-rate locked. It can usually be turned off through

Figure 7.5
An fps counter.

the video card settings, but the exact method for disabling V-Sync differs from card to card.

Profiling

The fps counter can be used for some basic profiling. The game is currently rendering about ten textured quads with color information (the fps text). A 2D game might use a quad per tile and quads for the player and game enemies. Let's be very generous and assume many particle systems, say, 10,000 quads. That's a lot of quads to be on screen at one time and should be okay for most games. A rough test can be done to see if the current sprite can handle this many quads.

```
renderer.DrawText(_fpsText);
for (int i = 0; i < 1000; i++)
{
  _renderer.DrawText(_fpsText);
}
```

This renders the fps text 1,000 times. That's about 10,000 quads total. On my computer, the fps goes from 1,000 plus to just over 30. Thirty is fine for most 2D games. This means most 2D games will probably be fine with the current efficiency of the sprite code. Computers with older graphics cards may not fair so well, so some efficiency measures will be covered toward the end of this chapter.

Refining the Text Class

The text class is quite functional now, but it could do with some more methods that will make it easier to use. For instance, there is no way to set the position of a text string. There really needs to be a way to measure the text so it can be aligned. Also, text often needs to be constrained to columns. This can be achieved by giving the text a maximum width. If the text overflows this width, it will be wrapped on the next line. This is a very desirable feature, especially when filling a text box in a game.

Here's the helper method to set the Text position.

```
public void SetPosition(double x, double y)
{
  CreateText(x, y);
}
```

To reposition the text, the quads are simply recalculated. This isn't the most optimal way, but it's very simple to code and highly unlikely to ever cause a bottleneck in game programming.

A function to alter the color of the entire text would also make things more convenient.

```
public void SetColor (Color color)
{
  _color = color;
  foreach (CharacterSprite s in _bitmapText)
  {
    s.Sprite.SetColor(color);
  }
}
```

In this snippet, the Text has a color member; this stores this current color of the text. When CreateText is called, all the vertices are remade including the color component. With the current color stored in the text class, the vertices can be remade maintaining the Text color. An overloaded SetColor function is added (doesn't require a color parameter) for use in the CreateText function.

```
public void SetColor()
{
  foreach (CharacterSprite s in _bitmapText)
  {
    s.Sprite.SetColor(_color);
  }
}
```

At the end of the CreateText function, an extra line needs to be added

```
SetColor();
```

The width and height of the text is very important when trying to align text on the screen; therefore, a way to measure a text string in pixels would be useful. A MeasureText method in the Font class will give this functionality.

```
public Vector MeasureFont (string text)
{
  return MeasureFont (text, -1);
}
```

```
public Vector MeasureFont (string text, double maxWidth)
{
  Vector dimensions = new Vector();
  foreach (char c in text)
  {
    CharacterData data = _characterData[c];
    dimensions.X += data.XAdvance;
    dimensions.Y = Math.Max(dimensions.Y, data.Height + data.YOffset);
  }
  return dimensions;
}
```

There are two MeasureFont methods: the first method is an overload that doesn't require a maximum width parameter, and the second is where all the measurement happens.

A vector is returned containing the width and height as the X and Y values. The Z component isn't used. It's returned as a vector, rather than some other data structure such as PointF because vectors store doubles and that's how position is stored. The width and height is going to be mostly used to alter the position of other pieces of text or sprites; doubles mean no casting needs to be done. Vectors are also easy to scale and transform.

The text is measured by iterating through the character data and adding up the X advance to get the width for the entire string. The height of the string is the height of the tallest character.

Rather than calculate the width and height every time they are needed, it's more convenient to store these dimensions in the Text class.

```
public class Text
{
  Font _font;
  List<CharacterSprite> _bitmapText = new List<CharacterSprite>();
  string _text;
  Vector _dimensions;
  public double Width
  {
    get { return _dimensions.X; }
  }
  public double Height
  {
```

```
      get { return _dimensions.Y; }
   }
}
```

The dimension member needs to be updated every time the text is changed. There is only one place in the code where the text gets changed: the `CreateText` method.

```
private void CreateText(double x, double y)
{
  _bitmapText.Clear();
  double currentX = x;
  double currentY = y;
  foreach (char c in _text)
  {
    CharacterSprite sprite = _font.CreateSprite(c);
    float xOffset = ((float)sprite.Data.XOffset) / 2;
    float yOffset = ((float)sprite.Data.YOffset) / 2;
    sprite.Sprite.SetPosition(currentX + xOffset, currentY - yOffset);
    currentX += sprite.Data.XAdvance;
    _bitmapText.Add(sprite);
  }
  _dimensions = _font.MeasureFont(_text);
  SetColor();
}
```

One more line is added at the end to measure the size of the string. To confirm this works, try centering the fps text, or render the fps text twice in a row, or twice in a column.

The final functionality to be added to the text class is the ability to set a max width. This will cause very long sentences to be wrapped onto a new line. This is very useful when attempting to keep text in a textbox or ensuring text doesn't go off the edge of the screen. Try to work through what the algorithm would need to do to format text with a max width.

- Split the text into words.

- Get the next word in the text.

- Measure the length of the word.

- If the current length is greater than the max width, start a new line.

The Text class needs to redefine the CreateText method to handle a maximum width parameter.

```
private void CreateText(double x, double y)
{
 CreateText(x, y, _maxWidth);
}
private void CreateText(double x, double y, double maxWidth)
{
  _bitmapText.Clear();
  double currentX = 0;
  double currentY = 0;
  string[] words = _text.Split(' ');
  foreach (string word in words)
  {
    Vector nextWordLength = _font.MeasureFont(word);
    if (maxWidth != -1 &&
      (currentX + nextWordLength.X) > maxWidth)
    {
      currentX = 0;
      currentY += nextWordLength.Y;
    }
    string wordWithSpace = word + " "; // add the space character that was
removed.
    foreach (char c in wordWithSpace)
    {
      CharacterSprite sprite = _font.CreateSprite(c);
      float xOffset = ((float)sprite.Data.XOffset) / 2;
      float yOffset = (((float)sprite.Data.Height) * 0.5f) + ((float)
sprite.Data.YOffset);
      sprite.Sprite.SetPosition(x + currentX + xOffset, y - currentY -
yOffset);
      currentX += sprite.Data.XAdvance;
      _bitmapText.Add(sprite);
    }
  }
  _dimensions = _font.MeasureFont(_text, _maxWidth);
  _dimensions.Y = currentY;
  SetColor(_color);
}
```

This code relies on a _maxWidth member. If _maxWidth equals −1 then no wrapping is done. Otherwise, the text is wrapped for the number of pixels specified in the _maxWidth value. Here's an extra constructor that will take in a maximum width.

```
int _maxWidth = -1;
public Text(string text, Font font) : this(text, font, -1) { }
public Text(string text, Font font, int maxWidth)
{
  _text = text;
  _font = font;
  _maxWidth = maxWidth;
  CreateText(0, 0, _maxWidth);
}
```

Figure 7.6 shows text being wrapped using the new maxWidth parameter. It's generated with the following piece of code.

```
Text longText = new Text("The quick brown fox jumps over the lazy dog",
  _font, 400);
_renderer.DrawText(longText);
```

This word wrapping code doesn't take account of new line characters or tab characters, but it wouldn't be hard to extend it.

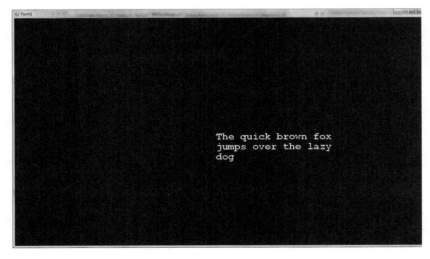

Figure 7.6
Wrapping text.

All the basic functionality to make the text class very usable has now been added. Another good feature to add would be a scale; this would scale the text up and down by a given amount.

```
longText.SetScale(0.5); // this would halve the text size
```

The `MeasureText` method could also be extended to take in a `maxWidth` parameter. This way even if text is wrapped the width and height can be correctly calculated.

Faster Rendering with glDrawArrays

Basic profiling using the frames per second count has shown that for 2D games, the current code isn't that bad. But with only small changes, the performance can be vastly improved.

```
public void DrawSprite(Sprite sprite)
{
  Gl.glBegin(Gl.GL_TRIANGLES);
  {
    for (int i = 0; i < Sprite.VertexAmount; i++)
    {
      Gl.glBindTexture(Gl.GL_TEXTURE_2D, sprite.Texture.Id);
      DrawImmediateModeVertex(
        sprite.VertexPositions[i],
        sprite.VertexColors[i],
        sprite.VertexUVs[i]);
    }
  }
  Gl.glEnd();
}
```

This is the current render code. It is executed once for each sprite. The problem with the above code is that every time `glEnd` is called, everything is sent to the graphics card and then the CPU stops; it does nothing until the graphics card sends back a message saying it received all the vertices. With 10,000 sprites, that mounts up to a lot of waiting. The more draw calls, the slower the game will run.

The solution to this problem is to draw as much as possible at once. Generally, this is known as batching. Instead of the CPU talking to the GPU like "Draw this, now draw this sprite, now draw this sprite," it instead makes a list of all the sprites and says to the GPU, "Draw all these sprites." There is a lot less waiting so the code is a lot faster. With the way the code is laid out, only a few changes need to be made to get this performance increase.

A new class is needed to collect all the vertex information before sending it to the graphics card. A good name for this class is `Batch`. The `Batch` will take the sprites and pack all the vertex information together in some big arrays. It then gives OpenGL pointers to these arrays and sends a draw command. This new class will use the Tao framework so remember to include the proper `using` statements.

```
public class Batch
{
  const int MaxVertexNumber  = 1000;
  Vector[] _vertexPositions  = new Vector[MaxVertexNumber];
  Color[] _vertexColors      = new Color[MaxVertexNumber];
  Point[] _vertexUVs         = new Point[MaxVertexNumber];
  int _batchSize = 0;
  public void AddSprite(Sprite sprite)
  {
    // If the batch is full, draw it, empty and start again.
    if (sprite.VertexPositions.Length + _batchSize > MaxVertexNumber)
    {
      Draw();
    }
    // Add the current sprite vertices to the batch.
    for (int i = 0; i < sprite.VertexPositions.Length; i++)
    {
      _vertexPositions[_batchSize + i]  = sprite.VertexPositions[i];
      _vertexColors[_batchSize + i]     = sprite.VertexColors[i];
      _vertexUVs[_batchSize + i]        = sprite.VertexUVs[i];
    }
    _batchSize += sprite.VertexPositions.Length;
  }
}
```

The max vertex number is how big a batch is allowed to get before it tells OpenGL to render all the vertices it has. The next members are the arrays that describe all the vertex information: its position, color, and U,V coordinates. The `_batchSize` member tracks how big the batch is becoming. This information needs to be passed on to OpenGL to draw the arrays. It's also compared with the max vertex number to decide when to draw the batch.

The batch collects `Sprites` and the function it uses to do this is `AddSprite`. `AddSprite` first checks if adding this sprite will make the batch too big. If that's the case, it forces the current batch to be drawn and emptied. The sprite vertex information is then iterated through and added to the batch arrays.

Two more functions handle the drawing of the batch.

```
const int VertexDimensions = 3;
const int ColorDimensions = 4;
const int UVDimensions = 2;
void SetupPointers()
{
  Gl.glEnableClientState(Gl.GL_COLOR_ARRAY);
  Gl.glEnableClientState(Gl.GL_VERTEX_ARRAY);
  Gl.glEnableClientState(Gl.GL_TEXTURE_COORD_ARRAY);
  Gl.glVertexPointer(VertexDimensions, Gl.GL_DOUBLE, 0,
_vertexPositions);
  Gl.glColorPointer(ColorDimensions, Gl.GL_FLOAT, 0, _vertexColors);
  Gl.glTexCoordPointer(UVDimensions, Gl.GL_FLOAT, 0, _vertexUVs);
}
public void Draw()
{
  if (_batchSize == 0)
  {
    return;
  }
  SetupPointers();
  Gl.glDrawArrays(Gl.GL_TRIANGLES, 0, _batchSize);
  _batchSize = 0;
}
```

The `Draw` function is the more important of the two here. If the batch is empty, the `Draw` function does nothing. Otherwise, it calls the `SetupPointers` function. `SetupPointers` first describes the vertex format using `glEnableClient-State`. In this case, the vertex described has color, position, and U,V information. Once this is done, OpenGL is told where this information exists using the `glPointer` calls.

All `glPointer` calls are of the same general format. The first argument is the number of elements. The `glVertexPointer` controls the position and has three elements; one each for X, Y, and Z. Texture is defined with two elements, one for U and one for V. Color is defined by four elements: red, green, blue, and alpha. These pointers will be used by OpenGL to fetch the graphics information that it's going to render.

The pointers need to point to the memory address at the start of each of the arrays. The memory from that point on will be read sequentially. It then uses the dimension information to decide when to stop reading the memory. This is why the `Vector`, `Color`, and `Point` structures each have the `[StructLayout (LayoutKind.Sequential)]` attribute in their definitions. The order of their members is very important; swap them around and the rendering won't work as expected.

To tell OpenGL to read from these pointers and render the data, the execution is returned to the `Draw` method. The `glDrawArrays` method is called; this takes in a type, a stride, and the number of vertices to draw. The type is `GL_TRIAN-GLES`, as each sprite is made from two triangles and this is how the vertex information should be interpreted. The stride is zero. The stride is how much memory to skip after reading each vertex. Sometimes for efficiency reasons different vertex information is all packed together in one continuous stretch of memory. The stride ensures the irrelevant bits can be skipped over. In the batch, all the data is relevant so no stride is needed. The final argument is how many vertices are to be rendered; this information has been recorded in the `_batch-Size` member.

The final command in `Draw` is to reset the `_batchSize`. The data in the arrays doesn't need to be emptied as none of it will be drawn without overwriting it with new sprite data.

Modifying the Renderer

Batched drawing has a little more setup than using `glBegin` and `glEnd`, but it's not that much more complicated. The final task is to replace the old `glBegin`, `glEnd` rendering in the `Renderer` with the new batch method.

```
class Renderer
{
  Batch _batch = new Batch();
  public void DrawSprite(Sprite sprite)
  {
    _batch.AddSprite(sprite);
  }
```

```
public void Render()
{
    _batch.Draw();
}
}
```

Converting the renderer class is very simple: a `Batch` object is added as a member, and sprites are added to this when drawn. There is one additional method called `Render`, which has been added; this needs to be called every frame. If there is anything left in the batch that hasn't been drawn by the end of the frame, then `Render` will ensure it gets drawn.

The `Renderer` currently doesn't handle different textures very well. As all the sprites are drawn in a big batch, all the sprites in that batch must have the same texture. An easy way to handle this is to do a texture check each addition, and if the texture is different draw the batch.

Profiling the Batch Draw Method

Text will render just as before, but now it will be faster. If the previous example of rendering around 10,000 sprites is repeated, the frame-rate on my computer jumps from around 30 fps to over 80 fps—a significant increase. This will mean older computers will be much more likely to run smoothly.

Summary

Now you've added text drawing capabilities to your code library and improved the sprite rendering code. It's nearly time to jump in and create a game, but before that, we'll take a closer look at the math used in games.

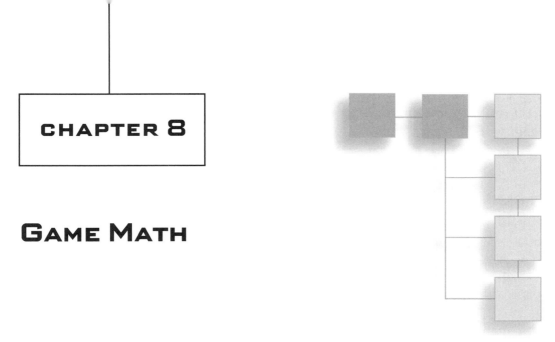

CHAPTER 8

GAME MATH

Games can be written without a lot of advanced math knowledge, but the more graphically advanced the game, the more math you'll need to know. There are many fields of mathematics; some are more commonly used than others when writing a game. Geometry is important to describe 3D and 2D worlds. Matrices and vectors are useful for describing worlds and the relationships between entities in these worlds. Trigonometric functions are great for special effects and making things act organically. Tween functions are a handy way to express movement over a constant time. The more math you know, the more tools you have to solve any problems that come up when programming games.

Trigonometric Functions

The trigonometric functions sine and cosine are often used in game programming. Applying sine and cosine to some number will return a value from −1 to 1. These returned values make up a wave form, a smoothly oscillating curve. This curve is of great use when moving something up and down smoothly—creating an organic pulsing color, smooth oscillating scaling, and many other game-like effects.

Plotting a Graph

The best way to get a feel for the uses of cosine and sine is to create a sandbox program where you can play with the values. A good starting point is a program that plots the sine and cosine waves on a graph. Here's a game state that will draw

some axis and plot a particular graph. You don't need to create a new project.
You can just add this state to your existing code and then set it as the default
state.

```
class WaveformGraphState : IGameObject
{
  double _xPosition = -100;
  double _yPosition = -100;
  double _xLength = 200;
  double _yLength = 200;
  double _sampleSize = 100;
  double _frequency = 2;
  public delegate double WaveFunction(double value);

  public WaveformGraphState()
  {
    Gl.glLineWidth(3);
    Gl.glDisable(Gl.GL_TEXTURE_2D);
  }

  public void DrawAxis()
  {
    Gl.glColor3f(1, 1, 1);

    Gl.glBegin(Gl.GL_LINES);
    {
      // X axis
      Gl.glVertex2d(_xPosition, _yPosition);
      Gl.glVertex2d(_xPosition + _xLength, _yPosition);
      // Y axis
      Gl.glVertex2d(_xPosition, _yPosition);
      Gl.glVertex2d(_xPosition, _yPosition + _yLength);
    }
    Gl.glEnd();
  }


  public void DrawGraph(WaveFunction waveFunction, Color color)
  {
    double xIncrement = _xLength / _sampleSize;
    double previousX = _xPosition;
    double previousY = _yPosition + (0.5 * _yLength);
```

```
Gl.glColor3f(color.Red, color.Green, color.Blue);
Gl.glBegin(Gl.GL_LINES);
{
  for (int i = 0; i < _sampleSize; i ++)
  {

    // Work out new X and Y positions
    double newX = previousX + xIncrement; // Increment one unit on the x
    // From 0-1 how far through plotting the graph are we?
    double percentDone = (i / _sampleSize);
    double percentRadians = percentDone * (Math.PI * _frequency);

    // Scale the wave value by the half the length
    double newY = _yPosition + waveFunction(percentRadians) *
(_yLength / 2);

    // Ignore the first value because the previous X and Y
    // haven't been worked out yet.
    if (i > 1)
    {
      Gl.glVertex2d(previousX, previousY);
      Gl.glVertex2d(newX, newY);
    }

    // Store the previous position
    previousX = newX;
    previousY = newY;
  }
}
Gl.glEnd();
} // Empty Update and Render methods omitted
}
```

The member variables _xPosition, _yPosition, _xLength, and _yLength are used to position and describe the size of the graph. The smoothness of the graph is determined by the _sampleSize variable. The sample size is the number of vertices used to draw the line of the graph. Each vertex y position is determined by a particular wave function such as sine or cosine. The _frequency variable is used to determine how often the wave will oscillate, the higher the frequency the greater the number of oscillations.

The default values describe a graph positioned at x:-100, y:-100 with each axis being 200 pixels long. This will make the graph big enough to easily read, but the DrawGraph function treats the graph as if the x and y axes run from 0 to 1.

After the member variables, a delegate is defined.

```
public delegate double WaveFunction(double value);
```

Graphs are often defined as $x = x'$, $y = f(x')$ where x' is the next value of x and plain x is the previous value. The x value is usually increased by a set number and the y value is calculated from the x. The WaveFunction delegate describes f in the formula; a function that takes in some double value and returns some double value. This is the same signature of the cosine and sine functions. By using a WaveFunction type, the DrawGraph function can take in cosine, sine, or any other wave function and no extra code needs to be written.

The state's constructor sets the line width to 3 pixels making the graph lines easy to see. It also turns off the texture state; if the texture state is turned on, the lines may appear dull because they are incorrectly being assigned an invalid texture.

The DrawGraph function is the most important function in the game state. It is responsible for plotting the graph. It uses the sample rate to work out how to space the vertices so that any line will totally fill the length graph. There are two common ways to define angles: degrees and radians. Degrees are quite commonly known; a full circle is 360°, and a half circle is 180°. Radians are a measurement of degrees using Pi, a full circle is two times Pi, and a half circle is Pi. The C# Sin and Cos functions expect to be given an angle in radians; for this reason, the 0-1 value of the X axis is scaled by Pi when the Y axis values are being calculated.

The inner loop of the DrawGraph function works out a new position from the old position and then plots a line from the old position to the new position. To demonstrate the code in action, a Render function needs to be written that calls DrawGraph for sine and cosine. The graph output can be seen in Figure 8.1.

```
public void Render()
{
  DrawAxis();
  DrawGraph(Math.Sin, new Color(1,0,0,1));
  DrawGraph(Math.Cos, new Color(0, 0.5f, 0.5f, 1));
}
```

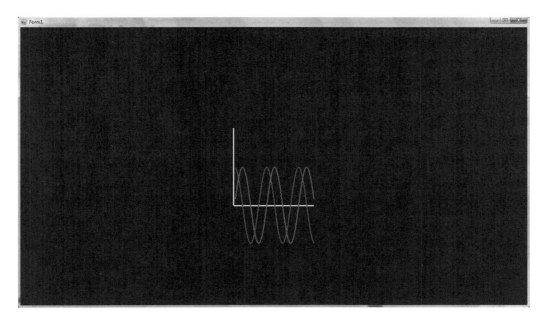

Figure 8.1
A plot of the sine and cosine functions.

The `DrawGraph` function takes in a function used to plot the graph and a color that decides what color the graph will be. Sine and cosine are waveforms, and it's easy to make interesting new wave forms by adding these waves together. A new waveform function can be created by using an anonymous method. This code snippet creates a graph that combines cosine and sine but scales the result down by a half.

```
DrawGraph(delegate(double value)
{
  return (Math.Sin(value) + Math.Cos(value)) *0.5;
}, new Color(0.5f, 0.5f, 1, 1));
```

Try the following snippet and observe the graph you get.

```
DrawGraph(delegate(double value)
{
  return (Math.Sin(value) + Math.Sin(value + value)) *0.5;
}, new Color(0.5f, 0.5f, 1, 1));
```

These graphs look interesting, but without a game application, they may seem academic and rather dull. Next, these functions will be used to animate sprites.

Trigonometric Functions for Special Effects

Create a new game state called `SpecialEffectsState`. This state will demonstrate how to use the sine and cosine functions that have just been covered to create cool special effects with the `text` class.

```
class SpecialEffectState : IGameObject
{
  Font _font;
  Text _text;
  Renderer _renderer = new Renderer();
  double _totalTime = 0;

  public SpecialEffectState(TextureManager manager)
  {
    _font = new Font(manager.Get("font"), FontParser.Parse("font.fnt"));
    _text = new Text("Hello", _font);
  }

  public void Update(double elapsedTime)
  {
  }

  public void Render()
  {
    Gl.glClearColor(0.0f, 0.0f, 0.0f, 1.0f);
    Gl.glClear(Gl.GL_COLOR_BUFFER_BIT);
    _renderer.DrawText(_text);
    _renderer.Render();
  }
}
```

The basic state just renders out the text "Hello." It's very easy to use the sine value to make this text pulse the opacity from 0–1 and back again. Text is used here, but it could just as easily be a sprite or model.

```
public void Update(double elapsedTime)
{
```

```
  double frequency = 7;
  float _wavyNumber = (float)Math.Sin(_totalTime*frequency);
  _wavyNumber = 0.5f + _wavyNumber * 0.5f; // scale to 0-1
  _text.SetColor(new Color(1, 0, 0, _wavyNumber));

  _totalTime += elapsedTime;
}
```

The total time keeps track of how long the state has been running. The number keeps increasing and will eventually become so big that it wraps around to 0. It's used to feed the sine function numbers that will produce a wave similar to the one plotted previously. The sine wave is scaled so that it oscillates between 0 and 1 rather than − 1 and 1. The frequency is increased as well to make the pulse occur more often. Run the code and check out the effect.

After pulsing in and out of sight, the next step is to have the text travel through a garish rainbow of all the colors. Each color channel is assigned a different sine or cosine wave and the strengths of each channel change over time.

```
public void Update(double elapsedTime)
{
  double frequency = 7;
  float _wavyNumberR = (float)Math.Sin(_totalTime*frequency);
  float _wavyNumberG = (float)Math.Cos(_totalTime*frequency);
  float _wavyNumberB = (float)Math.Sin(_totalTime+0.25*frequency);
  _wavyNumberR = 0.5f + _wavyNumberR * 0.5f; // scale to 0-1
  _wavyNumberG = 0.5f + _wavyNumberG * 0.5f; // scale to 0-1
  _wavyNumberB = 0.5f + _wavyNumberB * 0.5f; // scale to 0-1

  _text.SetColor(new Color(_wavyNumberR, _wavyNumberG,
_wavyNumberB, 1));

  _totalTime += elapsedTime;
}
```

It's very easy to play with this code to get a wide variety of different effects. The color channel isn't the only thing that can by modified using trigonometric functions; the next example will alter the position of the text. To change the text position a SetPosition method must be added to the Text class. To move the text, every vertex that makes up every character must have its position changed; the easiest way to do this is just to re-create all these characters at the new position.

```
public void SetPosition(double x, double y)
{
  CreateText(x, y);
}
```

With the `Text` classes `SetPosition` method defined, it can be used in the `Update` loop to create a new text-based special effect.

```
public void Update(double elapsedTime)
{
  double frequency = 7;
  double _wavyNumberX = Math.Sin(_totalTime*frequency)*15;
  double _wavyNumberY = Math.Cos(_totalTime*frequency)*15;

  _text.SetPosition(_wavyNumberX, _wavyNumberY);

  _totalTime += elapsedTime;
}
```

This will move the text in a rough circle. This time the numbers don't need to be scaled between 0 and 1; instead, they are increased so the movement of the text is very obvious. Different functions can be used to alter the position of the text as needed.

Finally, this last example takes each letter of the text and animates it as if a wave was passing along the word. To animate each individual character of the text, a new `GetPosition` method must be added to the `Sprite` class. The sprite position is taken from the center of the sprite.

```
public Vector GetPosition()
{
  return GetCenter();
}
```

With the above code added to the `Sprite` class, the new `GetPosition` method can be used in the `Update` loop.

```
public void Update(double elapsedTime)
{
  double frequency = 7;

  int xAdvance = 0;
  foreach (CharacterSprite cs in _text.CharacterSprites)
```

```
    {
        Vector position = cs.Sprite.GetPosition();
        position.Y = 0 + Math.Sin((_totalTime + xAdvance) * frequency)*25;
        cs.Sprite.SetPosition(position);
        xAdvance++;
    }

    _totalTime += elapsedTime;
}
```

Vectors

Vectors are a very common game programming tool. The easiest way to get a good feel for vector math is to use it in a game. Very quickly the possible uses will become second nature. A simple vector class has already been made in the previous chapters, but until now none of its properties have been defined.

What Is a Vector?

In game programming, vectors are used to manipulate and describe 3D game worlds. Mathematically, vectors are described as a direction with a magnitude. The magnitude is just the length of the vector. See Figure 8.2.

The most common vectors in game programming are 2D, 3D, and 4D. Four-dimension vectors are used when using projection matrices to translate vertices from 3D to 2D. On paper, vectors and positions are very similar. A position [0, 3, 0] and a vector [0, 3, 0] have the same internal values, but they represent different things. The position uses a coordinate system to define an absolute position in the world. A vector describes a direction (up in this case) and a magnitude or length (in this case, 3). See Figure 8.3 for a comparison. For example, "three miles in the air" is not a position; it's a description of a position using a direction and a length—a vector.

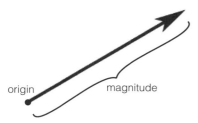

Figure 8.2
The anatomy of a vector.

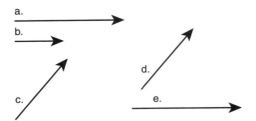

Figure 8.3
Comparing vectors and positions.

In Figure 8.3, vectors a and e are the same vector because they have the same direction and magnitude. They are at different origins so they appear different places on the diagram. Vectors c and d are also the same. Vector b is the same direction as a and e, but the magnitude is less so it is a different vector.

Vectors, in game programming, are used to answer questions such as:

- The enemy spaceship is at position [0, 0, 90]; the player spaceship is at [0, 80, −50]. What direction should the enemy launch a missile? Each frame, how is that missile's position updated to send it towards the player?

- Is the player's distance from the bomb a meter or less?

- Which side of the wall is the player?

- Is the player looking at the NPC?

- Given a quad that represents the end of a gun, which direction are the bullets going to fire?

- How should light reflect off this surface?

- Move the car three meters forward.

- A player has just hit an enemy; which direction should that enemy move?

- How do I increase the force of this bullet by 100?

- Which player is nearest the alien artifact?

To be able to answer these questions, the vector class will need to be expanded to add the basic vector methods. The examples in this chapter will build upon the code you have written in previous chapters. Most examples will require you to create a new game state and make this the activate state to test the code. All the example code is available on the CD in the Code\Chapter 8 directory. The next sections will explain the various vector operations and list the code that needs to be added to complete the vector class. Game engines sometimes have a Vector2d, Vector3d, and Vector4d, but I think it's simpler in this case to just have one vector structure; it can still be used for any 2D operations, and for the contents of this book, 4D vectors won't be used.

```
[StructLayout(LayoutKind.Sequential)]
public struct Vector
{
  public double X { get; set; }
  public double Y { get; set; }
  public double Z { get; set; }
  public Vector(double x, double y, double z) : this()
  {
    X = x;
    Y = y;
    Z = z;
  }
}
```

The Length Operation

The length operation takes a vector and returns that vector's magnitude. With a simple vector of [0, 1, 0], it's easy to see the length is 1, but with a vector of [1.6, −0.99, 8], the length is less apparent. Here is the formula to give a vector's length.

$$||v|| = \sqrt{x^2 + y^2 + z^2}$$

The two bars around the v are the mathematical notation for the length of a vector. The equation is the same for any dimension of vector: square the members, add them together, and take the square root.

This formula is simple to translate into code. It is broken into two functions: one function will square and add the members; the other will perform the square root.

```
public double Length()
{
  return Math.Sqrt(LengthSquared());
}
```

```
public double LengthSquared()
{
  return (X * X + Y * Y + Z * Z);
}
```

If you want to compare the length of two vectors the LengthSquared operation can be compared instead of the Length, saving a square root operation and making it slightly more efficient.

Vector Equality

Vectors are considered equal if all the members' values, X,Y, and Z, are equal. Vectors don't have a position; they are just a direction from some origin. Figure 8.3 has a number of vectors; even though some vectors are placed at different positions, they are still equal because all their members are equal. Three miles north is still three miles north if it's three miles north of your house, or three miles north of the Great Pyramid of Giza.

It is simple to create an Equals function for the vector.

```
public bool Equals(Vector v)
{
  return (X == v.X) && (Y == v.Y) && (Z == v.Z);
}
```

In code it would be convenient if the == operator was also overloaded. At the moment, the following cannot be written

```
// Cannot write this
if (vector1 == vector2)
{
  System.Console.WriteLine("They're the same")
}

// Instead must write
if (vector1.Equals(vector2))
{
  System.Console.WriteLine("They're the same")
}
```

To use the == operator, it needs to be overloaded and that requires a few more functions to be overridden as well, GetHashCode, !=, and Equals (Object obj).

```csharp
public override int GetHashCode()
{
  return (int)X ^ (int)Y ^ (int)Z;
}

public static bool operator ==(Vector v1, Vector v2)
{
  // If they're the same object or both null, return true.
  if (System.Object.ReferenceEquals(v1, v2))
  {
    return true;
  }

  // If one is null, but not both, return false.
  if (v1 == null || v2 == null)
  {
    return false;
  }

  return v1.Equals(v2);
}

public override bool Equals(object obj)
{
  if (obj is Vector)
  {
    return Equals((Vector)obj);
  }
  return base.Equals(obj);
}

public static bool operator !=(Vector v1, Vector v2)
{
  return !v1.Equals(v2);
}
```

A lot of code just to overload the equality operator! The only curious function is
GetHashCode. A hash is a number that tries, but is not guaranteed, to uniquely
identify an object; it's used in C# Dictionary structures. It needs to be overridden when overriding equality because if equality is overridden, it makes it
harder for the compiler to know what a good hash would be.

Vector Addition, Subtraction, and Multiplication

The vector addition operation is very simple; each member of the first vector is added to the respective member of the second vector. Here is the code to perform vector addition.

```
public Vector Add(Vector r)
{
  return new Vector(X + r.X, Y + r.Y, Z + r.Z);
}

public static Vector operator+(Vector v1, Vector v2)
{
  return v1.Add(v2);
}
```

When the binary addition operator + is overloaded, it automatically overloads +=. The same is true for *= and /=.

Figure 8.4 shows the result of adding two vectors together. Vectors are often added together when trying to get a certain offset in 3D space. For instance, say you wanted to put a 3D model of a halo above a player's head. The player origin is directly in between the feet of the character. You have a vector that represents an offset from the player's feet to the center of the player's head [0, 1.75, 0].

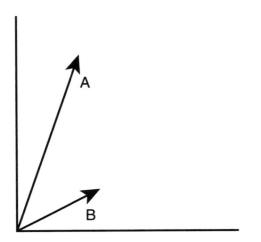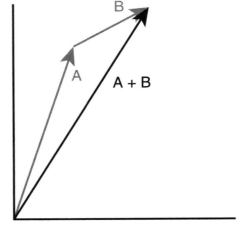

Figure 8.4
Vectors addition.

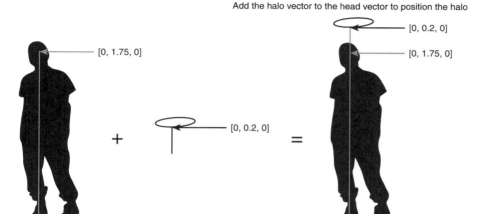

Figure 8.5
Adding a halo to a player.

If you add a vector [0, 0.2, 0] that should get you a position that's perfect for a hovering halo. This operation is shown in Figure 8.5.

Vector subtraction is used all the time to get the vector between two points in space. The calculation is very similar to addition, but the members are subtracted rather than added.

```
public Vector Subtract (Vector r)
{
  return new Vector (X - r.X, Y - r.Y, Z - r.Z);
}
public static Vector operator- (Vector v1, Vector v2)
{
  return v1.Subtract (v2);
}
```

The result of subtracting two vectors is shown in Figure 8.6. In a space battle, one spaceship might want to shoot another spaceship. Spaceship A can subtract its position, represented as a vector, from spaceship B's position; this will give a vector from A to B (see Figure 8.7). This vector's direction can be used to aim missiles or advance one craft towards the other.

Vector multiplication is when a vector is multiplied by a scalar number; a scalar number is a number like an int or double, just a normal number. If all a vector's

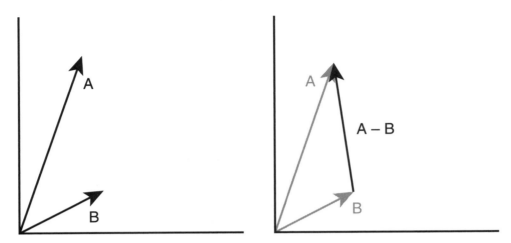

Figure 8.6
Vector subtraction.

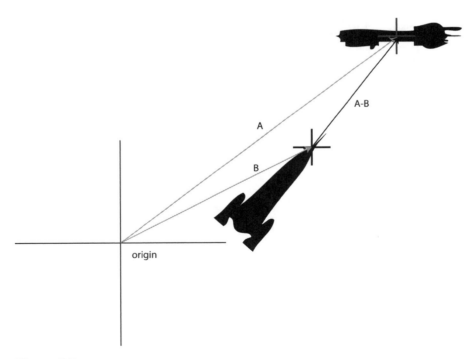

Figure 8.7
Getting the vector between two spaceships.

elements are multiplied against another element, this is known as the dot product and is covered here.

```
public Vector Multiply(double v)
{
  return new Vector(X * v, Y * v, Z * v);
}

public static Vector operator * (Vector v, double s)
{
  return v.Multiply(s);
}
```

Figure 8.8 shows what occurs when a vector is multiplied by a scalar. Multiplying by a vector scales the vector, so multiplying by 2 will double the length of the vector. Multiplying by −1 will make the vector point in the opposite direction it currently points. If a player character was shot in a 3D game, the vector the bullet was traveling can be multiplied by −1, reversing it. This vector will now point outwards from the body along the line of the bullet's entry, a perfect vector to use to play a blood splat effect (see Figure 8.9).

Normal Vectors

A normal vector is a vector that has a length of exactly 1. These vectors are also known as unit vectors. Unit vectors are an excellent way to represent a direction without caring about the magnitude. The normalize operation maintains the vector's direction but makes its magnitude equal 1. If a unit vector is multiplied

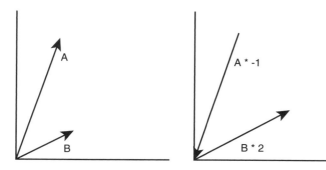

Figure 8.8
Vector, scalar multiplication.

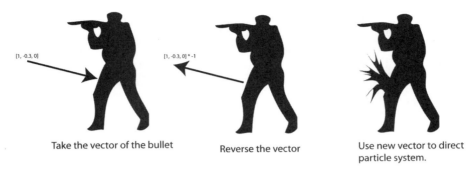

Take the vector of the bullet   Reverse the vector   Use new vector to direct
                                                                 particle system.

Figure 8.9
Using vectors for blood spray.

by a scalar, the resulting vector length will be the same as the scalar value. If you have a vector of some unknown length and you want it to be length 6, you can normalize the vector and then multiply by 6.

```
public Vector Normalize (Vector v)
{
  double r = v.Length();
  if (r != 0.0)        // guard against divide by zero
  {
    return new Vector(v.X / r, v.Y / r, v.Z / r);   // normalize and return
  }
  else
  {
    return new Vector(0, 0, 0);
  }
}
```

This code is not technically correct; it should be impossible to normalize a zero vector, but the code simply does nothing if a zero vector is normalized. Vectors are normalized by calculating their length and then dividing each element by that length. The effect of normalizing a vector can be seen in Figure 8.10.

In game programming, direction is often very important and normal vectors are used to define directions. You may have heard the term *normal mapping*. This is a texture where each pixel represents a normal vector, the texture is stretched over a 3D model, and the lighting calculations take into account the normal vector on each pixel of the rendered model. Normal mapping gives the surface of the final model a lot more detail than it would otherwise have.

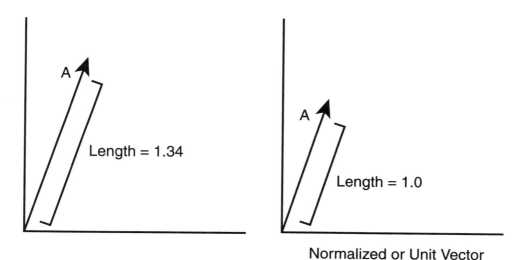

Figure 8.10
Normalizing a vector.

Imagine a two-dimensional vector with an X and Y element. Up, down, left, and right vectors can be created with $[0, 1]$, $[0, -1]$, $[-1, 0]$, and $[1, 0]$. This creates a cross-like shape. If you now created four more normal vectors between these up, down, left, and right vectors you would start to approximate a circle. This is the unit circle; it has a radius of 1. The unit circle can be seen in Figure 8.11. If a three-element vector $[X, Y, Z]$ is used, then a unit sphere is created. If you had all vectors of length 2, then you would have a sphere with a radius of 2 and so on.

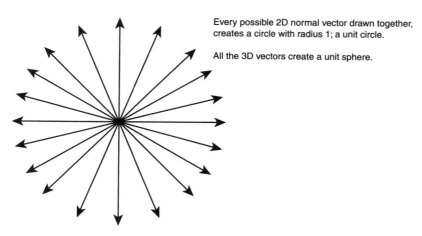

Every possible 2D normal vector drawn together, creates a circle with radius 1; a unit circle.

All the 3D vectors create a unit sphere.

Figure 8.11
Unit circle.

It is very easy to do a circle-point or sphere-point intersection test. This is a test that checks if a point is inside a certain circle or sphere. Let's take the circle example. A circle is defined by the circle position and a radius. If a unit circle exists at [5, 6] and there is a point [5.5, 6.5] the first step is to get the distance from the circle origin. This is done by vector subtraction of the circle origin from the point [5, 6] − [5.5, 6.5] = [0.5, 0.5] giving the vector from the point to the center of the circle. The distance between the point and the circle is then calculated by performing the length operation on that vector. This gives a length of 0.707 . . . . If this length is smaller than the circle radius, then the point is inside the circle; if it is greater, it is outside. If it is the same, it's on the very edge of the circle, as Figure 8.12 shows.

The same method works for sphere-point intersection. This is a quick way to see if the player is in a certain position or if the mouse has been used to click on a certain area. If you don't feel comfortable with it, try sketching out a few

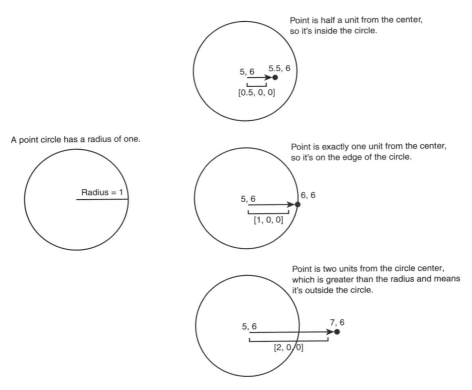

Figure 8.12
Circle-point intersection.

examples on a piece of paper until you do. Once you've got it, try to think how you might do a circle-circle intersection or a sphere-sphere intersection.

The Dot Product Operation

The dot product is an operation that takes two vectors and returns a number. The number returned is related to the angle between the two vectors.

$$A \bullet B = |A||B|\cos(\theta)$$

The dot product operation used on vector A and B returns the length of A and B multiplied by the cosine of the angle between the vectors. This is shown graphically in Figure 8.13. If vectors B and A are normalized, then their length values are 1 and the equation is simplified to $A \bullet B = \cos(\theta)$. To retrieve the angle, the arccosine operation can be used. In C#, the arccosine function is `Math.acos` and it returns the angle in radians.

The dot product operation is very good for determining if objects in the game are facing each other. It's also very useful for testing if an object is on one side of a plane or the other; this is used in 3D games to ensure the character doesn't walk through walls.

The operation itself is very simple: all the elements from the first vector are multiplied by the second vector, then all these values are added together to

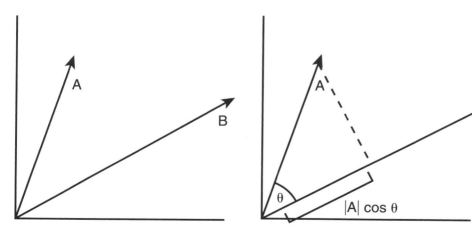

Figure 8.13
The dot product operation.

produce a scalar. The dot product is a very common operation in 3D graphics, so common the multiply operator * is often overloaded to represent it.

```
public double DotProduct(Vector v)
{
  return (v.X * X) + (Y * v.Y) + (Z * v.Z);
}

public static double operator *(Vector v1, Vector v2)
{
  return v1.DotProduct(v2);
}
```

Dot products are great for determining if a point is behind or in front of a plane. A plane is a two-dimensional surface, like a piece of paper. A piece of paper can be positioned and angled anywhere just like a geometric plane. The difference is that a piece of paper has an edge. Planes don't have edges; they keep going infinitely along their two dimensions—a piece of paper without end! A plane is defined using a point and a normalized vector. (See Figure 8.14.) The point positions the plane in space and the normal specifies the direction it's pointing.

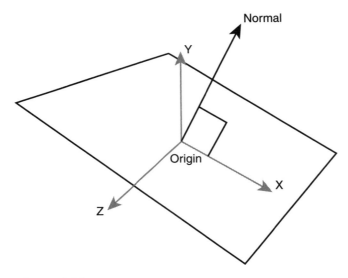

Figure 8.14
A plane.

In a game a 3D plane might be positioned somewhere to signify a change; if the player crosses this plane then he has finished the level, or a boss should spawn, or he has fallen to drown in the sea. The test to see which side a player is on goes like this.

- Create a vector from the plane position to the player position.

- Dot product the plane normal with the newly created vector.

- If the result is zero, the player position is exactly on the plane.

- If the result is above zero, the player is on the normal side of the plane.

- If the result is below zero, the player is on the other side of the plane.

This test can be seen graphically in Figure 8.15.

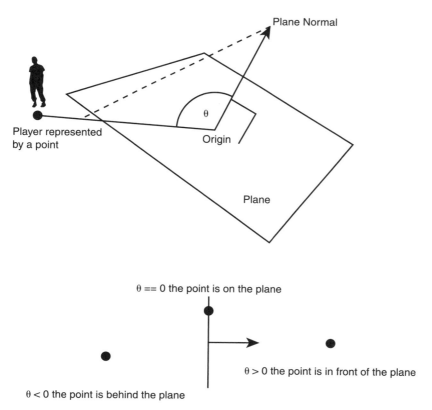

Figure 8.15
Player and plane position.

Dot product tests are used in back face culling. This is a technique to see if some polygon is facing away from the camera. By default, polygons are not double-sided; they only have one side indicated by the normal. If the polygons face away from the camera, they can't be seen. This means the graphics hardware doesn't need to be told about them. The dot product can be used to filter out all the polygons that are facing away from the camera.

The Cross-Product Operation

The last vector operation to be covered is the cross-product. Unlike the previous operations, this operation only works on vectors with three or more elements. This means there is no cross-product operation for a simple X,Y vector. The calculation is more complicated than previous operations but the results are quite intuitive. The cross-product takes two vectors and returns a vector per-pendicular to the passed in vectors. If you have a table with one side from $[0, 0, 0]$ to $[0, 0, 1]$ and another side from $[0, 0, 0]$ to $[1, 0, 0]$, then the resulting dot product vector will be a vector that is pointing upwards from the table's surface $[0, 1, 0]$. The operation can be seen in Figure 8.16.

Here is the formula for calculating the cross-product.

$$A = B \bullet C$$

$$A = \begin{bmatrix} A_x \\ A_y \\ A_z \end{bmatrix} \quad B = \begin{bmatrix} B_x \\ B_y \\ B_z \end{bmatrix} \quad C = \begin{bmatrix} C_x \\ C_y \\ C_z \end{bmatrix}$$

$$A_x = B_y C_z - B_z C_y$$

$$A_y = B_z C_x - B_x C_z$$

$$A_z = B_x C_y - B_y C_x$$

The formula looks rather intimidating; fortunately, once it's converted to code it can pretty much be ignored. When this formula is used, you won't be thinking about the particular mechanics of the code, just that you want a vector that points outwards from two cross-product vectors.

```
public Vector CrossProduct (Vector v)
{
    double nx = Y * v.Z - Z * v.Y;
```

```
    double ny = Z * v.X - X * v.Z;
    double nz = X * v.Y - Y * v.X;
    return new Vector(nx, ny, nz);
}
```

The cross-product is very useful for working out the normal of a surface. For instance, you may have a train that you want to move forward in the 3D world. The train could be at any angle, so it's hard to know what forward means. First, you really need a normal vector that faces the same way as the train. If you found a polygon on the train facing the way you want, the cross-product of two sides of this polygon will give you a vector that is facing outward from it along the train, as shown in Figure 8.17. This vector can be normalized so it is just a direction. This direction multiplied by some scalar can be added to the train's position and it will move forward that scalar amount.

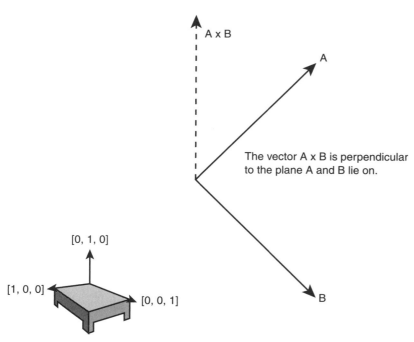

A x B

A

The vector A x B is perpendicular
to the plane A and B lie on.

B

[0, 1, 0]

[1, 0, 0]

[0, 0, 1]

The surface normal of the table can be found by
taking the cross product of its width and length.

Figure 8.16
The cross-product operation.

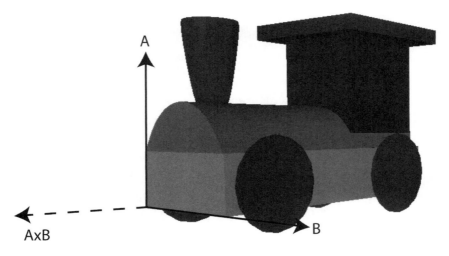

Figure 8.17
Calculating the forward normal of a train.

Finishing Touches to the Vector Structure

By now, quite an impressive, fully functional vector structure has been made, but there are a few final touches that will make it easier to work with. First, the ToString method can be overridden so it outputs something useful. The To-String method is automatically called when using the debugger in Visual Studio. Overriding this method will allow a vector to be understood at a glance, without needing to dig down into the definition and look at the individual values.

```
public override string ToString()
{
  return string.Format("X:{0}, Y:{1}, Z:{2}", X, Y, Z);
}
```

The zero vector is a special type of vector; it has no unit vector. It is a vector that represents no direction and has no magnitude. It is a little like the null of vectors. For that reason it is useful to have as a constant.

```
[StructLayout(LayoutKind.Sequential)]
public struct Vector
{
  public static Vector Zero = new Vector(0, 0, 0);
```

That is all the vector operations needed. With this simple structure a whole 3D world can be built and manipulated. Don't worry if you don't quite understand every little bit at the moment; the more you use the bits you do know the more the rest will fall into place.

Two-Dimensional Intersection

Intersection is a way of determining when two shapes overlap or intersect. This is essential in all graphical programming including games. Detecting if the mouse cursor is over a button is an intersection test. In games, detecting if a missile has hit a ship is also an intersection test. 2D intersection is very simple and a great place to start.

Circles

Circles are defined with a position and a radius. Intersection is best shown graphically, so let's create a new game state called `CircleIntersectionState` and make it load by default.

```
class CircleIntersectionState : IGameObject
{
  public CircleIntersectionState()
  {
    Gl.glLineWidth(3);
    Gl.glDisable(Gl.GL_TEXTURE_2D);
  }
  #region IGameObject Members

  public void Update(double elapsedTime)
  {
  }

  public void Render()
  {
  }
  #endregion
}
```

The state currently does nothing apart from getting OpenGL ready to draw lines. Next, a circle class needs to be created.

```
public class Circle
{
  Vector Position { get; set; }
  double Radius { get; set; }

  public Circle()
  {
    Position = Vector.Zero;
    Radius = 1;
  }

  public Circle(Vector position, double radius)
  {
    Position = position;
    Radius = radius;
  }

  public void Draw()
  {
    // Determines how round the circle will appear.
    int vertexAmount = 10;
    double twoPI = 2.0 * Math.PI;

    // A line loop connects all the vertices with lines
    // The last vertex is connected to the first vertex
    // to make a loop.
    Gl.glBegin(Gl.GL_LINE_LOOP);
    {
      for (int i = 0; i <= vertexAmount; i++)
      {
        double xPos = Position.X + Radius * Math.Cos(i * twoPI /
vertexAmount);
        double yPos = Position.Y + Radius * Math.Sin(i * twoPI /
vertexAmount);
        Gl.glVertex2d(xPos, yPos);
      }
    }
    Gl.glEnd();
  }
}
```

By default, a circle is defined to be at the origin and to have a radius of 1 unit. The drawing code is currently missing. The circle will be drawn using OpenGL immediate mode—just the outline will be drawn. The sine and cosine functions are used to determine where to plot each vertex that will make up the circle's perimeter.

To test the drawing function in the `CircleIntersectionState`, add a `_circle` member to the class.

```
Circle _circle = new Circle(Vector.Zero, 200);
```

This creates a circle of radius 200 around the origin. To see the circle, the render method needs to be modified.

```
public void Render()
{
  _circle.Draw();
}
```

Run the program and you should see something similar to Figure 8.18.

The circle is made from only 10 vertices so it doesn't appear very smooth. To increase the smoothness increase the number of vertices used in the Draw method of the Circle class.

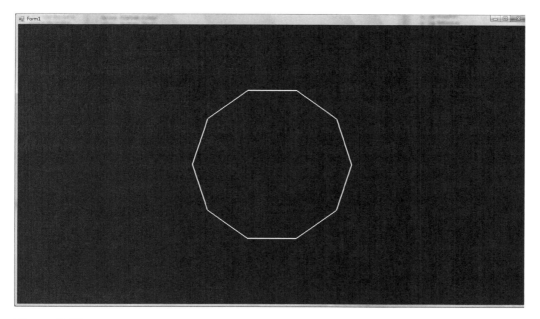

Figure 8.18
Rendering a circle.

For the purposes of demonstrating intersection, it would be nice to able to color the circles. A white circle could be a non-intersected circle and a red circle could indicate that it intersects with something. This is an easy addition to make. In the `Circle` class, modify the code so it has a color member that is used in the `Draw` function.

```
Color _color = new Color(1, 1, 1, 1);
public Color Color
{
  get { return _color; }
  set { _color = value; }
}

public void Draw()
{
  Gl.glColor3f(_color.Red, _color.Green, _color.Blue);
```

By default, all circles will be rendered white but the color can be changed at any time.

Circle-point intersection was covered in the vector section. The distance of the point from the circle origin is calculated; if that distance is greater than the circle radius, then it lies outside of the circle. To test this graphically, the mouse pointer can be used as the point.

Getting the position of the mouse pointer is a little tricky because of the different coordinate systems involved. The OpenGL origin is in the middle of the form but the cursor's position is not in the same coordinate system; its origin is the very top left of the form. This means OpenGL considers the position 0, 0 to be a point in the middle of the form while the cursor considers 0,0 to be the very top left of the form. These different coordinate systems are shown in Figure 8.19. The form coordinate origin is labeled a, the control coordinate is labeled b, and the OpenGL coordinate origin is labeled c. To convert the mouse pointer from the form coordinate system to the OpenGL coordinate system a little more code needs to be added to the form.

The first thing we need is a simple `Input` class to record the mouse input.

```
public class Input
{
  public Point MousePosition { get; set; }
}
```

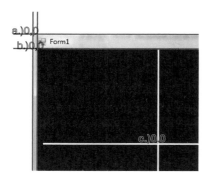

Figure 8.19
Coordinate systems of the form.

The `Input` class will be initiated and updated in the form. `GameStates` that wish to know about the mouse position need to take the `Input` object into their constructors. Add an `Input` object to the form class now.

```
public partial class Form1 : Form
{
  Input _input = new Input();
```

In the form a new function needs to be created that will update the Input class; this will be called every frame.

```
private void UpdateInput()
{
  System.Drawing.Point mousePos = Cursor.Position;
  mousePos = _openGLControl.PointToClient(mousePos);

  // Now use our point definition,
  Point adjustedMousePoint = new Point();
  adjustedMousePoint.X = (float)mousePos.X - ((float)ClientSize.Width
/ 2);
  adjustedMousePoint.Y = ((float)ClientSize.Height / 2) - (float)mouse-
Pos.Y;
  _input.MousePosition = adjustedMousePoint;
}

private void GameLoop(double elapsedTime)
{
  UpdateInput();
```

`UpdateInput` translates the mouse position from the form's coordinate system to the control coordinate system by using the `PointToClient` function. The mouse position is then finally converted to the OpenGL coordinate system based on the center of the OpenGL control. This is done by taking away half the width and height of the control from its X and Y position. The final coordinate now correctly maps the mouse position from the form coordinates to OpenGL co-ordinates. If the mouse was placed in the center of the OpenGL control, it would have the Input class report the position (0,0).

There is one last thing that needs to be written before leaving the form code. The new input object must be added to the constructor of the circle state.

```
_system.AddState("circle_state", new CircleIntersectionState(_input));
```

The state's constructor must also be modified.

```
Input _input;
public CircleIntersectionState(Input input)
{
  _input = input;
```

Once the input is being passed to the state then the mouse position can be used. It's worth confirming that everything is working correctly. The easiest way to do this is to draw a dot where the cursor is in OpenGL.

```
public void Render()
{
  Gl.glClearColor(0.0f, 0.0f, 0.0f, 1.0f);
  Gl.glClear(Gl.GL_COLOR_BUFFER_BIT);
  _circle.Draw();

  // Draw the mouse cursor as a point
  Gl.glPointSize(5);
  Gl.glBegin(Gl.GL_POINTS);
  {
    Gl.glVertex2f(_input.MousePosition.X,
      _input.MousePosition.Y);
  }
  Gl.glEnd();
}
```

Run the program and a small square will follow the pointer of the cursor. You may note that I've added the glClear commands. Try removing the glClear commands and see what happens.

Now that the mouse pointer is working, we can return to the intersection code. The update loop for the state will do the intersection check.

```
public void Update(double elapsedTime)
{
  if (_circle.Intersects(_input.MousePosition))
  {
    _circle.Color = new Color(1, 0, 0, 1);
  }
  else
  {
    // If the circle's not intersected turn it back to white.
    _circle.Color = new Color(1, 1, 1, 1);
  }
}
```

This shows how the `intersect` function will be used; all that's left is to write it. The test requires a number of vector operations; therefore, the point object is converted to a vector.

```
public bool Intersects(Point point)
{
  // Change point to a vector
  Vector vPoint = new Vector(point.X, point.Y, 0);
  Vector vFromCircleToPoint = Position - vPoint;
  double distance = vFromCircleToPoint.Length();

  if (distance > Radius)
  {
    return false;
  }
  return true;
}
```

Run the program and observe what happens when the cursor is moved in and out of the circle.

Rectangles

The rectangle intersection code doesn't need to be completed. The only rectangles we need are buttons, and they'll always be axis aligned. This makes the code far simpler than dealing with arbitrarily aligned rectangles.

If the point is more right than the leftmost edge of the rectangle, more left than the rightmost edge, and lower than the top and higher than the bottom, then the point is in the rectangle. It can be shown visually just like the circle example.

```
class RectangleIntersectionState : IGameObject
{
  Input _input;
  Rectangle _rectangle = new Rectangle(new Vector(0,0,0), new Vector
(200, 200,0));
  public RectangleIntersectionState(Input input)
  {
    _input = input;
  }

  #region IGameObject Members

  public void Update(double elapsedTime)
  {
    if (_rectangle.Intersects(_input.MousePosition))
    {
      _rectangle.Color = new Color(1, 0, 0, 1);
    }
    else
    {
      // If the circle's not intersected turn it back to white.
      _rectangle.Color = new Color(1, 1, 1, 1);
    }
  }

  public void Render()
  {
    _rectangle.Render();
  }
  #endregion
}
```

Here is the state; it's very similar to the circle example before. Remember to make it load as the default state. The rectangle itself is made using a line loop like the circle.

```
public class Rectangle
{
  Vector BottomLeft { get; set; }
  Vector TopRight { get; set; }
  Color _color = new Color(1, 1, 1, 1);
  public Color Color
  {
    get { return _color; }
    set { _color = value; }
  }

  public Rectangle(Vector bottomLeft, Vector topRight)
  {
    BottomLeft = bottomLeft;
    TopRight = topRight;
  }

  public void Render()
  {
    Gl.glColor3f(_color.Red, _color.Green, _color.Blue);
    Gl.glBegin(Gl.GL_LINE_LOOP);
    {
      Gl.glVertex2d(BottomLeft.X, BottomLeft.Y);
      Gl.glVertex2d(BottomLeft.X, TopRight.Y);
      Gl.glVertex2d(TopRight.X, TopRight.Y);
      Gl.glVertex2d(TopRight.X, BottomLeft.Y);
    }
    Gl.glEnd();
  }
}
```

The `rectangle` class can create and draw rectangles. The only function missing is the all important `intersect` function.

```
public bool Intersects(Point point)
{
  if (
    point.X >= BottomLeft.X &&
    point.X <= TopRight.X &&
    point.Y <= TopRight.Y &&
    point.Y >= BottomLeft.Y)
```

```
    {
      return true;
    }
    return false;
}
```

Run the program and move the mouse over the rectangle. Like the circle example, it will turn red demonstrating that the intersection code works.

Tweens

A tween is a method of changing one value to another over time. This can be used for animating, changing position, color, scale, or any other value you can think of. Tweening is probably most well known for its use in Adobe Flash, which comes with many tween functions already built in.

An Overview of Tweening

It's probably easiest to show an example to give a rough idea how it works and then dive into the details. This state can be used in your existing code base, but if you want to create a new project then you'll need to remember to add references to Tao.DevIL and add the Sprite, Texture, and TextureManager classes.

```
class TweenTestState: IGameObject
{
  Tween _tween = new Tween(0, 256, 5);
  Sprite _sprite = new Sprite();

  public SpriteTweenState(TextureManager textureManager)
  {
    _sprite.Texture = textureManager.Get("face");
    _sprite.SetHeight(0);
    _sprite.SetWidth(0);
  }

  public void Render()
  {
    // Rendering code goes here.
  }

  public void Update(double elapsedTime)
```

```
  {
    if (_tween.IsFinished() != true)
    {
      _tween.Update(elapsedTime);
      _sprite.SetWidth((float)_tween.Value());
      _sprite.SetHeight((float)_tween.Value());
    }
  }
}
```

The tween object is used to make a sprite grow from nothing to a size of 256 over a period of 5 seconds. Here, the tween constructor takes three arguments. The first argument is the start value, the second is the destination value, and the final argument is the time to go from the start value to the second value.

The Update loop checks if the tween has finished. If it hasn't, it updates the tween. The width and height are set to the tween's value—somewhere from 0 to 256.

With the above example, the tween linearly moves from start to end. This means after 2.5 seconds the value of the tween will be 128. Tweens don't have to be linear; they accelerate or decelerate to their destinations. This power to change the type of tween comes from representing position as a function over time.

```
public void function(double time)
{
// Create a position using the time value
return position;
}
```

The actual tween function is a little more complicated than that. Here is the function that performs linear interpolation.

```
public static double Linear(double timePassed, double start, double dis-
tance, double duration)
{
  return distance * timePassed / duration + start;
}
```

The tween code uses a linear tween by default, but many different tweens can be added. Figure 8.20 shows a number of these tweens.

There are many Flash tween functions available on the internet, and it's very easy to convert these to C# code.

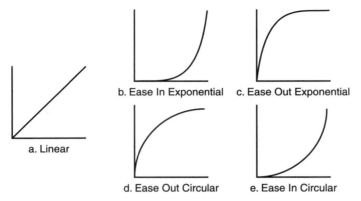

b. Ease In Exponential   c. Ease Out Exponential

a. Linear

d. Ease Out Circular   e. Ease In Circular

Figure 8.20
Five types of tween functions.

The Tween Class

The Tween class encapsulates the idea of representing a variable's value over time. Here is the full working class.

```
public class Tween
{
  double _original;
  double _distance;
  double _current;
  double _totalTimePassed = 0;
  double _totalDuration = 5;
  bool _finished = false;
  TweenFunction _tweenF = null;
  public delegate double TweenFunction(double timePassed, double start,
double distance, double duration);

  public double Value()
  {
    return _current;
  }
  public bool IsFinished()
  {
    return _finished;
  }
```

```
  public static double Linear(double timePassed, double start, double
distance, double duration)
  {
    return distance * timePassed / duration + start;
  }

  public Tween(double start, double end, double time)
  {
    Construct(start, end, time, Tween.Linear);
  }

  public Tween(double start, double end, double time, TweenFunction
tweenF)
  {
    Construct(start, end, time, tweenF);
  }

  public void Construct(double start, double end, double time, TweenFunc-
tion tweenF)
  {
    _distance = end - start;
    _original = start;
    _current = start;
    _totalDuration = time;
    _tweenF = tweenF;
  }

  public void Update(double elapsedTime)
  {
    _totalTimePassed += elapsedTime;
    _current = _tweenF(_totalTimePassed, _original, _distance,
_totalDuration);

    if (_totalTimePassed > _totalDuration)
    {
      _current = _original + _distance;
      _finished = true;
    }
  }
}
```

There are two constructors and both call the `Construct` method. The constructors allow a user to specify the type of tween function, or alternatively just use the default linear change over time. A tween function is defined by the `TweenFunction` delegate. The only implementation of the `TweenFunction` delegate in this class is the `Linear` function. Its use can be seen in the default constructor.

```
Construct(start, end, time, Tween.Linear);
```

The `Construct` method records the start value of the tween, the end value, and the time in which the tween can perform this operation. A tween function can also be passed in to determine how the value will be changed over time. The `Construct` method records these values and works out the distance from the start value to the end value. This distance is passed on to the relevant tween function.

The `Tween` object is updated every frame and the time elapsed is summed each `Update` call. This way the `Tween` object knows how far through the tween it is. The tween function delegate modifies the current value of the tween. Finally, the `Update` method checks if the tween has finished, and if it has, it sets the finish flag to true.

With only a linear function, the `Tween` class isn't very exciting, so here are some more functions that can be added. These are shown in Figure 8.20.

```
public static double EaseOutExpo(double timePassed, double start, double
distance, double duration)
{
if (timePassed == duration)
{
  return start + distance;
}
return distance * (-Math.Pow(2, -10 * timePassed / duration) + 1) + start;
}

public static double EaseInExpo(double timePassed, double start, double
distance, double duration)
{
  if (timePassed == 0)
  {
    return start;
  }
```

```
  else
  {
    return distance * Math.Pow(2, 10 * (timePassed / duration - 1)) + start;
  }
}

public static double EaseOutCirc(double timePassed, double start, double
distance, double duration)
{
  return distance * Math.Sqrt(1 - (timePassed = timePassed / duration - 1) *
timePassed) + start;
}

public static double EaseInCirc(double timePassed, double start, double
distance, double duration)
{
  return -distance * (Math.Sqrt(1 - (timePassed /= duration) * timePassed)
- 1) + start;
}
```

Using Tweens

Now that the `tween` class has been created, it is time to show off some of its power. As always, this begins with a new game state being created. This one is named `TweenTestState`.

This state requires the face texture used earlier in the book to be added to the project and its "Copy To Output Directory" property set to "Copy if newer". In the form constructor the face texture should be loaded into the `TextureManager`.

```
_textureManager.LoadTexture("face", "face_alpha.tif");
```

With the texture loaded it can be now be used to make a sprite in the `Tween-TestState` class.

```
class TweenTestState : IGameObject
{
  Sprite _faceSprite = new Sprite();
  Renderer _renderer = new Renderer();
  Tween _tween = new Tween(0, 256, 5);
  public TweenTestState(TextureManager textureManager)
```

```
    {
      _faceSprite.Texture = textureManager.Get ("face");
    }

    #region IGameObject Members

    public void Process (double elapsedTime)
    {
      if (_tween.IsFinished () != true)
      {
        _tween.Process (elapsedTime);
        _faceSprite.SetWidth ((float)_tween.Value ());
        _faceSprite.SetHeight ((float)_tween.Value ());
      }
    }

    public void Render ()
    {
      Gl.glClearColor (0.0f, 0.0f, 0.0f, 1.0f);
      Gl.glClear (Gl.GL_COLOR_BUFFER_BIT);
      _renderer.DrawSprite (_faceSprite);
      _renderer.Render ();
    }
    #endregion
}
```

The tween increases the width and height of the sprite from 0 all the way up to 256. Run the code and check out the animation. The sprite will enlarge in a smooth pleasing way. The next change is only a tiny modification to the code but results in a big change.

```
Tween _tween = new Tween (0, 256, 5, Tween.EaseInExpo);
```

Run the program again and now the sprite will slowly expand. Then the change will accelerate as it comes to full size. One small change has totally changed the way the animation plays out. This is a great way to tweak existing animations. Try the rest of the tween functions and see what they do, play around with the rest of the arguments, and get a feel for how it all works.

```
Tween _alphaTween = new Tween (0, 1, 5, Tween.EaseInCirc);
Color _color = new Color (1, 1, 1, 0);
public void Process (double elapsedTime)
```

```
{
  if (_tween.IsFinished() != true)
  {
    _tween.Process(elapsedTime);
    _faceSprite.SetWidth((float)_tween.Value());
    _faceSprite.SetHeight((float)_tween.Value());
  }

  if (_alphaTween.IsFinished() != true)
  {
    _alphaTween.Process(elapsedTime);
    _color.Alpha = (float)_alphaTween.Value();
    _faceSprite.SetColor(_color);
  }
}
```

Another tween has been added. This tween takes the transparency of the sprite from zero up to full opacity. This is a great method to use to fade in text. The position of the sprite can also be altered with a tween. Try tweening the sprite from off-screen to the center. Another good exercise would be to tween the sprite opacity from zero to one and then set off a tween that will reverse it; tweening from one to zero. These can then be called one after another, looping the tween.

Matrices

Matrices are used throughout graphics programming. There are many different applications of matrices, but this section will concentrate only on those related to graphics and game programming.

Matrices are mathematical structures that provide a convenient way to describe and perform a number of operations on a 3D model or sprite made from a quad. These operations include transforming (moving the models around 3D space), rotating, scaling, sheering (making the shape *lean* in a certain direction), and projecting (the conversion of a point in 3D space to 2D space, for example). Many of these operations can be done manually; for instance, our sprite class already performs the translation operation by adding vectors to each vertex position.

A matrix has several advantages over a vector when performing such operations. Different matrices can be combined with their operation into a single matrix that defines the combination of all those operations. For instance, a matrix that rotates a model 90 degrees, a matrix that scales a model up two times, and a matrix that moves the model two miles to the left can all be combined into a single matrix that does all these operations at once. This is done by matrix multiplication—multiply the matrices together and the result will be a matrix that is the combination of all the operations.

Combining operations is not the only advantage to matrices. A matrix can be inverted; this will perform the opposite operation that the original matrix would have performed. If a rotation matrix was created to rotate 5 degrees around the Z axis, and it was then applied to a model, the model's original position could be restored by inverting the matrix and applying it again. Matrices are applied to a model by multiplying each vertex by the matrix.

Matrix math can be quite dense; few game developers would be able to write the code for matrix multiplication immediately when asked. The actual matrix operations are quite simple, but it can take a while to understand them completely. Don't be discouraged, and if you want a more thorough understanding check the recommended reading section in Appendix A.

What Is a Matrix?

A matrix is a grid of numbers. Like vectors, matrices come in many dimensions. The vector we have defined has a dimension of three—X, Y, and Z. The most commonly used matrix in 3D graphics is 4x4, as is shown in Figure 8.21.

Figure 8.21 shows the matrix described as three axis vectors and one position vector: the origin. $X_xX_yX_z$ describes the x vector, $Y_xY_yY_z$ the y vector, $Z_xZ_yZ_z$ the z vector, and the origin vector is described as $O_xO_yO_z$. These three vectors are the axis of the model and its origin. These can be used to quickly determine an object's position and the direction it faces on the X, Y, and Z axes. If the axes are all normalized, then the object isn't scaled; if the axes all have a length of two, then the object is scaled to be twice as big. This is a visual way of thinking about matrices that makes them easier to use.

The final column in Figure 8.21 is [0, 0, 0, 1]. The values in this column will never change; they are only used when computing projections (from 3D to 2D space). Such projection operations aren't that common so the matrix we'll use will be 4x3. The end column will always be [0, 0, 0, 1].

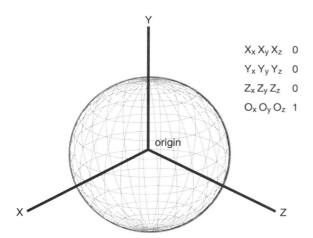

$$\begin{matrix} X_x & X_y & X_z & 0 \\ Y_x & Y_y & Y_z & 0 \\ Z_x & Z_y & Z_z & 0 \\ O_x & O_y & O_z & 1 \end{matrix}$$

Figure 8.21
A visual representation of a matrix.

Before covering matrix operations, it's time to make the basic class.

```
public class Matrix
{
    double _m11, _m12, _m13;
    double _m21, _m22, _m23;
    double _m31, _m32, _m33;
    double _m41, _m42, _m43;
}
```

Here is the `Matrix` class based on a 4x3 layout. Its member variables are laid out in a similar way to Figure 8.18 but there is no fourth column (we know the fourth column will always be [0, 0, 0, 1] so the values don't need to be stored). The `Vector`, `Color`, and `Point` components were all structures, but the `Matrix` is a larger component so it has been declared as a class.

In the following sections, we'll flesh out the `Matrix` class and add some operations to it.

The Identity Matrix

The identity matrix is the matrix that when multiplied by any other matrix will not modify it in any way. The number 1 is an example of an identity in real numbers; any number multiplied by 1 results in the original number unchanged.

All matrix identities are square. Here are the identities for a 3×3 matrix and a 4×4 matrix.

$$\begin{bmatrix} 1 & 0 & 0 \\ 0 & 1 & 0 \\ 0 & 0 & 1 \end{bmatrix} \qquad \begin{bmatrix} 1 & 0 & 0 & 0 \\ 0 & 1 & 0 & 0 \\ 0 & 0 & 1 & 0 \\ 0 & 0 & 0 & 1 \end{bmatrix}$$

When creating a matrix operation, the identity is the perfect starting place. It doesn't do anything to the vertices it's applied to so only the changes you apply on top of the identity will be performed. If a matrix of all zeros was applied to any model, then that model would disappear; all its vertices would be collapsed down to a singularity like a black hole. The matrix class should by default be initialized to the identity matrix.

Add these definitions to your matrix class.

```
public static readonly Matrix Identity =
  new Matrix(new Vector(1, 0, 0),
            new Vector(0, 1, 0),
            new Vector(0, 0, 1),
            new Vector(0, 0, 1));

public Matrix() : this (Identity)
{

}

public Matrix(Matrix m)
{
  _m11 = m._m11;
  _m12 = m._m12;
  _m13 = m._m13;

  _m21 = m._m21;
  _m22 = m._m22;
  _m23 = m._m23;
  _m31 = m._m31;
  _m32 = m._m32;
  _m33 = m._m33;
  _m41 = m._m41;
```

```
  _m42 = m._m42;
  _m43 = m._m43;
}

public Matrix(Vector x, Vector y, Vector z, Vector o)
{
  _m11 = x.X; _m12 = x.Y; _m13 = x.Z;
  _m21 = y.X; _m22 = y.Y; _m23 = y.Z;
  _m31 = z.X; _m32 = z.Y; _m33 = z.Z;
  _m41 = o.X; _m42 = o.Y; _m43 = o.Z;
}
```

This code adds a constant identity matrix and a number of constructors. The default constructor initializes the members to the identity matrix by passing the identity matrix to a copy constructor. The second constructor is the copy constructor. A copy constructor is a constructor that is called with one parameter, which is the same type as the object being constructed. The copy constructor copies all its member data so that the created object is exactly the same. The final constructor takes in a vector for each axis and one vector for the origin.

Matrix-Matrix and Vector-Matrix Multiplication

The most important methods of the `Matrix` class are its multiplication methods; these are used to combine matrices and transform on vertex positions. Matrix multiplication can only be performed if the width of the first matrix equals the height of the second. Matrix-matrix and vector-matrix multiplication is performed using the same algorithm.

Here is the definition.

$$C_{i,k} = A_{i,j}B_{j,k}$$

`C` is the result from the multiplication, `i` is the length of the rows in matrix `A`, and `k` is the length of the columns in matrix `B`. The `j` is the number of possible summations of `i` and `k`. In matrix multiplication, different-shaped matrices can result from the original shapes of the matrices that are multiplied. Again, don't worry if the math all seems a little intimidating; knowing how and when to use a matrix is the most important lesson to take away.

The width of our matrix equals its height if we remember to include the final column of $[0, 0, 0, 1]$. Therefore, using the multiplication definition, the code for the matrix-matrix multiplication is as follows:

```
public static Matrix operator * (Matrix mA, Matrix mB)
{
  Matrix result = new Matrix();

  result._m11 = mA._m11 * mB._m11 + mA._m12 * mB._m21 + mA._m13 * mB._m31;
  result._m12 = mA._m11 * mB._m12 + mA._m12 * mB._m22 + mA._m13 * mB._m32;
  result._m13 = mA._m11 * mB._m13 + mA._m12 * mB._m23 + mA._m13 * mB._m33;

  result._m21 = mA._m21 * mB._m11 + mA._m22 * mB._m21 + mA._m23 * mB._m31;
  result._m22 = mA._m21 * mB._m12 + mA._m22 * mB._m22 + mA._m23 * mB._m32;
  result._m23 = mA._m21 * mB._m13 + mA._m22 * mB._m23 + mA._m23 * mB._m33;

  result._m31 = mA._m31 * mB._m11 + mA._m32 * mB._m21 + mA._m33 * mB._m31;
  result._m32 = mA._m31 * mB._m12 + mA._m32 * mB._m22 + mA._m33 * mB._m32;
  result._m33 = mA._m31 * mB._m13 + mA._m32 * mB._m23 + mA._m33 * mB._m33;

  result._m41 = mA._m41 * mB._m11 + mA._m42 * mB._m21 + mA._m43 * mA._m31 +
mB._m41;
  result._m42 = mA._m41 * mB._m12 + mA._m42 * mB._m22 + mA._m43 * mB._m32 +
mB._m42;
  result._m43 = mA._m41 * mB._m13 + mA._m42 * mB._m23 + mA._m43 * mB._m33 +
mB._m43;

  return result;
}
```

The vector matrix multiplication is similar.

```
public static Vector operator * (Vector v, Matrix m)
{

  return new Vector(v.X * m._m11 + v.Y * m._m21 + v.Z * m._m31 + m._m41,
          v.X * m._m12 + v.Y * m._m22 + v.Z * m._m32 + m._m42,
          v.X * m._m13 + v.Y * m._m23 + v.Z * m._m33 + m._m43);
}
```

Translating and Scaling

Translation is a pretty simple operation. The last row of the vector is the origin of
the object; it is the translation. Creating a matrix to alter the translation is just the
identity matrix with the last row altered. Here is the translation matrix.

$$\begin{bmatrix} 1 & 0 & 0 & 0 \\ 0 & 1 & 0 & 0 \\ 0 & 0 & 1 & 0 \\ t_x & t_y & t_z & 1 \end{bmatrix}$$

The code is also simple.

```
public void SetTranslation(Vector translation)
{
  _m41 = translation.X;
  _m42 = translation.Y;
  _m43 = translation.Z;
}
```

```
public Vector GetTranslation()
{
  return new Vector(_m41, _m42, _m43);
}
```

The scaling matrix is also quite easy to understand. Remember, each row represents an axis. The first row of the matrix can be thought of as a vector. This vector is the X axis of whatever is being scaled; the greater its X_x dimension the greater it's scaled in that direction. The second row is the Y axis, the third row is the Z axis, and they too can be thought of as vectors. If each of the vectors has a length of 2, then the object is scaled uniformly along each axis.

$$\begin{bmatrix} S_x & 0 & 0 & 0 \\ 0 & S_y & 0 & 0 \\ 0 & 0 & S_z & 0 \\ 0 & 0 & 0 & 1 \end{bmatrix}$$

```
public void SetScale(Vector scale)
{
  _m11 = scale.X;
  _m22 = scale.Y;
  _m33 = scale.Z;
}
```

```
public Vector GetScale()
{
  Vector result = new Vector();
  result.X = (new Vector(_m11, _m12, _m13)).Length();
  result.Y = (new Vector(_m21, _m22, _m23)).Length();
  result.Z = (new Vector(_m31, _m32, _m33)).Length();
  return result;
}
```

The scale can also be non-uniform. It can be scaled more along one axis than the others. To find out the scale along a particular axis, just get the row and convert it to a vector; then apply the vector length operation, and this will give you the scaling amount.

Rotation

The math for rotating around an arbitrary axis is a lot more complicated than the previous matrices. It's not important to know exactly how this works; it's more important to know the result. The rotation matrix is made from an axis u which is defined as a normalized vector and a scalar value (θ) that describes the amount of rotation in radians. If the model you wanted to rotate was a wine cork then the normalized vector u could be represented by a needle pushed through the cork. The angle (θ) represents the amount the needle is rotated which in turn rotates the cork.

$$\begin{bmatrix} 1+(1-\cos\theta)(u_x^2-1) & (1-\cos\theta)u_xu_y-u_z\sin\theta & (1-\cos\theta)u_xu_z+u_y\sin\theta & 0 \\ (1-\cos\theta)u_xu_y+u_z\sin\theta & 1+(1-\cos\theta)(u_y^2-1) & (1-\cos\theta)u_yu_z-u_x\sin\theta & 0 \\ (1-\cos\theta)u_xu_z-u_y\sin\theta & (1-\cos\theta)u_yu_z+u_x\sin\theta & 1+(1-\cos\theta)(u_z^2-1) & 0 \\ 0 & 0 & 0 & 1 \end{bmatrix}$$

```
public void SetRotate(Vector axis, double angle)
{
  double angleSin = Math.Sin(angle);
  double angleCos = Math.Cos(angle);
  double a = 1.0 - angleCos;
  double ax = a * axis.X;
  double ay = a * axis.Y;
  double az = a * axis.Z;
```

```
   _m11 = ax * axis.X + angleCos;
   _m12 = ax * axis.Y + axis.Z * angleSin;
   _m13 = ax * axis.Z - axis.Y * angleSin;

   _m21 = ay * axis.X - axis.Z * angleSin;
   _m22 = ay * axis.Y + angleCos;
   _m23 = ay * axis.Z + axis.X * angleSin;

   _m31 = az * axis.X + axis.Y * angleSin;
   _m32 = az * axis.Y - axis.X * angleSin;
   _m33 = az * axis.Z + angleCos;
}
```

Sine and cosine can be expensive operations if they are used many times a frame, and for that reason, their use in the code is minimized. The axis vector should be normalized, but there is no check in the SetRotate function.

Inverse

The inverse is very useful for reversing the operations of a given matrix. To calculate the inverse, the determinate of the matrix is required. Every square matrix has its own determinate. A matrix is invertible only if the determinate doesn't equal zero.

```
public double Determinate()
{
  return _m11 * (_m22 * _m33 - _m23 * _m32) +
         _m12 * (_m23 * _m31 - _m21 * _m33) +
         _m13 * (_m21 * _m32 - _m22 * _m31);
}
```

The determinate can then be used to calculate the inverse of the top 3×3 of the matrix—the scale and rotation parts. The translation part of the matrix is calculated manually.

```
public Matrix Inverse()
{
  double determinate = Determinate();
  System.Diagnostics.Debug.Assert(Math.Abs(determinate) >
Double.Epsilon,
```

```
"No determinate");

  double oneOverDet = 1.0 / determinate;

  Matrix result = new Matrix();
  result._m11 = (_m22 * _m33 - _m23 * _m32) * oneOverDet;
  result._m12 = (_m13 * _m32 - _m12 * _m33) * oneOverDet;
  result._m13 = (_m12 * _m23 - _m13 * _m22) * oneOverDet;

  result._m21 = (_m23 * _m31 - _m21 * _m33) * oneOverDet;
  result._m22 = (_m11 * _m33 - _m13 * _m31) * oneOverDet;
  result._m23 = (_m13 * _m21 - _m11 * _m23) * oneOverDet;

  result._m31 = (_m21 * _m32 - _m22 * _m31) * oneOverDet;
  result._m32 = (_m12 * _m31 - _m11 * _m32) * oneOverDet;
  result._m33 = (_m11 * _m22 - _m12 * _m21) * oneOverDet;

  result._m41 = -(_m41 * result._m11 + _m42 * result._m21 + _m43 *
result._m31);
  result._m42 = -(_m41 * result._m12 + _m42 * result._m22 + _m43 *
result._m32);
  result._m43 = -(_m41 * result._m13 + _m42 * result._m23 + _m43 *
result._m33);

  return result;
}
```

With this code, any matrix we will be using can be inverted.

That's it for the Matrix class; it's now useful for both 2D and 3D applications. Next, we will apply it.

Matrix Operations on Sprites

Create a new game state called MatrixTestState. This state will draw a sprite and apply various matrices to that sprite. Here is the code to just draw the sprite, which should be quite familiar to you by now.

```
class MatrixTestState : IGameObject
{
  Sprite _faceSprite = new Sprite();
```

```
Renderer _renderer = new Renderer();
public MatrixTestState(TextureManager textureManager)
{
  _faceSprite.Texture = textureManager.Get("face");
  Gl.glEnable(Gl.GL_TEXTURE_2D);
}
public void Render()
{
  Gl.glClearColor(0.0f, 0.0f, 0.0f, 1.0f);
  Gl.glClear(Gl.GL_COLOR_BUFFER_BIT);
  _renderer.DrawSprite(_faceSprite);
  _renderer.Render();
}
public void Update(double elapsedTime)
{
}
}
```

This code uses the face sprite from the earlier chapters. The matrices will be applied to the sprite in the `MatrixTestState` constructor.

```
Matrix m = new Matrix();
m.SetRotate(new Vector(0, 0, 1), Math.PI/5);

for (int i = 0; i < _faceSprite.VertexPositions.Length; i++)
{
  _faceSprite.VertexPositions[i] *= m;
}
```

Run the code and you will notice that the face has been rotated. The rotation is done along the Z axis (0, 0, 1); this is the axis that comes out of the screen. Imagine the face sprite is a piece of paper on the screen. To rotate it, you stick a pin through it, attaching it to the screen and damaging your monitor! The pin represents the Z axis. Spinning the paper sprite now will spin it around that axis. For 2D objects in an orthographic projection, the Y axis and Z axis aren't very useful for rotations, but they would be useful in a 3D game. Any normalized axis can be used to rotate an object, not just the major X, Y, and Z axes.

In the code example, the rotation amount is given in radians `Math.PI/5`, which is equivalent to 36 degrees. The rotation matrix is applied to each vertex that makes up the sprite. We've now used one matrix that slightly rotates the sprite;

let's add another matrix that will scale it. The scale matrix will be combined with the rotation matrix by multiplying them. Modify the existing code in the constructor so it looks like the code here:

```
Matrix m = new Matrix();
m.SetRotate(new Vector(0, 0, 1),Math.PI/5);

Matrix mScale = new Matrix();
mScale.SetScale(new Vector(2.0, 2.0, 0.0));

m *= mScale;

for (int i = 0; i < _faceSprite.VertexPositions.Length; i++ )
{
  _faceSprite.VertexPositions[i] *= m;
}
```

This code creates a scale matrix that scales the X and Y axis by 2. This is combined with the rotation matrix by multiplying them together and assigning the result to the matrix m. This new combined m matrix is then applied to the face sprite, scaling and rotating it. The order of matrix multiplication is important; multiplying matrix a by matrix b is not guaranteed to have the same result as matrix b by matrix a. Play around with different matrices to get a good idea of how they work together.

The final code snippet will demonstrate the inverse matrix. The inverse matrix reverses a matrix operation. If rotate-scale matrix was multiplied by its inverse matrix, then the result would be the identity matrix. The identity matrix will not have any effect on the sprite when it is applied to it.

```
Matrix m = new Matrix();
m.SetRotate(new Vector(0, 0, 1),Math.PI/5);

Matrix mScale = new Matrix();
mScale.SetScale(new Vector(2.0, 2.0, 2.0));

m *= mScale;
Vector scale = m.GetScale();
m *= m.Inverse();

for (int i = 0; i < _faceSprite.VertexPositions.Length; i++ )
```

```
{
  _faceSprite.VertexPositions[i] *= m;
}
```

Experiment with the translation matrix as well, and try combining the matrices in different orders.

Modifying the Sprite to Use Matrices

The sprite currently has a translation method `SetPosition`, but it doesn't have similar `SetScale` or `SetRotation` methods. These would be very useful functions to add and would be great to use with the tween functions. Modifying the sprite class is quite simple but some additional members and methods need to be added.

```
double _scaleX = 1;
double _scaleY = 1;
double _rotation = 0;
double _positionX = 0;
double _positionY = 0;

public void ApplyMatrix(Matrix m)
{
  for (int i = 0; i < VertexPositions.Length; i++)
  {
    VertexPositions[i] *= m;
  }
}
public void SetPosition(Vector position)
{
  Matrix m = new Matrix();
  m.SetTranslation(new Vector(_positionX, _positionY, 0));
  ApplyMatrix(m.Inverse());
  m.SetTranslation(position);
  ApplyMatrix(m);
  _positionX = position.X;
  _positionY = position.Y;
}
```

```
public void SetScale(double x, double y)
{
  double oldX = _positionX;
  double oldY = _positionY;
  SetPosition(0, 0);
  Matrix mScale = new Matrix();
  mScale.SetScale(new Vector(_scaleX, _scaleY, 1));
  mScale = mScale.Inverse();
  ApplyMatrix(mScale);
  mScale = new Matrix();
  mScale.SetScale(new Vector(x, y, 1));
  ApplyMatrix(mScale);
  SetPosition(oldX, oldY);
  _scaleX = x;
  _scaleY = y;
}

public void SetRotation(double rotation)
{
  double oldX = _positionX;
  double oldY = _positionY;
  SetPosition(0, 0);
  Matrix mRot = new Matrix();
  mRot.SetRotate(new Vector(0, 0, 1), _rotation);
  ApplyMatrix(mRot.Inverse());
  mRot = new Matrix();
  mRot.SetRotate(new Vector(0, 0, 1), rotation);
  ApplyMatrix(mRot);
  SetPosition(oldX, oldY);
  _rotation = rotation;
}
```

These extra functions allow the sprite to be rotated and scaled as needed. They are a little more expensive, but it's very easy to transfer these functions to a 3D model. These functions can be trimmed down quite a bit to gain a performance boost.

Optimization

It's important to focus on games and only optimize when it's needed. For most games, the matrix class is already as fast as it needs to be, but programmers, as a rule, like to optimize, so here are some pointers. Matrices involve a lot of arithmetic so reducing the use of matrices is generally a good thing. The most optimized code is the code that never runs.

At the moment, each sprite is made of two triangles, making a total of six vertices, but really, a sprite could be made with a mere four vertices. A good starting point to address this would be investigating the index buffer functions in the OpenGL documentation.

Modern CPUs have specialized hardware, SIMD (which stands for Single Instruction, Multiple Data), to do matrix and vector operations. The SIMD instructions dramatically increase the speed of matrix calculations. Unfortunately, at the time of writing, SIMD operations are only supported under the Mono implementation of C#.

Most of your test programs will be built in debug mode. Release mode is much faster. There is also an option to turn on optimization if you right-click the project in the solution explorer and choose Properties.

Garbage collection is one thing that can make C# slower than a language like C++. The best way to avoid slow down from the garbage collection is to reduce the amount of objects created in the main loop. You are creating an object any time you use the keyword new. Objects are best created once in the constructor or defined as a member of the object and not in the process or render loops.

Some of the matrix operations create matrices. It makes them convenient to use and a lot of the object creation will be optimized away, but they can be made more efficient. When debugging, if you right-click the window, there's an option called "Go to Disassembly." This shows the IL (intermediate language) generated by each line of the C# code. The fewer IL instructions, the faster the code will run, provided the release build optimization doesn't already remove these IL instructions for you. Unfortunately, any optimizations the compiler performs will generally not be shown in the disassembly.

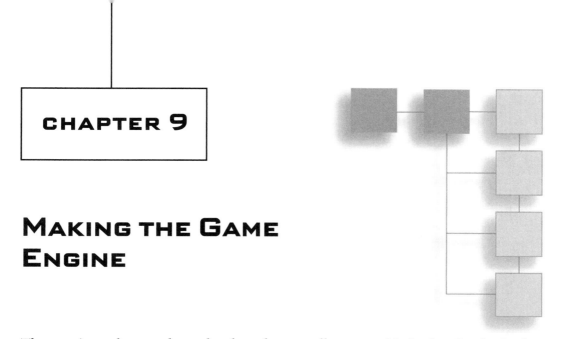

CHAPTER 9

MAKING THE GAME ENGINE

The previous chapters have developed an excellent reusable body of code. Rather than copy this code from project to a project, it should be collected together in its own awesome engine library. It can then be shared by several game projects so that all changes and improvements happen in one place.

A New Game Engine Project

The game engine project will be unlike any of the projects we've created so far. The game engine doesn't run by itself; instead, it is used by a separate game project. This means the game engine is more correctly referred to as a library rather than a program. As you learn more techniques, you can add more code to this library and tune it to your needs. Figure 9.1 shows how the library can be used by several projects at once.

Close any projects in Visual Studio and start a new project by going to File > New Project. This will bring up a dialog box, as shown in Figure 9.2. Choose the Class Library option. The game engine will be a library used by other projects. Next to the name, I've chosen simply "Engine," but this is your game engine so name it whatever you like.

If you are using Visual Studio 2008 it's important to remember to change the build type to ×86. This is because the DevIL libraries are currently only available for 32-bit projects. Right-click the project, choose Properties, and click the Build tab. On the Configuration drop-down box, choose All Configurations, then on

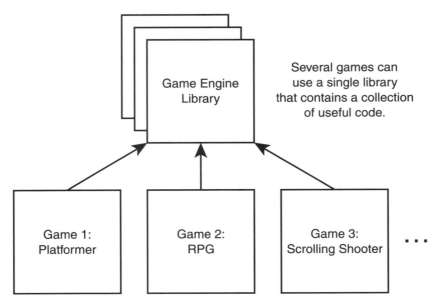

Figure 9.1
Using the game engine library.

the Platform Target drop-down box chose ×86. The settings can be seen in Figure 9.3. If your result doesn't look like Figure 9.3, you're already set up for 32 bit. In Visual Studio 2010, these settings should be handled automatically. If you

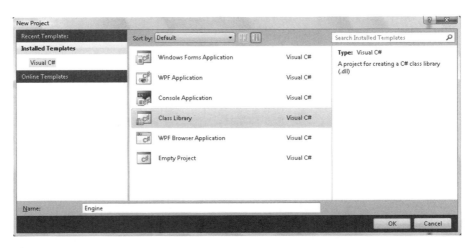

Figure 9.2
Create a class library project.

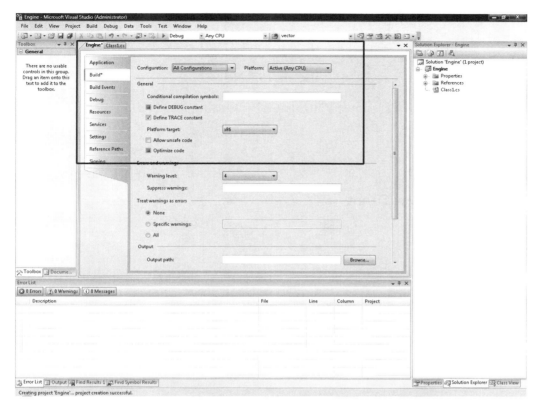

Figure 9.3
Settings for a 32-bit project.

do need to edit the build targets in 2010, then right-click the solution in the solution explorer and open the Properties window. In the Properties dialog, click on Configuration and then click Configuration Manager. In the Configuration Manager, you can add the ×86 platform and then select it for the engine project.

The next step is to add all the classes, tests, and references that make up the engine and then add the new project to source control. You can add the Tao references by clicking the browse tab of the Add References dialog and manually browsing to the dll files, which should be in the Tao framework install directory (with Vista and Windows 7 it will probably be C:\Program Files (×86)\TaoFramework\bin and for Windows XP it should be C:\Program Files\TaoFramework\bin). Alternatively, you may find the libraries already exist under the Recent tab in Add References dialog.

The references required are

- Tao framework OpenGL binding for .NET

- Tao framework Tao.DevIL binding for .NET

- Tao framework Windows Platform API binding for .NET

- nuint.framework

- System.Drawing

- System.Windows.Forms

The core engine components are

- Batch

- CharacterData

- CharacterSprite

- Color

- FastLoop

- Font

- FontParser

- IGameObject

- Input

- Matrix

- Point

- PreciseTimer

- Renderer

- Sprite

- StateSystem

- Text

- Texture

- TextureManager

- Tween

- Vector

These core engine classes should all be set to `public`. If they are `private`, `protected`, or `internal` then any game using the engine library will not be able to access them. There may also be `private`, `protected`, or `internal` functions that now need to be made `public` so that they may be accessed from the library; change these to public as you encounter them.

As you develop games, you can extend the engine with useful code you create. The engine should never have any gameplay code for a specific game; the engine should be general enough to form the basis of many different games.

Extending the Game Engine

The classes we've created so far cover a good deal of what is desirable in a game engine. There are a few omissions: the input library could be better developed, there is no support for handling multiple textures, and there is no support for sound. These are all simple changes that will round out the engine.

You may notice that if you try to run the game engine project, you'll receive this error: "A project with an Output Type of Class Library cannot be started directly." Class libraries have no main function; they do not directly run code. Instead, other projects make use of the code they contain. That means if you want to test part of the engine you'll need to make a new project that uses the engine.

Using the Game Engine in a Project

A new project needs to be created that will make use of the new engine class. This project will be used to run the engine code and test the various improvements we'll be making.

Close the engine project in Visual Studio and start a new project by selecting File > New > Project. This time choose a Windows Form Application instead of a

Class Library. This project is going to be used to test the engine library so call it "EngineTest." Click OK and a new project will be generated.

This project now needs to load the engine library. Visual Studio uses two terms: Solution and Project. Each time we've started a new project, Visual Studio has created a solution to contain that project. The solution usually shares the same name as the main project; in this case, there is a solution called EngineTest that contains a project with the same name. This can be seen in the solution explorer shown in Figure 9.4.

A solution can contain several different projects. Our EngineTest solution needs to contain the engine project so that it can use the engine code. It's very simple to add new projects. Right-click the EngineTest solution in the solution explorer;

Figure 9.4
A solution with one project.

this will display a context menu as can be seen in Figure 9.5. Choose Add > Existing Project and the Add Existing Project dialog box will appear.

The dialog will provide a view of the project directory on your machine (see Figure 9.6). One of these subdirectories will contain your engine library. Visual Studio displays the solution and its projects using a directory structure. Open the Engine folder (if you named your game engine some other name, then find the corresponding folder). Inside this folder is another folder called Engine. (The first Engine folder is the solution and the second engine folder is the project.) Open the second Engine folder. Inside this folder is a file called Engine.csproj; this is the file that represents the C# program. Open this file.

The solution explorer will now have two projects: Engine, the class library, and EngineTest, the project that will use the engine library. The engine library project

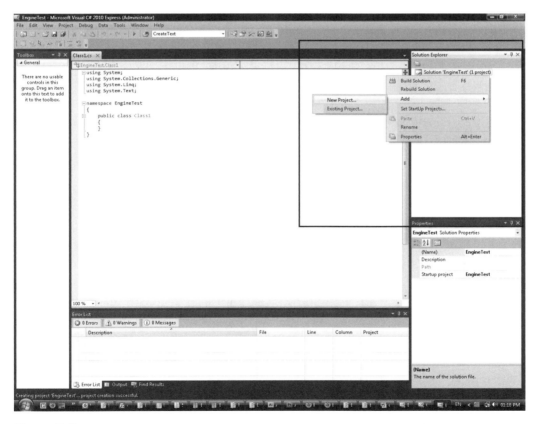

Figure 9.5
Adding a project to a solution.

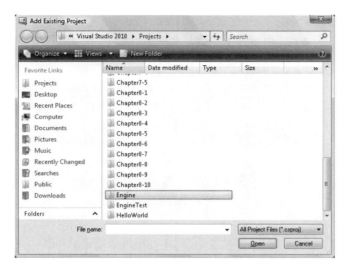

Figure 9.6
List of Solution folders.

hasn't been copied across to the EngineTest solution; it's just a reference. All its code stays in the same place. This makes it easier to work with several projects using the engine library but without duplicating the code. The Engine code can be edited from any solution and all the changes will be shared with all projects using the library.

You may notice that the font for the EngineTest project is in bold. This is because when you run the solution, the EngineTest project will be executed. A solution might contain several projects that could generate executables, and the Solution Explorer needs to know which project you want to run and debug. You can make the Engine project the start-up project by right-clicking its name in the Solution Explorer and choosing Set as Start Up Project. The Engine project's name will now turn bold, and the EngineTest project name will turn non-bold. Running the project will produce an error stating class libraries are not executable. Right-click the TestEngine project and set that as the start-up project again so you can once again run the solution. This functionality is useful if you also wanted to develop a level editor or other tool for your game. It could be added to the solution as an additional project that makes use of the engine and game project.

Engine and TestEngine exist in the same solution, but at the moment they do not have access to each other. TestEngine needs to access the code in Engine, but Engine should never need to know about the TestEngine project. In the Solution

Figure 9.7
The References folder.

Explorer, expand the EngineTest project; beneath the project is a References folder, as shown in Figure 9.7.

Right-click the Folder icon and choose Add Reference from the context menu. This will bring up the dialog box that we've used before to add references to NUnit and the Tao libraries. The Add Reference dialog box has a number of tabs along its top; by default, the .NET tab is selected. The .NET tab lists all the references to .NET libraries that are installed on the computer. This time we want to include a reference to the Engine project. Click the Projects tab, as shown in Figure 9.8.

There is only one project; select it and press OK. Now the EngineTest project has a reference to the Engine project. It also needs the following .NET references added; `System.Drawing`, `Tao.OpenGL`, `Tao.DevIL`, and

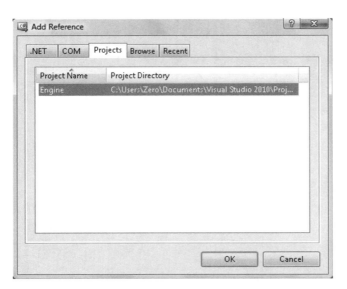

Figure 9.8
Adding a project as a reference.

`Tao.Platforms.Window`. This is so the `SimpleOpenGL` control can be added to the form and OpenGL can be set up. Some of this could be moved into the engine library using a default set up class. The dll files for `DevIL`, `ILU`, and `ILUT` need to be copied to the `bin/debug/` and `bin/release/` directories of the EngineTest project.

Drop a `SimpleOpenGL` control on to the EngineTest form and set its `dock` property to `fill`, the same way that you have done for earlier projects. Now view the form.cs code.

```
using System;
using System.Collections.Generic;
using System.ComponentModel;
using System.Data;
using System.Drawing;
using System.Linq;
using System.Text;
using System.Windows.Forms;

namespace EngineTest
{
  public partial class Form1 : Form
```

```
  {
    public Form1()
    {
      InitializeComponent();
    }
  }
}
```

This is default code created by Visual Studio for a Windows Form project. The using statements at the top refer to the different libraries the form is using. Now that we have an Engine project, a new using statement can be added.

```
using Engine;
```

This will provide access to all the classes in the engine library. The normal setup code also needs to be written. Here is the default setup code for a new game project.

```
using System;
using System.Collections.Generic;
using System.ComponentModel;
using System.Data;
using System.Drawing;
using System.Linq;
using System.Text;
using System.Windows.Forms;
using Tao.OpenGl;
using Tao.DevIl;
using Engine;

namespace EngineTest
{
  public partial class Form1 : Form
  {
    bool            _fullscreen      = false;
    FastLoop        _fastLoop;
    StateSystem     _system          = new StateSystem();
    Input           _input           = new Input();
    TextureManager  _textureManager  = new TextureManager();

    public Form1()
```

```
{
  InitializeComponent();
  simpleOpenGlControl1.InitializeContexts();

  InitializeDisplay();
  InitializeTextures();
  InitializeGameState();

  _fastLoop = new FastLoop(GameLoop);
}

private void InitializeGameState()
{
  // Load the game states here
}

private void InitializeTextures()
{
  // Init DevIl
  Il.ilInit();
  Ilu.iluInit();
  Ilut.ilutInit();
  Ilut.ilutRenderer(Ilut.ILUT_OPENGL);

  // Load textures here using the texture manager.
}

private void UpdateInput()
{
  System.Drawing.Point mousePos = Cursor.Position;
  mousePos = simpleOpenGlControl1.PointToClient(mousePos);

  // Now use our point definition,
  Engine.Point adjustedMousePoint = new Engine.Point();
  adjustedMousePoint.X = (float)mousePos.X - ((float)ClientSize.
    Width / 2);
  adjustedMousePoint.Y = ((float)ClientSize.Height / 2) - (float)
    mousePos.Y;
  _input.MousePosition = adjustedMousePoint;
}

private void GameLoop(double elapsedTime)
```

```
    {
      UpdateInput();
      _system.Update(elapsedTime);
      _system.Render();
      simpleOpenGlControl1.Refresh();
    }

    private void InitializeDisplay()
    {
      if (_fullscreen)
      {
        FormBorderStyle = FormBorderStyle.None;
        WindowState = FormWindowState.Maximized;
      }
      else
      {
        ClientSize = new Size(1280, 720);
      }
      Setup2DGraphics(ClientSize.Width, ClientSize.Height);
    }

    protected override void OnClientSizeChanged(EventArgs e)
    {
      base.OnClientSizeChanged(e);
      Gl.glViewport(0, 0, this.ClientSize.Width, this.ClientSize.
        Height);
      Setup2DGraphics(ClientSize.Width, ClientSize.Height);
    }

    private void Setup2DGraphics(double width, double height)
    {
      double halfWidth = width / 2;
      double halfHeight = height / 2;
      Gl.glMatrixMode(Gl.GL_PROJECTION);
      Gl.glLoadIdentity();
      Gl.glOrtho(-halfWidth, halfWidth, -halfHeight, halfHeight,
        -100, 100);
      Gl.glMatrixMode(Gl.GL_MODELVIEW);
      Gl.glLoadIdentity();
    }
  }
}
```

This same type of setup code can be used to start any number of projects, so it's worth keeping it as a file somewhere or refactoring it into the engine. The Up-dateInput code has had to change from our earlier examples. There are two classes with the same name—Point. One Point is from System.Drawing and the other is from our Engine library. To let the compiler know which point we mean, the fully qualified name is used; for example:

```
// Using the fully qualified name removes potential confusion.
System.Drawing.Point point = new System.Drawing.Point();
Engine.Point point = new Engine.Point();
```

Running this test program will produce a blank screen, which means that everything is working as expected. This project can now be used to run any engine tests required. Extra game states can be added as required. The engine currently doesn't support multiple textures very well so that will be the next change.

Multiple Textures

The engine library currently handles sprites with differing textures poorly. To demonstrate how it handles different textures, create a new game state called MultipleTexturesState. As with earlier states, this should implement IGameObject and be loaded using the StateSystem. This state will be testing the texture system; therefore, it will also need to take a TextureManager object in its constructor. The loading code can be placed in the In-itializeGameState method in form.cs.

```
private void InitializeGameState()
{
  // Load the game states here
  _system.AddState("texture_test", new MultipleTexturesState
(_textureManager));

  _system.ChangeState("texture_test");
}
```

This new state will need to create sprites with different textures. Two new textures are provided on the CD in the Assets directory: spaceship.tga and space-ship2.tga. These are large low detail sprites of two different spaceships. Add these .tga files to the solution and set the properties so that they will be copied into the build directory.

The new textures need to be loaded into the `TextureManager`; this is done in the `IntializeTextures` method.

```
// Load textures here using the texture manager.
_textureManager.LoadTexture("spaceship", "spaceship.tga");
_textureManager.LoadTexture("spaceship2", "spaceship2.tga");
```

Now that the textures are loaded, they can be used in the `MultipleTextures State`.

```
class MultipleTexturesState : IGameObject
{
  Sprite _spaceship1 = new Sprite();
  Sprite _spaceship2 = new Sprite();
  Renderer _renderer = new Renderer();

  public MultipleTexturesState(TextureManager textureManager)
  {
    _spaceship1.Texture = textureManager.Get("spaceship");
    _spaceship2.Texture = textureManager.Get("spaceship2");

    // Move the first spaceship, so they're not overlapping.
    _spaceship1.SetPosition(-300, 0);
  }

  public void Update(double elapsedTime) {}

  public void Render()
  {
    _renderer.DrawSprite(_spaceship1);
    _renderer.DrawSprite(_spaceship2);
    _renderer.Render();
  }
}
```

The state creates two sprites, one for each of the spaceship textures. The first spaceship is moved back 300 pixels on the X axis. This prevents the spaceships from overlapping. Run this state and you will see something similar to Figure 9.9.

In Figure 9.9, the second spaceship is drawn correctly, but the first one has the wrong texture. The first spaceship's sprite is the correct dimensions for its

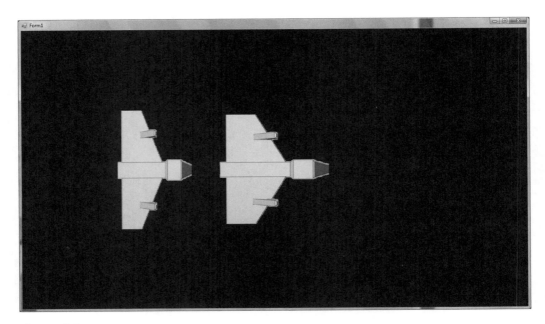

Figure 9.9
Incorrect texturing.

texture so it seems squashed compared to the second spaceship sprite, which has both correct dimensions and the correct texture.

The problem here is that the OpenGL is never being told when the texture changes. If it doesn't know, it uses whatever texture was set last. In the game loop a lot of texture changing per frame can slow things down, but a moderate amount of texture changing is nothing to worry about and indeed is essential for most games.

The class that needs to be modified is the Renderer class. The Renderer class batches up all the sprites so that they can be sent to the graphics card all at once. At the moment the Renderer class doesn't check which texture a sprite uses. It needs to check to see if it's drawing something with a new texture. If it is, then it can tell OpenGL to draw whatever has been batched so far with the old texture and then start a new batch using this new texture.

Here's the current Renderer.DrawSprite code.

```
public void DrawSprite(Sprite sprite)
{
    _batch.AddSprite(sprite);
}
```

The extra logic transforms it to this code.

```
int _currentTextureId = -1;
public void DrawSprite(Sprite sprite)
{
  if (sprite.Texture.Id == _currentTextureId)
  {
    _batch.AddSprite(sprite);
  }
  else
  {
    _batch.Draw(); // Draw all with current texture

    // Update texture info
    _currentTextureId = sprite.Texture.Id;
    Gl.glBindTexture(Gl.GL_TEXTURE_2D, _currentTextureId);
    _batch.AddSprite(sprite);
  }
}
```

Rerun the project and you should see something similar to Figure 9.10.

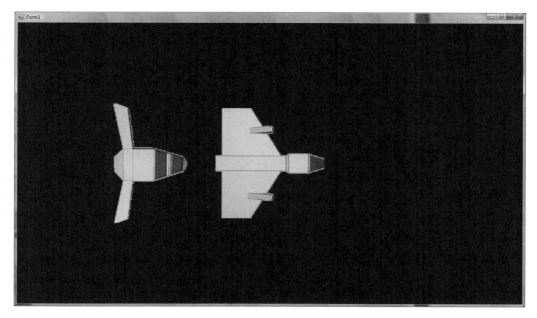

Figure 9.10
Correct texturing.

The code isn't quite as simple as before, but it now allows the engine to support sprites with different textures. You might be thinking about the worst case situation for this code; every single sprite that's drawn may force a texture change. The way to avoid this is to sort out the things being drawn and ensure that the maximum numbers of vertices that are using the same texture are sent together. There is another way to minimize the number of texture changes. Instead of using lots of separate small textures, textures are grouped together and combined into a bigger texture; this is often referred to as a texture atlas. Sprites can then reference this big texture but change the U,V coordinates of their vertices so they only use a small part of it (this is how the font rendering works). Generally, if it's not a problem, then don't try to fix it!

Adding Sound Support

Sound is very easy to ignore, but it can change the feeling of how a game plays. Sound is also very easy to add using the excellent OpenAL library. Before worrying about the details, think about how a very simple sound library interface might work using a code sketch.

```
SoundManager soundManager = new SoundManager();
soundManager.Add("zap", "zap.wav");
Sound zapSound = soundManager.Play("zap")
if (soundManager.IsSoundPlaying("zap"))
{
    soundManager.StopPlaying(zapSound);
}
```

This code indicates that a sound library should manage sounds in a similar way to the texture manager. When a sound is played, a reference will be returned. The reference can be used to control the sound; check if it's playing with the IsSoundPlaying method or stop it playing with the StopPlaying method. It would also be nice to have looping sounds and a volume control.

Creating Sound Files

To test the new sound code, some sounds will be needed. Broadly speaking, games have two categories of sound: sound effects like a gun shooting and background music or ambient sound.

A great way to generate sound effects is to use the hard to pronounce sfxr program created by Tomas Pettersson. It's available on the CD and be can seen in Figure 9.11.

Sfxr is a program that randomly generates sound effects for games. The sound effects sound a little like those that might have been generated by NES consoles. Keep clicking the Randomize button and new sounds will be generated. Once you've found a sound you like, it can be exported as a wave file. I've included two generated sound effects called soundeffect1.wav and soundeffect2.wav in the Assets directory on the CD. These should be added to the TestEngine project in the same way the textures were added. Sfxr sounds are great for retro-style games or placeholder sounds.

Developing a SoundManager

OpenAL is a professional-level library used by many modern games, so it has a wide range of support for more advanced sound effects, such as playing sounds from a 3D position. It also has functions to generate the Doppler Effect.

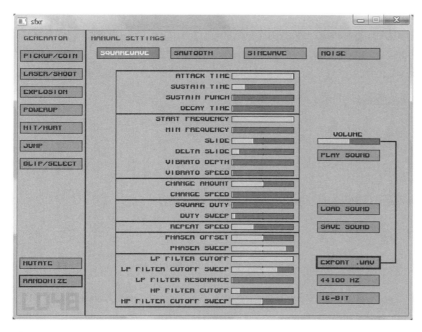

Figure 9.11
Creating sound effects with sfxr.

A common example of the Doppler Effect is a police car or ambulance driving past—as the vehicle passes, the frequency of the siren changes. Because the game we'll be making will be 2D, we won't use this functionality, but it can be very useful. Dig around the documentation and experiment with the library to get the full benefit from it.

To start using OpenAL the reference needs to be added to the engine library project. It's called "Tao Framework Tao.OpenAl Binding for .NET." If it is not listed under the .NET tab of the Add Reference dialog then choose the Browse tab and navigate to the Tao framework install directory \TaoFramework\bin and choose it from there. OpenAL also requires alut.dll, ILU.dll, and OpenAL32.dll to be copied to the bin/debug and bin/release directories. These dll files can be found in your Tao Framework install directory, \TaoFramework\lib. A skeleton class can then be created based on the simple idealized API and how the TextureManager works. First, a sound class needs to be made. This class will represent a sound being played.

```
public class Sound
{
}
```

This sound class can then be used to build up the sound manager skeleton class. Remember these classes should be added to the engine project because this code can be used by many games.

```
public class SoundManager
{
  public SoundManager()
  {
  }

  public void LoadSound(string soundId, string path)
  {
  }

  public Sound PlaySound(string soundId)
  {
    return null;
  }

  public bool IsSoundPlaying(Sound sound)
```

```
  {
    return false;
  }

  public void StopSound(Sound sound)
  {
  }
}
```

Sound hardware can only play a limited number of sounds at the same time. The number of sounds that can be played is known as the number of channels. Modern sound hardware can often play up to 256 sounds at the same time. The OpenAL way to discover how many sound channels are available is to keep requesting channels and when the hardware can't give any more, then you have the maximum number.

```
readonly int MaxSoundChannels = 256;
List <int> _soundChannels = new List<int>();

public SoundManager()
{
  Alut.alutInit();
  DicoverSoundChannels();
}

private void DicoverSoundChannels()
{
  while (_soundChannels.Count < MaxSoundChannels)
  {
    int src;
    Al.alGenSources(1, out src);
    if (Al.alGetError() == Al.AL_NO_ERROR)
    {
      _soundChannels.Add(src);
    }
    else
    {
      break; // there's been an error - we've filled all the channels.
    }
  }
}
```

Each sound channel is represented by a number so the available sound channels can simply be stored as a list of integers. The SoundManager constructor initializes OpenAL and then discovers all the sound channels up to a maximum of 256. The OpenAL function alGenSources generates a sound source that reserves one of the channels. The code then checks for errors; if an error is detected that means that OpenAL is unable to generate anymore sound sources so it's time to break out of the loop.

Now that sound sources are being discovered, it's time to start adding this to the EngineTest project. The sound manager should exist in the form.cs class and then be passed through to any state that wants to use it.

```
public partial class Form1 : Form
{
  bool            _fullscreen    = false;
  FastLoop        _fastLoop;
  StateSystem     _system        = new StateSystem();
  Input           _input         = new Input();
  TextureManager  _textureManager = new TextureManager();
  SoundManager    _soundManager   = new SoundManager();
```

The last line creates the sound manager object and it will discover the number of sound channels available. The next step is to load files from the hard disk into memory. A new structure needs to be created to hold the data for the sound files loaded from the disk.

```
public class SoundManager
{
  struct SoundSource
  {
    public SoundSource(int bufferId, string filePath)
    {
      _bufferId = bufferId;
      _filePath = filePath;
    }
    public int _bufferId;
    string _filePath;
  }
  Dictionary<string, SoundSource> _soundIdentifier = new
    Dictionary<string, SoundSource>();
```

The `SoundSource` structure stores information about the loaded sounds. It will only ever be used internally by the sound manager so the structure exists inside the `SoundManager` class. When sound data is loaded in OpenAL an integer will be returned; this is used to keep a reference of the sound for when it needs to be played. The sound identifier maps a sound's name onto the sound data in memory. The dictionary will be a big table of all the sounds available to the game with an easy English language string to identify each one.

To load a sound file the `using System.IO;` statement needs to added to the top of the file. The `LoadSound` function will fill up the `_soundIdentifier` dictionary with game sounds.

```
public void LoadSound(string soundId, string path)
{
  // Generate a buffer.
  int buffer = -1;
  Al.alGenBuffers(1, out buffer);

  int errorCode = Al.alGetError();
  System.Diagnostics.Debug.Assert(errorCode == Al.AL_NO_ERROR);

  int format;
  float frequency;
  int size;
  System.Diagnostics.Debug.Assert(File.Exists(path));
  IntPtr data = Alut.alutLoadMemoryFromFile(path, out format, out size,
    out frequency);
  System.Diagnostics.Debug.Assert(data != IntPtr.Zero);
  // Load wav data into the generated buffer.
  Al.alBufferData(buffer, format, data, size, (int)frequency);
  // Everything seems ok, add it to the library.
  _soundIdentifier.Add(soundId, new SoundSource(buffer, path));
}
```

The `LoadSound` method first generates a buffer. This buffer is an area in memory where the sound data from the disk will be stored. The OpenAL utility function `alutLoadMemoryFromFile` is used to read the data for a .wav into memory. The memory containing the file data is then put into the buffer along with the format, size, and frequency data that was also read in. This buffer is then put into our dictionary using the `soundId` to identify it later.

The sounds added to the project can now be loaded up using the sound manager.

```
public Form1()
{
  InitializeComponent();
  simpleOpenGlControl1.InitializeContexts();

  InitializeDisplay();
  InitializeSounds();            // Added
  InitializeTextures();
  InitializeGameState();
```

The `InitializeSound` method will be responsible for loading in all the sound files.

```
private void InitializeSounds()
{
  _soundManager.LoadSound("effect", "soundEffect1.wav");
  _soundManager.LoadSound("effect2", "soundEffect2.wav");
}
```

To test the sound manager, we really need some code that will let these sounds be played. When OpenAL plays a sound, it returns an integer that is used to reference the sound being played. For our sound manager we are going to wrap that integer up in the `Sound` class; this gives it more context in the code. Instead of just being a random integer, it's now a typed sound object. If there is an error playing the sound, then minus one will be returned. Here's the `Sound` class that will wrap up OpenAL's reference integer.

```
public class Sound
{
  public int Channel { get; set; }

  public bool FailedToPlay
  {
    get
    {
      // minus is an error state.
      return (Channel == -1);
    }
  }
}
```

```
public Sound(int channel)
{
  Channel = channel;
}
}
```

Now that the sound wrapper class is properly defined a `PlaySound` method can be added. A sound has to be played on a channel. There are only a limited number of channels so it is possible that all the channels are full. In this case the sound won't be played. This is a very simple heuristic, but for games with hundreds of sounds going off at once, it may be better to give each sound a priority and then the sounds of high priority can take over the channels of those sounds with a lower priority. The priority value would probably be linked to the sound's volume and distance from the player.

A method needs to be written that will determine if a given channel is free or not. An easy way to determine if a channel is free is to ask OpenAL if it is currently playing anything on that channel. If nothing is being played on the channel then it is free. This new `IsChannelPlaying` method should be added to the `SoundManager` class.

```
private bool IsChannelPlaying(int channel)
{
  int value = 0;
  Al.alGetSourcei(channel, Al.AL_SOURCE_STATE, out value);
  return (value == Al.AL_PLAYING);
}
```

The OpenAL function `alGetSourcei` queries a particular channel about some property. The property is determined by the second argument; in this case we're asking what the current state of the source is. The size and speed of the sound on the channel can also be queried in this way. The `IsChannelPlaying` function checks to see if the channel's current state is set to playing; if so it returns true, otherwise false.

With the `IsChannelPlaying` function defined we can now use it to build up another function that will return a free channel. This new function will be called `GetNextFreeChannel` and will iterate through the list of channels that the function `DicoverSoundChannels` made in the constructor. If it can't find a sound channel free it will return minus one as an error flag.

```
private int FindNextFreeChannel()
{
  foreach (int slot in _soundChannels)
  {
    if (!IsChannelPlaying(slot))
    {
      return slot;
    }
  }

  return -1;
}
```

This function finds a free channel for our sounds to be played on. This makes it easy to write a robust `PlaySound` method that will be able to deal with a limited number of sound channels.

```
public Sound PlaySound(string soundId)
{
  // Default play sound doesn't loop.
  return PlaySound(soundId, false);
}
public Sound PlaySound(string soundId, bool loop)
{
  int channel = FindNextFreeChannel();
  if (channel != -1)
  {
    Al.alSourceStop(channel);
    Al.alSourcei(channel, Al.AL_BUFFER, _soundIdentifier[soundId].
      _bufferId);
    Al.alSourcef(channel, Al.AL_PITCH, 1.0f);
    Al.alSourcef(channel, Al.AL_GAIN, 1.0f);

    if (loop)
    {
      Al.alSourcei(channel, Al.AL_LOOPING, 1);
    }
    else
    {
      Al.alSourcei(channel, Al.AL_LOOPING, 0);
    }
    Al.alSourcePlay(channel);
```

```
    return new Sound(channel);
  }
  else
  {
    // Error sound
    return new Sound(-1);
  }
}
```

There are two `PlaySound` methods implemented here; one takes a flag to indicate if the sound should be looped, the other takes one less parameter and assumes the sound should only be played once by default. The `PlaySound` method finds a free channel and loads the buffered data from the `SoundSource` on to the channel. It then resets the default properties on the sound channel, including the pitch and gain and the looping flag is set. This determines if the sound will finish after being played once or if it just repeats. Finally it's told to play the sound and a `Sound` object is returned.

The sound system is now working well enough to test. It can load files from the disk and play them as needed. Here is a new test state that will demonstrate the functionality.

```
class SoundTestState : IGameObject
{
  SoundManager _soundManager;
  double _count = 3;

  public SoundTestState(SoundManager soundManager)
  {
    _soundManager = soundManager;
  }

  public void Render()
  {
    // The sound test doesn't need to render anything.
  }

  public void Update(double elapsedTime)
  {
    _count -= elapsedTime;
```

```
    if (_count < 0)
    {
      _count = 3;
      _soundManager.PlaySound("effect");
    }
  }
}
```

Load it in the normal way and make sure it's the default state being run. Every 3 seconds it will play the first sound effect. Feel free to change the numbers around or play both effects at once.

This code snippet plays both sounds at the same time, demonstrating that the SoundManager uses hardware channels correctly.

```
public void Update(double elapsedTime)
{
  _count -= elapsedTime;

  if (_count < 0)
  {
    _count = 3;
    _soundManager.PlaySound("effect");
    _soundManager.PlaySound("effect2");
  }
}
```

The SoundManager class needs a few final functions to make it more complete. It needs to be able test if a sound is playing and also to stop a sound. Volume control would also be useful.

```
public bool IsSoundPlaying(Sound sound)
{
  return IsChannelPlaying(sound.Channel);
}
public void StopSound(Sound sound)
{
  if (sound.Channel == -1)
  {
    return;
  }
  Al.alSourceStop(sound.Channel);
}
```

The check to see if a sound is playing reuses the code that checks if a sound is playing on a particular channel. The stop sound function uses an OpenAL method to stop the sound on a certain channel. These new functions can be tested in the sound state again.

```
public void Update (double elapsedTime)
{
  _count -= elapsedTime;

  if (_count < 0)
  {
    _count = 3;
    Sound soundOne = _soundManager.PlaySound("effect");
    Sound soundTwo = _soundManager.PlaySound("effect2");

    if (_soundManager.IsSoundPlaying(soundOne))
    {
      _soundManager.StopSound(soundOne);
    }
  }
}
```

Here the first sound is told to play, then immediately after there's a check to see if it is playing. This returns true and another call stops the sound. The first is never heard as it's always stopped by the end of the game loop.

```
float _masterVolume = 1.0f;
public void MasterVolume(float value)
{
  _masterVolume = value;
  foreach (int channel in _soundChannels)
  {
    Al.alSourcef(channel, Al.AL_GAIN, value);
  }
}
```

In OpenAL the volume can be altered by specifying the gain on a channel. The gain goes from 0 to 1. Here the master volume is set for every channel. The volume is also stored in a class variable. When a new sound is played it will overwrite the current gain setting for the channel so it needs to be reapplied. This can be done at the bottom of the PlaySound method.

```
{
  Al.alSourcef(channel, Al.AL_GAIN, _masterVolume);
  Al.alSourcePlay(channel);
  return new Sound(channel);
}
```

This now gives a master volume control for all the sound channels. The volume can also be set per channel; this is useful when fading out music or making one sound effect more or less noticeable.

```
public void ChangeVolume(Sound sound, float value)
{
  Al.alSourcef(sound.Channel, Al.AL_GAIN, _masterVolume * value);
}
```

Here the volume of a particular sound is scaled by the master volume; this ensures that if the player sets his master volume to low setting then a new sound isn't going to suddenly be very loud. The value should be between 0 and 1. Here's some more test code that shows these volume changes.

```
public SoundTestState(SoundManager soundManager)
{
  _soundManager = soundManager;
  _soundManager.MasterVolume(0.1f);
}
```

This will set the volume to be one tenth its previous value. If you run the test state again the difference should be immediately noticeable. The final task for the sound manager is to make sure it closes down correctly. It creates a lot of references to sound files and data and it needs to free these when it is destroyed. The best way to do this is to implement the IDisposable interface.

```
public class SoundManager : IDisposable
 public void Dispose()
 {
   foreach (SoundSource soundSource in _soundIdentifier.Values)
   {
     SoundSource temp = soundSource;
     Al.alDeleteBuffers(1, ref temp._bufferId);
   }
   _soundIdentifier.Clear();
   foreach (int slot in _soundChannels)
```

```
{
  int target = _soundChannels[slot];
  Al.alDeleteSources(1, ref target);
}
Alut.alutExit();
}
```

This function goes through all the sound buffers and frees them and then through all the sound card channels and frees those too.

Improving Input

The engine has very limited input support at the moment. The input class can be queried to find the mouse cursor position, but there is no other support. The ideal input for arcade-style games is a gamepad—a purpose-built piece of hardware to play games. First-person shooter games, strategy, and simulation games tend to work best with a mouse and keyboard combination. For this reason the mouse should be more fully supported by the engine and the state of keyboard should also be queryable.

Wrapping Game Controllers

For arcade games there's no better controller than a gamepad. PCs have always been behind the curve when compared to console controllers, but recent console controllers have begun to use USB connections. This makes it very easy to add support for console controllers on the PC. These controllers also tend to be the most popular for users as they're high quality, widely supported, and very easy to find.

Controller support in the TaoFramework is good but not excellent. There is support for control sticks and analog buttons but no support for haptic effects like rumble or more exotic controllers like the Wiimote. External C# libraries for these newer controls do exist if they tickle your interest but they will require some research to use.

The controller support in this engine will be limited to the more standard controllers. For PC gamers the most popular controller is likely to be the Xbox 360 controller because it's immediately recognized by Windows and has a large selection of buttons and control sticks. The gamepad code will be flexible enough that any standard joypad could be used, but for testing purposes, it's the Xbox 360 pad that will be targeted. It can be seen in Figure 9.12.

Figure 9.12
Xbox 360 controller.

The Xbox 360 controller has a few different types of controls. It has two control sticks on the front. We'll want to be able to get a value from −1 to 1 on the X and Y axis to determine where the player moves the control stick. The D-pad supports basic left, right, up, and down commands. The rest of the controls on the face of the controller are made from simple buttons: Back, Start, A, B, X, and Y. These are quite simple with only two states, pressed and not pressed, which can be represented by a boolean variable. On the top of the controller are four shoulder buttons, the buttons nearest the face of the controller are simple buttons, but the back two buttons are triggers. The triggers are special because they are not digital on/off buttons; they have a range of values from 0 to 1, depending on how hard they are pressed. All these controls together make quite a complicated gamepad, and a number of classes will be needed to describe the different functionality of each type of control.

To begin, a new game test state needs to be made. Call this state `InputTestState` and make it the default loaded state in the normal way. The gamepad wrappings exist in the SDL section of the Tao Framework; this means another reference needs to be added—Tao framework SDL Binding for .NET (if you don't have this reference then select the Browse tab, navigate to the

TaoFramework\lib directory, and choose `Tao.Sdl.dll`). Another dll also needs to be copied to the bin directories—`sdl.dll`. We'll go through the various controls one by one and then finally build up a fully supported controller. If you're not using an Xbox 360 controller, you should still be able to follow this section with any other controller. Just substitute the controls used where necessary.

The controller is the main way that the player interacts with the game. For that reason we always want to know the current state of the controller. Every frame will include code that asks the controller the state of all its controls, and we'll update our representation in memory. The constant querying of a device is sometimes known as polling.

The SDL library requires its joypad subsystem to be initiated before it can be used. For now this code can be placed in the `InputTestState`, but it will eventually need to be moved to the input class.

```
bool _useJoystick = false;
public InputTestState()
{
  Sdl.SDL_InitSubSystem(Sdl.SDL_INIT_JOYSTICK);
  if (Sdl.SDL_NumJoysticks() > 0)
  {
    // Start using the joystick code
    _useJoystick = true;
  }
}
```

The setup code is quite readable. The joystick subsystem of SDL is initiated, and if it works, then we can use joysticks. Next in the engine library project, a class needs to be made to represent the controller. Because a very specific controller is going to be represented, I'm going to call this class `XboxController`.

```
using System;
using System.Collections.Generic;
using System.Linq;
using System.Text;
using Tao.Sdl;

namespace Engine
{
  public class XboxController : IDisposable
```

```
  {
    IntPtr _joystick;
    public XboxController(int player)
    {
      _joystick = Sdl.SDL_JoystickOpen(player);
    }

    #region IDisposable Members

    public void Dispose()
    {
      Sdl.SDL_JoystickClose(_joystick);
    }

    #endregion
  }
}
```

This code creates the joystick using a player index. You might want to create a game that supports two or more players; in this case, you'd need to create a controller for each player. The joystick is also disposable so it will release its reference to the controller once it's destroyed.

The controller can now be created in the test state.

```
XboxController _controller;
public InputTestState()
{
  Sdl.SDL_InitSubSystem(Sdl.SDL_INIT_JOYSTICK);
  if (Sdl.SDL_NumJoysticks() > 0)
  {
    // Start using the joystick code
    _useJoystick = true;
    _controller = new XboxController(0);
  }
}
```

The first type of control we're going to wrap is the control stick. Control sticks are great for moving the character and positioning the camera. Control sticks aren't made perfectly. They will often report that they're being pushed even when they are centered and the controller is resting on the desk. The solution to this problem is to ignore all output from the control stick unless it's pushed over a certain threshold. The part that is ignored is known as the dead zone and can vary from controller to controller (for this reason it's best to be a little generous when specifying your dead zone).

The control stick is treated as two axes—an X axis from left to right and a Y axis from top to bottom. SDL returns the axis information as `short` number value but a more convenient representation would be a `float` from -1 to 1. The -1 value is the control stick pushed far to the left (or down) and 1 would be fully pushed in the opposite direction.

```
using System;
using System.Collections.Generic;
using System.Linq;
using System.Text;
using Tao.Sdl;

namespace Engine
{
  public class ControlStick
  {
    IntPtr _joystick;
    int _axisIdX = 0;
    int _axisIdY = 0;
    float _deadZone = 0.2f;

    public float X { get; private set; }
    public float Y { get; private set; }

    public ControlStick(IntPtr joystick, int axisIdX, int axisIdY)
    {
      _joystick = joystick;
      _axisIdX = axisIdX;
      _axisIdY = axisIdY;
    }

    public void Update()
    {
      X = MapMinusOneToOne(Sdl.SDL_JoystickGetAxis(_joystick,
        _axisIdX));
      Y = MapMinusOneToOne(Sdl.SDL_JoystickGetAxis(_joystick,
        _axisIdY));
    }
```

```
    private float MapMinusOneToOne(short value)
    {
      float output = ((float)value / short.MaxValue);

      // Be careful of rounding error
      output = Math.Min(output, 1.0f);
      output = Math.Max(output, -1.0f);

      if (Math.Abs(output) < _deadZone)
      {
        output = 0;
      }

      return output;
    }
  }


}
```

SDL represents analog controls using axes that can be polled with `SDL_JoystickGetAxis`. The control sticks are made from two axes. A controller might have a number of different axes, so in the constructor, two indices are passed in to identify which axis we want this control stick to represent. These identifying numbers will change for each type of controller. The numbers that represent the different controls on the gamepad aren't guaranteed to be the same for every type of gamepad. One gamepad's left control stick might have the index one, but another type of gamepad might index the left control stick with the index five. For this reason, it's often a good idea to allow the player to remap his controls.

The `Update` method is called once per frame, and it updates the X and Y values with values from –1 to 1, depending on the position of the stick. There's also a little buffer for the dead zone that ignores small movements of the control stick.

The Xbox controller has two control sticks so the controller class can now be updated to represent this.

```
public ControlStick LeftControlStick { get; private set; }
public ControlStick RightControlStick { get; private set; }
public XboxController(int player)
{
  _joystick = Sdl.SDL_JoystickOpen(player);
```

```
  LeftControlStick = new ControlStick(_joystick, 0, 1);
  RightControlStick = new ControlStick(_joystick, 4, 3);
}

public void Update()
{
  LeftControlStick.Update();
  RightControlStick.Update();
}
```

Now that there are some controls on the controller, it can be used in the test state to move things around. The Update function of InputTestState updates the SDL joystick system and then updates the controller, updating all of its control values.

```
public void Update(double elapsedTime)
{
  if (_useJoystick == false)
  {
    return;
  }

  Sdl.SDL_JoystickUpdate();
  _controller.Update();
}

public void Render()
{
  if (_useJoystick == false)
  {
    return;
  }
  Gl.glDisable(Gl.GL_TEXTURE_2D);
  Gl.glClearColor(1, 1, 1, 0);

  Gl.glClear(Gl.GL_COLOR_BUFFER_BIT);
  Gl.glPointSize(10.0f);
  Gl.glBegin(Gl.GL_POINTS);
  {
    Gl.glColor3f(1, 0, 0);
    Gl.glVertex2f(
      _controller.LeftControlStick.X * 300,
```

```
    _controller.LeftControlStick.Y * -300);
  Gl.glColor3f(0, 1, 0);
  Gl.glVertex2f(
    _controller.RightControlStick.X * 300,
    _controller.RightControlStick.Y * -300);
  }
  Gl.glEnd();
}
```

The Render function draws a white background and a green and red dot representing each of the control sticks. The point size is increased and texture mode is disabled to make the dots more visible. Run the program and move the dots around the screen. The control stick's values only go from –1 to 1, which isn't a large enough number to visually move the dots around the screen; therefore, the value is multiplied by 300. The Y axis is multiplied by –300 to invert it; try removing the minus sign and see which control scheme you prefer.

The next control to wrap is the button. There are actually ten buttons on the Xbox 360 controller. The X, Y, A, B buttons, start and back, the two shoulder buttons, and pushing in the two control sticks. As before, add the following control class to the engine library project.

```
using System;
using System.Collections.Generic;
using System.Linq;
using System.Text;
using Tao.Sdl;

namespace Engine
{
  public class ControllerButton
  {
    IntPtr _joystick;
    int _buttonId;

    public bool Held { get; private set; }

    public ControllerButton(IntPtr joystick, int buttonId)
    {
      _joystick = joystick;
      _buttonId = buttonId;
    }
```

```
    public void Update ()
    {
      byte buttonState = Sdl.SDL_JoystickGetButton (_joystick,
_buttonId);
      Held = (buttonState == 1);
    }

  }
}
```

The Update function of the button updates the Held variable. The controller class can now have its buttons added.

```
public ControllerButton ButtonA { get; private set; }
public ControllerButton ButtonB { get; private set; }
public ControllerButton ButtonX { get; private set; }
public ControllerButton ButtonY { get; private set; }

// Front shoulder buttons
public ControllerButton ButtonLB { get; private set; }
public ControllerButton ButtonRB { get; private set; }

public ControllerButton ButtonBack { get; private set; }
public ControllerButton ButtonStart { get; private set; }

// If you press the control stick in
public ControllerButton ButtonL3 { get; private set; }
public ControllerButton ButtonR3 { get; private set; }
public XboxController (int player)
{
  _joystick = Sdl.SDL_JoystickOpen (player);
  LeftControlStick = new ControlStick (_joystick, 0, 1);
  RightControlStick = new ControlStick (_joystick, 4, 3);
  ButtonA = new ControllerButton (_joystick, 0);
  ButtonB = new ControllerButton (_joystick, 1);
  ButtonX = new ControllerButton (_joystick, 2);
  ButtonY = new ControllerButton (_joystick, 3);
  ButtonLB = new ControllerButton (_joystick, 4);
  ButtonRB = new ControllerButton (_joystick, 5);
  ButtonBack = new ControllerButton (_joystick, 6);
  ButtonStart = new ControllerButton (_joystick, 7);
  ButtonL3 = new ControllerButton (_joystick, 8);
```

```
        ButtonR3 = new ControllerButton (_joystick, 9);
}
```

The buttons all need to update their state.

```
public void Update()
{
LeftControlStick.Update();
RightControlStick.Update();
ButtonA.Update();
ButtonB.Update();
ButtonX.Update();
ButtonY.Update();
ButtonLB.Update();
ButtonRB.Update();
ButtonBack.Update();
ButtonStart.Update();
ButtonL3.Update();
ButtonR3.Update();
}
```

To represent these buttons on screen we need a new function in the test state.

```
private void DrawButtonPoint (bool held, int yPos)
{
  if (held)
  {
    Gl.glColor3f (0, 1, 0);
  }
  else
  {
    Gl.glColor3f (0, 0, 0);
  }
  Gl.glVertex2f (-400, yPos);
}
```

This function makes it easy for all the buttons to be rendered, the color changing as they're pressed. The function calls can go in the test state Render function just under where the control stick axes are rendered but still before the Gl.glEnd(); statement.

```
DrawButtonPoint (_controller.ButtonA.Held, 300);
DrawButtonPoint (_controller.ButtonB.Held, 280);
```

```
DrawButtonPoint(_controller.ButtonX.Held, 260);
DrawButtonPoint(_controller.ButtonY.Held, 240);
DrawButtonPoint(_controller.ButtonLB.Held, 220);
DrawButtonPoint(_controller.ButtonRB.Held, 200);
DrawButtonPoint(_controller.ButtonBack.Held, 180);
DrawButtonPoint(_controller.ButtonStart.Held, 160);
DrawButtonPoint(_controller.ButtonL3.Held, 140);
DrawButtonPoint(_controller.ButtonR3.Held, 120);
```

Run the test state and the now the buttons and axes are both displayed on the screen. Each button pressed will be represented visually on screen.

There are only two types of controls left that need to be handled—the trigger buttons and the D-pad. The triggers are actually represented by a single axis—the left trigger represents 0 to 1 on the axis and the right trigger represents 0 to −1. This means the code to wrap the trigger can be quite similar to the control pad.

```
using System;
using System.Collections.Generic;
using System.Linq;
using System.Text;
using Tao.Sdl;

namespace Engine
{
  public class ControlTrigger
  {
    IntPtr _joystick;
    int _index;
    bool _top = false; // The triggers are treated as axes and need split-
ting up
    float _deadZone = 0.24f;
    public float Value { get; private set; }

    public ControlTrigger(IntPtr joystick, int index, bool top)
    {
      _joystick = joystick;
      _index = index;
      _top = top;
    }
```

```
public void Update()
{
  Value = MapZeroToOne(Sdl.SDL_JoystickGetAxis(_joystick, _index));
}

private float MapZeroToOne(short value)
{
  float output = ((float)value / short.MaxValue);

  if (_top == false)
  {
    if (output > 0)
    {
      output = 0;

    }
    output = Math.Abs(output);
  }

  // Be careful of rounding error
  output = Math.Min(output, 1.0f);
  output = Math.Max(output, 0.0f);

  if (Math.Abs(output) < _deadZone)
  {
    output = 0;
  }

  return output;
}
  }

}
```

The ControlTrigger class operates on an axis but only takes half the value of
it. There are only two triggers so it's not much to add to the controller class. In
the constructor, the two triggers are set up using the same axis.

Finally, both the triggers must be added to the Update function of the
controller.

```
public ControlTrigger RightTrigger { get; private set; }
```

```
public ControlTrigger LeftTrigger { get; private set; }
// in the constructor
RightTrigger = new ControlTrigger(_joystick, 2, false);
LeftTrigger = new ControlTrigger(_joystick, 2, true);
// in the update function
RightTrigger.Update();
LeftTrigger.Update();
```

These triggers can be visualized very simply; two more points are rendered, each representing one of the triggers. The more the trigger is pressed, the further the point moves. The colors are slightly different so that they can be distinguished from the control sticks. This code should be added to the test state near the button and control stick visualizations but between the glBegin and glEnd statements.

```
Gl.glColor3f(0.5f, 0, 0);
Gl.glVertex2f(50, _controller.LeftTrigger.Value * 300);
Gl.glColor3f(0, 0.5f, 0);
Gl.glVertex2f(-50, _controller.RightTrigger.Value * 300);
```

The final control to be added is the D-pad. The D-pad will be treated as four buttons: up, down, left, and right.

```
using System;
using System.Collections.Generic;
using System.Linq;
using System.Text;
using Tao.Sdl;

namespace Engine
{
  public class DPad
  {
    IntPtr _joystick;
    int _index;

    public bool LeftHeld { get; private set; }
    public bool RightHeld { get; private set; }
    public bool UpHeld { get; private set; }
    public bool DownHeld { get; private set; }
    public DPad(IntPtr joystick, int index)
```

```
    {
      _joystick = joystick;
      _index = index;
    }

    public void Update()
    {
      byte b = Sdl.SDL_JoystickGetHat(_joystick, _index);
      UpHeld = (b == Sdl.SDL_HAT_UP);
      DownHeld = (b == Sdl.SDL_HAT_DOWN);
      LeftHeld = (b == Sdl.SDL_HAT_LEFT);
      RightHeld = (b == Sdl.SDL_HAT_RIGHT);
    }
  }
}
```

The controller only has one D-pad, but it still needs to be added.

```
public DPad Dpad { get; private set; }

public XboxController(int player)
{
  _joystick = Sdl.SDL_JoystickOpen(player);
  Dpad = new DPad(_joystick, 0);
// ... later in the code
public void Update()
{
  Dpad.Update();
```

The D-pad also needs to be added to the update loop, and that completes all the controls on the controller. Finally, it can be visualized by reusing the button display code.

```
DrawButtonPoint(_controller.Dpad.UpHeld, 80);
DrawButtonPoint(_controller.Dpad.DownHeld, 60);
DrawButtonPoint(_controller.Dpad.LeftHeld, 40);
DrawButtonPoint(_controller.Dpad.RightHeld, 20);
```

All the controls of the Xbox 360 controller are now supported and it's relatively easy to construct any other type of controller from these control pieces. The controller is quite easy to use, but the buttons could do with a little more work. At the moment, the button reports if it is held down or not; in games it's often more useful to know if the button was just pressed. Pressing the button once for instance can be used for selecting a menu option or firing a gun. It's a simple piece of code to add. This code should be added to the `ControllerButton` class.

```
bool _wasHeld = false;
public bool Pressed { get; private set; }
public void Update()
{
  // reset the pressed value
  Pressed = false;

  byte buttonState = Sdl.SDL_JoystickGetButton(_joystick, _buttonId);
  Held = (buttonState == 1);

  if (Held)
  {
    if (_wasHeld == false)
    {
      Pressed = true;
    }
    _wasHeld = true;
  }
  else
  {
    _wasHeld = false;
  }
}
```

The `Pressed` value is only true for one frame when the button is pressed, the `Held` value is true for as long as the button is pressed. The controller class and the various controls it uses have resulted in quite a lot of code. This code is all related and could be better organized by separating it into its own namespace, `Engine.Input`. Reorganizing your code is an important part of building up a reusable library. All the controller classes are involved with input so a separate input sub-library can be created.

Right-click the engine project and choose New Folder on the context menu, as shown in Figure 9.13.

Call the new folder Input and drag and drop all the control classes into the folder. The `input` class should also be added to this folder so you end with something

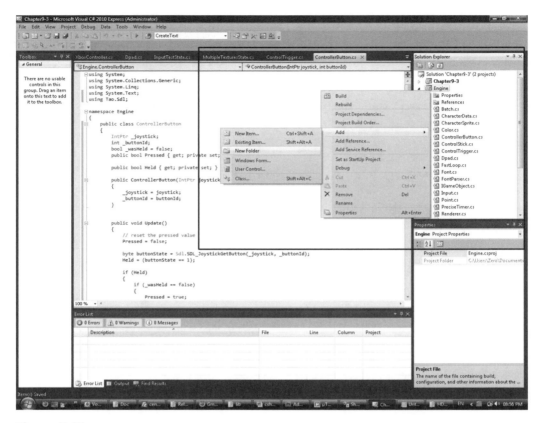

Figure 9.13
Creating a new project subfolder.

similar to Figure 9.14. Anytime you create a new class in the Input folder it will automatically use the namespace `Engine.Input`. The classes we've just added however need their namespaces changed manually. For each of the classes, change the line `namespace Engine` to `namespace Engine.Input`.

Try running the code. There will probably be a few errors complaining that the input classes cannot be found. To resolve these errors, add the statement `using Engine.Input;` to the top of the file.

Finally, the controller should be added to the `Input` class. In this case the Xbox 360 controller is used and the assumption is that if any user wants to use a different controller, it will have equivalent functionality to an Xbox 360 controller.

Figure 9.14
Separating out the input classes.

```csharp
public class Input
{
  public Point MousePosition { get; set; }
  bool _usingController = false;
  XboxController Controller { get; set; }

  public Input()
  {
    Sdl.SDL_InitSubSystem(Sdl.SDL_INIT_JOYSTICK);
    if (Sdl.SDL_NumJoysticks() > 0)
    {
      Controller = new XboxController(0);
      _usingController = true;
    }
  }
}
```

```
public void Update(double elapsedTime)
{
  if (_usingController)
  {
    Sdl.SDL_JoystickUpdate();
    Controller.Update();
  }
}
}
```

The `Input` class only supports one controller here, but it would be simple to extend to several controllers if you wanted to support that.

Adding Better Mouse Support

The mouse support at the moment is quite minor. The position of the cursor relative to the form is calculated in the form.cs and then this updates the input class mouse position. The mouse input is bound to the form and so to some extent the input class must be aware of the form. Make a new class called `Mouse` in the `Engine.Input` namespace; this class will store information about the current state of the mouse.

```
using System;
using System.Collections.Generic;
using System.Linq;
using System.Text;
using System.Windows.Forms;

namespace Engine.Input
{
  public class Mouse
  {
    Form _parentForm;
    Control _openGLControl;

    public Point Position { get; set; }

    public Mouse(Form form, Control openGLControl)
    {
      _parentForm = form;
      _openGLControl = openGLControl;
    }
```

```
public void Update (double elapsedTime)
{
  UpdateMousePosition () ;
}

private void UpdateMousePosition ()
{
  System.Drawing.Point mousePos = Cursor.Position;
  mousePos = _openGLControl.PointToClient (mousePos) ;

  // Now use our point definition,
  Engine.Point adjustedMousePoint = new Engine.Point () ;
  adjustedMousePoint.X = (float)mousePos.X - ((float)_parentForm.
    ClientSize.Width / 2) ;
  adjustedMousePoint.Y = ((float)_parentForm.ClientSize.Height / 2)
    - (float)mousePos.Y;
  Position = adjustedMousePoint;
  }
 }
}
```

The Mouse class updates its own position using the form and OpenGL control that are passed into the constructor. This new Mouse class needs to be added to the Input class.

```
public class Input
{
  public Mouse Mouse { get; set; }
```

It replaces the previous code to get the mouse position. The new Mouse class also needs to have its Update function called from the Input class.

```
public void Update (double elapsedTime)
{
  if (_usingController)
  {
    Sdl.SDL_JoystickUpdate () ;
    Controller.Update () ;
  }
  Mouse.Update (elapsedTime) ;
}
```

The `Mouse` class isn't constructed in the `Input` class because the `Input` class shouldn't have to know about the form or simple OpenGL control; instead, the mouse object is constructed in the form.cs constructor.

```
public Form1()
{
  InitializeComponent();
  simpleOpenGlControl1.InitializeContexts();
  _input.Mouse = new Mouse(this, simpleOpenGlControl1);
```

Now that the `Mouse` class exists, the `UpdateInput` function in the form class can be simplified.

```
private void GameLoop(double elapsedTime)
{
  UpdateInput(elapsedTime);
  _system.Update(elapsedTime);
  _system.Render();
  simpleOpenGlControl1.Refresh();
}

private void UpdateInput(double elapsedTime)
{
  // Previous mouse code removed.
  _input.Update(elapsedTime);
}
```

The `elapsedTime` is passed from the main `GameLoop` method into the `UpdateInput` method.

The `elapsedTime` has been passed to both the `UpdateInput` and `Update` functions in case we ever want the mouse to support a hover event. For instance, in a real-time strategy game, you might hover the mouse over a unit for a second or two, and on detecting that hover behavior, the game might pop up a tool tip displaying the unit's name and stats.

The mouse buttons can be treated in the same way as the controller buttons. The button will have `Held` and `Pressed` members. For the mouse, the state of the `Pressed` member corresponds to a Windows Forms click event. The gamepad works by polling, which means every frame the program queries the gamepad to find out what buttons are pressed and where the control sticks are. The mouse works a little differently than the gamepad, and it's not as straightforward to poll. Windows Form controls are associated with mouse events. An event is a way to call code when something happens; for instance, when the mouse moves, a button is clicked or double-clicked. These events can be hooked up to functions. We'll use the click event to determine when the mouse buttons are pressed and the up and down events to determine when the mouse button is held.

```
bool _leftClickDetect = false;
bool _rightClickDetect = false;
bool _middleClickDetect = false;

public bool MiddlePressed { get; private set; }
public bool LeftPressed { get; private set; }
public bool RightPressed { get; private set; }

public bool MiddleHeld { get; private set; }
public bool LeftHeld { get; private set; }
public bool RightHeld { get; set; }

public Mouse(Form form, Control openGLControl)
{
  _parentForm = form;
  _openGLControl = openGLControl;
  _openGLControl.MouseClick += delegate(object obj, MouseEventArgs e)
  {
    if (e.Button == MouseButtons.Left)
    {
      _leftClickDetect = true;
    }
    else if (e.Button == MouseButtons.Right)
    {
      _rightClickDetect = true;
    }
    else if (e.Button == MouseButtons.Middle)
    {
      _middleClickDetect = true;
    }
  };

  _openGLControl.MouseDown += delegate(object obj, MouseEventArgs e)
  {
```

```
    if (e.Button == MouseButtons.Left)
    {
      LeftHeld = true;
    }
    else if (e.Button == MouseButtons.Right)
    {
      RightHeld = true;
    }
    else if (e.Button == MouseButtons.Middle)
    {
      MiddleHeld = true;
    }
  };

  _openGLControl.MouseUp += delegate(object obj, MouseEventArgs e)
  {
    if (e.Button == MouseButtons.Left)
    {
      LeftHeld = false;
    }
    else if (e.Button == MouseButtons.Right)
    {
      RightHeld = false;
    }
    else if (e.Button == MouseButtons.Middle)
    {
      MiddleHeld = false;
    }
  };

  _openGLControl.MouseLeave += delegate(object obj, EventArgs e)
  {
    // If you move the mouse out the window then release all held buttons
    LeftHeld = false;
    RightHeld = false;
    MiddleHeld = false;
  };
}

public void Update(double elapsedTime)
{
  UpdateMousePosition();
```

```
  UpdateMouseButtons();
}

private void UpdateMouseButtons()
{
  // Reset buttons
  MiddlePressed = false;
  LeftPressed = false;
  RightPressed = false;

  if (_leftClickDetect)
  {
    LeftPressed = true;
    _leftClickDetect = false;
  }

  if (_rightClickDetect)
  {
    RightPressed = true;
    _rightClickDetect = false;
  }

  if (_middleClickDetect)
  {
    MiddlePressed = true;
    _middleClickDetect = false;
  }
}
```

In the constructor of the mouse, four OpenGL control events have an anonymous delegate attached to them. The mouse click event detects if the left, right, or middle mouse buttons have been pressed, and this sets a boolean to report if the event occurred. In the UpdateMouseButtons function, the detect booleans are used to set the public MiddlePressed, LeftPressed, and RightPressed variables. Presses should only occur for one frame, so at the start of the function all the button press flags are set to false. After the reset, the detect variables are checked, and if a press is detected, they are set back to true. The double-click event could be supported in a similar way.

The next three events determine if any of the mouse buttons are being held down. The down event detects when the mouse button is pressed down, and the up event detects when it's released again. These events are pretty straightforward, and they toggle the held flags for each button. The third event detects when the mouse leaves the control. This is important because once the mouse button leaves, no more events will be reported. This means the user could click down inside the control, leave the control, and release the mouse button. The release event would never be passed on and the held flags would get out of sync with the actual state of the mouse. For this reason, if the mouse leaves the control's area, then all the held flags are set to false.

The mouse input can be tested by creating a new game state—MouseTest-State—and loading it as the default game state in the EngineTest project.

```
class MouseTestState : IGameObject
{
  Input _input;

  bool _leftToggle = false;
  bool _rightToggle = false;
  bool _middleToggle = false;

  public MouseTestState(Input input)
  {
    _input = input;
  }


  private void DrawButtonPoint(bool held, int yPos)
  {
    if (held)
    {
      Gl.glColor3f(0, 1, 0);
    }
    else
    {
      Gl.glColor3f(0, 0, 0);
    }
    Gl.glVertex2f(-400, yPos);
  }

  public void Render()
  {
```

```
    Gl.glDisable(Gl.GL_TEXTURE_2D);
    Gl.glClearColor(1, 1, 1, 0);

    Gl.glClear(Gl.GL_COLOR_BUFFER_BIT);
    Gl.glPointSize(10.0f);
    Gl.glBegin(Gl.GL_POINTS);
    {
      Gl.glColor3f(1, 0, 0);
      Gl.glVertex2f(_input.Mouse.Position.X, _input.Mouse.Position.Y);

      if (_input.Mouse.LeftPressed)
      {
        _leftToggle = !_leftToggle;
      }

      if (_input.Mouse.RightPressed)
      {
        _rightToggle = !_rightToggle;
      }

      if (_input.Mouse.MiddlePressed)
      {
        _middleToggle = !_middleToggle;
      }

      DrawButtonPoint(_leftToggle, 0);
      DrawButtonPoint(_rightToggle, -20);
      DrawButtonPoint(_middleToggle, -40);

      DrawButtonPoint(_input.Mouse.LeftHeld, 40);
      DrawButtonPoint(_input.Mouse.RightHeld, 60);
      DrawButtonPoint(_input.Mouse.MiddleHeld, 80);
    }
    Gl.glEnd();
  }

  public void Update(double elapsedTime)
  {
  }
}
```

This test state reuses the DrawButtonPoint function from the earlier In-putTestState that was used to test the gamepad. This test state renders a dot beneath the mouse cursor and six other dots represent the button states. The top three dots represent the held state of each button. Hold down a button and its dot will light up; release the button and it will go black. The bottom three buttons represent the press state of the buttons. Each time a button is clicked, the dot that represents it will toggle its color.

This is all that's required for basic mouse support. There is still more work that can be done; for instance, detecting double-clicks of the mouse and having a way to poll the scroll wheel, but for most games what has been covered so far will be fine. The only remaining control method left to add is the keyboard.

Adding Keyboard Support

The keyboard is unlike the gamepad and the mouse because the method of interacting with it depends on the situation. If you have a screen that asks the user to enter his name, then you want a callback function that will tell you each character pressed by the user. But if you are in the middle of a fighting game, then you just want to be able to ask if a certain key has just been pressed; you don't care about the rest of the keys. These are two different modes of interaction and both are important and need to be supported.

The keyboard has an event-based system like the mouse. The form has `OnKey-Down` and `OnKeyUp` events that can have delegates attached. Unfortunately, these events ignore the arrow keys, and the arrow keys are very important in games because they are often used to control movement. The Alt key is also ignored as are a few other keys known collectively as the control keys. These keys generally have some meaning in the form and are therefore hidden from general use. Games need to use these keys so an alternative method of polling these keys needs to be implemented.

```
using System;
using System.Collections.Generic;
using System.Linq;
using System.Text;
using System.Runtime.InteropServices;
using System.Windows.Forms;

namespace Engine.Input
{
  public class Keyboard
```

```csharp
{
  [DllImport("User32.dll")]
  public static extern short GetAsyncKeyState(int vKey);

  Control _openGLControl;
  public KeyPressEventHandler KeyPressEvent;

  class KeyState
  {
    bool _keyPressDetected = false;
    public bool Held { get; set; }
    public bool Pressed { get; set; }

    public KeyState()
    {
      Held = false;
      Pressed = false;
    }

    internal void OnDown()
    {
      if (Held == false)
      {
        _keyPressDetected = true;
      }
      Held = true;
    }

    internal void OnUp()
    {
      Held = false;
    }

    internal void Process()
    {
      Pressed = false;
      if (_keyPressDetected)
      {
        Pressed = true;
        _keyPressDetected = false;
      }
    }
  }
}
```

```csharp
Dictionary<Keys, KeyState> _keyStates = new Dictionary<Keys,
  KeyState>();

public Keyboard(Control openGLControl)
{
  _openGLControl = openGLControl;
  _openGLControl.KeyDown += new KeyEventHandler(OnKeyDown);
  _openGLControl.KeyUp += new KeyEventHandler(OnKeyUp);
  _openGLControl.KeyPress += new KeyPressEventHandler(OnKeyPress);
}

void OnKeyPress(object sender, KeyPressEventArgs e)
{
  if (KeyPressEvent != null)
  {
    KeyPressEvent(sender, e);
  }
}

void OnKeyUp(object sender, KeyEventArgs e)
{
  EnsureKeyStateExists(e.KeyCode);
  _keyStates[e.KeyCode].OnUp();
}

void OnKeyDown(object sender, KeyEventArgs e)
{
  EnsureKeyStateExists(e.KeyCode);
  _keyStates[e.KeyCode].OnDown();
}

private void EnsureKeyStateExists(Keys key)
{
  if (!_keyStates.Keys.Contains(key))
  {
    _keyStates.Add(key, new KeyState());
  }
}

public bool IsKeyPressed(Keys key)
{
  EnsureKeyStateExists(key);
```

```
    return _keyStates[key].Pressed;
}

public bool IsKeyHeld(Keys key)
{
  EnsureKeyStateExists(key);
  return _keyStates[key].Held;
}

public void Process()
{
  ProcessControlKeys();
  foreach (KeyState state in _keyStates.Values)
  {
    // Reset state.
    state.Pressed = false;
    state.Process();
  }
}

private bool PollKeyPress(Keys key)
{
  return (GetAsyncKeyState((int)key) != 0);
}

private void ProcessControlKeys()
{
  UpdateControlKey(Keys.Left);
  UpdateControlKey(Keys.Right);
  UpdateControlKey(Keys.Up);
  UpdateControlKey(Keys.Down);
  UpdateControlKey(Keys.LMenu); // this is the left alt key
}

private void UpdateControlKey(Keys keys)
{
  if (PollKeyPress(keys))
  {
    OnKeyDown(this, new KeyEventArgs(keys));
  }
```

```
      else
      {
        OnKeyUp(this, new KeyEventArgs(keys));
      }
    }
  }

}
```

The keyboard state treats each key as a button with a `Pressed` and `Held` member. A subclass called `KeyState` contains the state of each key on the keyboard. The `Keyboard` constructor takes in a reference to the OpenGL control and adds delegates to its `KeyUp` and `KeyDown` events. These events are then used to update the state of the entire keyboard. The `KeyPress` event is also given a delegate, and this in turn fires another event called `KeyPressEvent`, passing on the data. `KeyPressEvent` is used when the user is typing the player name or entering data. When using the keyboard as a gaming device, the keys can be treated as buttons and queried with the functions `IsKeyPressed` and `IsKeyHeld`.

The slightly complicated part of the keyboard class is the polling of keys. This requires a C function to be imported from `User32.dll` and the `using System.Runtime.InteropServices;` needs to be added to the top of the file. The `KeyUp` and `KeyDown` events aren't fired for the arrow keys so the state of these keys is determined by `GetAsyncKeyState`. The `PollKeyPress` function uses `GetAsyncKeyState` to return true if the key is pressed and false if it isn't. Each frame the arrow keys and the Alt key are polled and the state is updated.

Create a new test state to confirm that the keyboard works. There's no code listing for this test state as it's very similar to the mouse state. Test out some of the keys and the arrow keys to confirm everything is working nicely. Once you are satisfied—that ends the modifications to the engine. The next step now is to create a game!

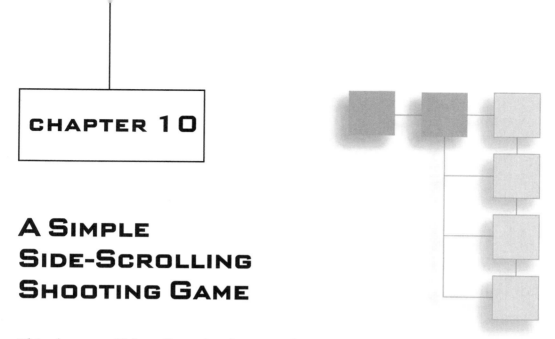

CHAPTER 10

A SIMPLE SIDE-SCROLLING SHOOTING GAME

This chapter will describe a simple game, develop a basic plan, and then cover its implementation. The implementation will be done in a pragmatic iterative style. A high-level first pass will get the game structure working. This will then be refined until it approaches the original description of the game.

A Simple Game

A simple game will demonstrate all the techniques that have been covered so far. We'll build a 2D scrolling shooter game. This type of game is quite simple to make and then easy to expand by adding more features. The pragmatic way to develop this game is to create a working game as quickly as possible, but it's still important to plan up front what these first stages will be. Figure 10.1 shows a high-level overview of the game flow.

The idea for this game is to create a simple yet complete game. Therefore, there will be a start screen, then an inner game, and finally a game over screen. The inner game will have a spaceship the player can move. The player should be able to press a button to fire a bullet that comes out of the front of the ship. There only needs to be one level, but more would be nice. The level will begin when the player goes from the start state to the inner game. After a set amount of time, the level ends. If the player is still alive at the end of the level, then that counts as a win; otherwise, the player loses the game. The level needs a number of enemies that advance towards the player and are able to shoot bullets. Enemies

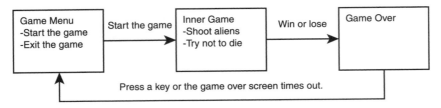

Figure 10.1
High-level game flow.

can be given a health value and take multiple shots to be destroyed. When destroyed they should explode.

By reading this quick description of the game, it's easy to start building up a list of classes and interactions. A good way to start the technical plan is to draw some boxes for the main classes and some arrows for the major interactions. We'll need three main game states, and the inner game state will be the most complicated. By looking at the game description, you can see that some of the important classes needed include `Player`, `Level`, `Enemy`, and `Bullet`. The level needs to contain and update the players, enemies, and bullets. Bullets should collide with enemies and players.

The inner game is where the player will fly the spaceship and blow up the oncoming enemies. The player ship will not actually move through space; instead, the movement will be faked. The player can move the player anywhere on the screen but the "camera" will stay fixed dead center. To give the impression of speeding through space, the background will be scrolled in the opposite direction the player is traveling. This greatly simplifies any player tracking or camera code.

This is a small game so we can start coding with this rather informal description. All game code goes in the game project and any code we generate that might be useful for multiple projects can go in the engine library. A more ambitious game plan might require a few small test programs—game states are very good for sketching out such code ideas.

The First Implementation Pass

The high-level view has broken the game down into three states. This first coding pass will create these three states and make them functional.

Create a new Windows Forms Application project. I've called the project Shooter, but feel free to choose whatever name you want. You are probably familiar with how to set up a project, but here is a quick overview. The solution will be set up in a very similar way to the EngineTest project in the previous chapters. The Shooter project uses the following references: Tao.DevIL, Tao. OpenGL, Tao.Platform.Windows, and System.Drawing. It will also need a reference to the Engine project. To do this, the Engine project should be added to the solution (right-click the Solution folder, choose Add > Existing Project, find the Engine project, and select it). Once the Engine project exists in the solution then the Shooter project can add it as a reference. To add the Engine project as a reference right-click the Shooter project references folder and choose Add Reference, navigate to the Projects tab, and choose the Engine project.

The Shooter project will use OpenGL, so in the Form editor, drag and drop a `SimpleOpenGLControl` onto the form and set its `Dock` property to "Fill." Right-click the Form1.cs and choose View Code. This file needs a game loop and initialization code added, which is supplied below.

```csharp
using System;
using System.Collections.Generic;
using System.ComponentModel;
using System.Data;
using System.Drawing;
using System.Linq;
using System.Text;
using System.Windows.Forms;
using Engine;
using Engine.Input;
using Tao.OpenGl;
using Tao.DevIl;

namespace Shooter
{
  public partial class Form1 : Form
  {
    bool            _fullscreen     = false;
    FastLoop        _fastLoop;
    StateSystem     _system         = new StateSystem();
    Input           _input          = new Input();
    TextureManager  _textureManager = new TextureManager();
    SoundManager    _soundManager   = new SoundManager();
```

```
public Form1()
{
  InitializeComponent();
  simpleOpenGlControl1.InitializeContexts();

  _input.Mouse = new Mouse(this, simpleOpenGlControl1);
  _input.Keyboard = new Keyboard(simpleOpenGlControl1);

  InitializeDisplay();
  InitializeSounds();
  InitializeTextures();
  InitializeFonts();
  InitializeGameState();

  _fastLoop = new FastLoop(GameLoop);
}

private void InitializeFonts()
{
  // Fonts are loaded here.
}

private void InitializeSounds()
{
  // Sounds are loaded here.
}

private void InitializeGameState()
{
  // Game states are loaded here
}

private void InitializeTextures()
{
  // Init DevIl
  Il.ilInit();
  Ilu.iluInit();
  Ilut.ilutInit();
  Ilut.ilutRenderer(Ilut.ILUT_OPENGL);

  // Textures are loaded here.
}
```

```csharp
    private void UpdateInput(double elapsedTime)
    {
      _input.Update(elapsedTime);
    }

    private void GameLoop(double elapsedTime)
    {
      UpdateInput(elapsedTime);
      _system.Update(elapsedTime);
      _system.Render();
      simpleOpenGlControl1.Refresh();
    }

    private void InitializeDisplay()
    {
      if (_fullscreen)
      {
        FormBorderStyle = FormBorderStyle.None;
        WindowState = FormWindowState.Maximized;
      }
      else
      {
        ClientSize = new Size(1280, 720);
      }
      Setup2DGraphics(ClientSize.Width, ClientSize.Height);
    }

    protected override void OnClientSizeChanged(EventArgs e)
    {
      base.OnClientSizeChanged(e);
      Gl.glViewport(0, 0, this.ClientSize.Width, this.ClientSize.
Height);
      Setup2DGraphics(ClientSize.Width, ClientSize.Height);
    }
    private void Setup2DGraphics(double width, double height)
    {
      double halfWidth = width / 2;
      double halfHeight = height / 2;
      Gl.glMatrixMode(Gl.GL_PROJECTION);
      Gl.glLoadIdentity();
      Gl.glOrtho(-halfWidth, halfWidth, -halfHeight, halfHeight,
-100, 100);
```

```
    Gl.glMatrixMode(Gl.GL_MODELVIEW);
    Gl.glLoadIdentity();
  }


  }
}
```

In this Form.cs code, a `Keyboard` object is created and assigned to the `Input` object. For the code to work a `Keyboard` member must be added to the `Input` class as below.

```
public class Input
{
  public Mouse Mouse { get; set; }
  public Keyboard Keyboard { get; set; }
  public XboxController Controller { get; set; }
```

The following DLL files will need to be added to the bin\Debug and bin\Release folders: alut.dll, DevIL.dll, ILU.dll, ILUT.dll, OpenAL32.dll, and SDL.dll. The project is now ready to use for developing a game.

This is the first game we've created, and it would be nice if the form title bar said something other than "Form1" when the game was running. It's easy to change this text in Visual Studio. In the solution explorer double-click the file Form1.cs; this will open the form designer. Click the form and go to the properties window. (If you can't find the properties window then go to the menu bar and choose View > Properties Window.) This will list all the properties associated with the form. Find the property labeled Text, and change the value to Shooter, as shown in Figure 10.2.

The Start Menu State

The first state to create is the start menu. For a first pass, the menu only needs two options: Start Game and Exit. These options are a kind of button; this state therefore needs two buttons and some title text. A mock-up for this screen is shown in Figure 10.3.

The title will be created using the `Font` and `Text` classes defined earlier in the book. There's a font on the CD called "title font"; it's a 48pt font with a suitably video game look. Add the .fnt and .tga files to the project and set the properties of each so that they are copied to the bin directory when the project is built.

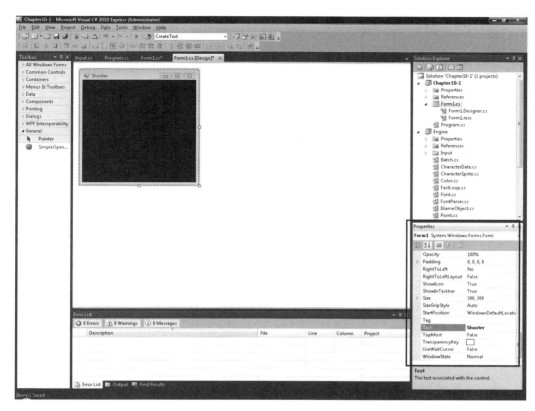

Figure 10.2
Changing the form title.

Figure 10.3
Title Screen mock-up.

The font file needs to be loaded in the Form.cs. If we were dealing with many fonts, it might be worth creating a `FontManager` class, but because we're only using one or two they can just be stored as member variables. Here is the code to load the font files.

```
private void InitializeTextures()
{
  // Init DevIl
  Il.ilInit();
  Ilu.iluInit();
  Ilut.ilutInit();
  Ilut.ilutRenderer(Ilut.ILUT_OPENGL);

  // Textures are loaded here.
  _textureManager.LoadTexture("title_font", "title_font.tga");
}

Engine.Font _titleFont;
private void InitializeFonts()
{
  _titleFont = new Engine.Font(_textureManager.Get("title_font"),
          FontParser.Parse("title_font.fnt"));
}
```

The font texture is loaded in the `IntializeTextures` function and this is used when the font object is created in the `IntializeFonts` method.

The title font can then be passed into the `StartMenuState` constructor. Add the following new `StartMenuState` to the Shooter project.

```
class StartMenuState : IGameObject
{
  Renderer  _renderer = new Renderer();
  Text     _title;

  public StartMenuState(Engine.Font titleFont)
  {
    _title = new Text("Shooter", titleFont);
    _title.SetColor(new Color(0, 0, 0, 1));
    // Center on the x and place somewhere near the top
    _title.SetPosition(-_title.Width/2, 300);
  }
```

```
  public void Update (double elapsedTime) { }

  public void Render ()
  {
    Gl.glClearColor (1, 1, 1, 0);

    Gl.glClear (Gl.GL_COLOR_BUFFER_BIT);
    _renderer.DrawText (_title);
    _renderer.Render ();
  }
}
```

The `StartMenuState` uses the font passed into the constructor to make the title text. The text is colored black, and then it's centered horizontally. The render loop clears the screen to white and draws the text. To run the state it needs to be added to the state system and set as the default state.

```
private void InitializeGameState ()
{
  // Game states are loaded here
  _system.AddState ("start_menu", new StartMenuState (_titleFont));
  _system.ChangeState ("start_menu");
}
```

Run the program and you should see something similar to Figure 10.4.

This stage is just a first pass. The title page can be refined and made prettier later. At the moment, functionality is the most important thing. To finish the title screen, the start and exit options are needed. These will be buttons, which means a button class will need to be made.

The buttons will be presented in a vertical list. At all times one of the buttons will be the selected button. If the user presses Enter on the keyboard or the A button on the gamepad, then the currently selected button will be pressed.

A button needs to know when it's selected; this is also known as having focus. Buttons also need to know what to do when they've been pressed; this is a great place to use a delegate. A button can be passed a delegate in the constructor and call that when it's pressed, executing any code we want. The button will also need methods to set its position. These requirements for the button describe something like the following class. The `Button` class is reusable so it can be added to the Engine project so it may be used in future projects.

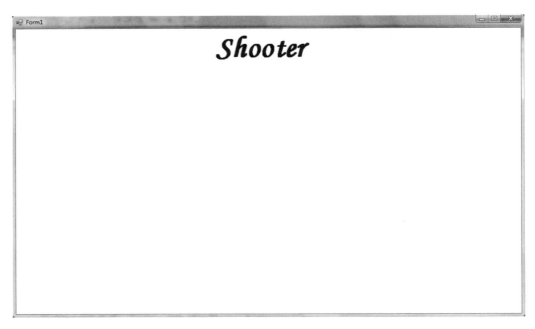

Figure 10.4
Rendering in the title.

```
public class Button
{
  EventHandler _onPressEvent;
  Text _label;
  Vector _position = new Vector();

  public Vector Position
  {
    get { return _position; }
    set
    {
      _position = value;
      UpdatePosition();
    }
  }

  public Button(EventHandler onPressEvent, Text label)
  {
    _onPressEvent = onPressEvent;
```

```
    _label = label;
    _label.SetColor(new Color(0, 0, 0, 1));
    UpdatePosition();
  }

  public void UpdatePosition()
  {
    // Center label text on position.
    _label.SetPosition(_position.X - (_label.Width / 2),
            _position.Y + (_label.Height / 2));
  }

  public void OnGainFocus()
  {
    _label.SetColor(new Color(1, 0, 0, 1));
  }

  public void OnLoseFocus()
  {
    _label.SetColor(new Color(0, 0, 0, 1));
  }

  public void OnPress()
  {
    _onPressEvent(this, EventArgs.Empty);
  }

  public void Render(Renderer renderer)
  {
    renderer.DrawText(_label);
  }
}
```

The button class doesn't directly handle the user input; instead, it relies on whichever piece of code uses it to pass on relevant input events. The OnGain-Focus and OnLoseFocus methods will be used to change the appearance of the button depending on the focus. This will let the user know which button he currently has selected. When the button position is changed, the label text position is also updated and centered. EventHandler is used to hold the function that will be called when the button is pressed. EventHandler describes a delegate that takes an object and event argument's enum.

Player input is detected by a class called Menu; it informs the buttons if they are selected or pressed. The Menu class contains a list of buttons, and only one button may have focus at any one time. The user can navigate the menu with the control pad or keyboard. The OnGainFocus and OnLoseFocus will change the button label text; this will let us know which button currently has the focus.

The color will be red when focused; otherwise, it will be black. Alternatively, the text could be enlarged, a background image could change, or some other values could be tweened in or out, but not now as this is the very first pass.

The menu will list the buttons vertically in a column, so a good name might be VerticalMenu. VerticalMenu is another reusable class so it can be added to the Engine project. The menu will need methods for adding buttons and a Render method.

```
using System;
using System.Collections.Generic;
using System.Linq;
using System.Text;
using Engine.Input; // Input needs to be added for gamepad input.
using System.Windows.Forms; // Used for keyboard input

namespace Engine

{
  public class VerticalMenu
  {
    Vector _position = new Vector();
    Input.Input _input;
    List<Button> _buttons = new List<Button>();
    public double Spacing { get; set; }

    public VerticalMenu(double x, double y, Input.Input input)
    {
      _input = input;
      _position = new Vector(x, y, 0);
      Spacing = 50;
    }


    public void AddButton(Button button)
```

```
  {
    double _currentY = _position.Y;

    if (_buttons.Count != 0)
    {
      _currentY = _buttons.Last().Position.Y;
      _currentY -= Spacing;
    }
    else
    {
      // It's the first button added it should have
      // focus
      button.OnGainFocus();
    }

    button.Position = new Vector(_position.X, _currentY, 0);
    _buttons.Add(button);
  }
  public void Render(Renderer renderer)
  {
    _buttons.ForEach(x => x.Render(renderer));
  }
  }
}
```

The position of the buttons is handled automatically. Each time a button is added, it is put below the other buttons on the Y axis. The Spacing member determines how far apart the buttons are spaced, and this defaults to 50 pixels. The menu itself also has a position that allows the buttons to be moved around as a group. The position is only set in the constructor. The VerticalMenu doesn't allow its position to be changed after it is constructed because this would require an extra method to rearrange all the buttons for the new position. This would be nice functionality to have, but it's not necessary. The Render method uses C#'s new lamba operator to render all the buttons.

The menu class doesn't handle user input yet, but before adding that, let's hook the menu up to StartMenuState so we can see if everything is working. The label on buttons will use a different font than the one used for the title. Find general_font.fnt and general_font.tga on the CD and add them to the project. Then this new font needs to be set up in the Form.cs file.

```csharp
// In form.cs
private void InitializeTextures()
{
  // Init DevIl
  Il.ilInit();
  Ilu.iluInit();
  Ilut.ilutInit();
  Ilut.ilutRenderer(Ilut.ILUT_OPENGL);

  // Textures are loaded here.
  _textureManager.LoadTexture("title_font", "title_font.tga");
  _textureManager.LoadTexture("general_font", "general_font.tga");
}

Engine.Font _generalFont;
Engine.Font _titleFont;
private void InitializeFonts()
{
  // Fonts are loaded here.
  _titleFont = new Engine.Font(_textureManager.Get("title_font"),
          FontParser.Parse("title_font.fnt"));

  _generalFont = new Engine.Font(_textureManager.Get("general_font"),
      FontParser.Parse("general_font.fnt"));
}
```

This new general font can now be passed through to the StartMenuState in the constructor and will be used to construct the vertical menu. The Input class is also passed along at this point and therefore the using Engine.Input statement must be added to the other using statements at the top of the Start-MenuState.cs file.

```csharp
Engine.Font _generalFont;
Input _input;
VerticalMenu _menu;

public StartMenuState(Engine.Font titleFont, Engine.Font generalFont,
Input input)
{
  _input = input;
  _generalFont = generalFont;
  InitializeMenu();
```

The actual menu creation is done in the `InitializeMenu` function because this stops it from cluttering up the `StartMenuState` constructor. The `StartMenuState` creates a vertical menu centered on the X axis and 150 pixels up on the Y axis. This positions the menu neatly below the title text.

```
private void InitializeMenu()
{
  _menu = new VerticalMenu(0, 150, _input);
  Button startGame = new Button(
    delegate(object o, EventArgs e)
    {
      // Do start game functionality.
    },
    new Text("Start", _generalFont));

  Button exitGame = new Button(
    delegate(object o, EventArgs e)
    {
      // Quit
      System.Windows.Forms.Application.Exit();
    },
    new Text("Exit", _generalFont));

  _menu.AddButton(startGame);
  _menu.AddButton(exitGame);
}
```

Two buttons are created: one for exit and one for start. It's easy to see how additional buttons could be added (e.g., load saved game, credits, settings, or website would all be fairly trivial to add using this system). The exit button delegate is fully implemented, and when called, it will exit the program. The start menu button functionality is empty for the time being; it will be filled in when we make the inner game state.

The vertical menu is now being successfully created, but it won't be visible until it's added to the render loop.

```
public void Render()
{
  Gl.glClearColor(1, 1, 1, 0);
  Gl.glClear(Gl.GL_COLOR_BUFFER_BIT);
  _renderer.DrawText(_title);
```

```
  _menu.Render(_renderer);
  _renderer.Render();
}
```

Run the program and the menu will be rendered under the title.

Only the input handling remains to be implemented. The gamepad will navigate the menu with the left control stick or the keyboard. This requires some extra logic to decide when a control stick has been flicked up or down. This logic is shown below in the HandleInput function, which belongs to the Verti-calMenu class. You may have to make a change to the Input class to make the Controller member public so it's accessible from outside the Engine project.

```
bool _inDown = false;
bool _inUp = false;
int _currentFocus = 0;
public void HandleInput()
{
  bool controlPadDown = false;
  bool controlPadUp = false;

  float invertY = _input.Controller.LeftControlStick.Y * -1;

  if (invertY < -0.2)
  {
    // The control stick is pulled down
    if (_inDown == false)
    {
      controlPadDown = true;
      _inDown = true;
    }
  }
  else
  {
    _inDown = false;
  }

  if (invertY > 0.2)
  {
    if (_inUp == false)
    {
      controlPadUp = true;
```

```
        _inUp = true;
    }
  }
  else
  {
    _inUp = false;
  }

  if (_input.Keyboard.IsKeyPressed(Keys.Down)
  || controlPadDown)
  {
    OnDown();
  }
  else if (_input.Keyboard.IsKeyPressed(Keys.Up)
    || controlPadUp)
  {
    OnUp();
  }
}
```

The `HandleInput` function needs to be called in the `StartMenuState`.
`Update` method. If you don't add this call then none of the input will be
detected. `HandleInput` detects the particular input that the vertical menu is
interested in and then calls other functions to deal with it. At the moment there
are only two functions, `OnUp` and `OnDown`; these will change the currently
focused menu item.

```
private void OnUp()
{
  int oldFocus = _currentFocus;
  _currentFocus++;
  if (_currentFocus == _buttons.Count)
  {
    _currentFocus = 0;
  }
  ChangeFocus(oldFocus, _currentFocus);
}

private void OnDown()
{
  int oldFocus = _currentFocus;
```

```
  _currentFocus-;
  if (_currentFocus == -1)
  {
    _currentFocus = (_buttons.Count - 1);
  }
  ChangeFocus(oldFocus, _currentFocus);
}

private void ChangeFocus(int from, int to)
{
  if (from != to)
  {
    _buttons[from].OnLoseFocus();
    _buttons[to].OnGainFocus();
  }
}
```

By pressing up or down on the keyboard, the focus is moved up and down the buttons on the vertical menu. The focus also wraps around. If you are at the top of the menu and press up, then the focus will wrap around and go to the bottom of the menu. The ChangeFocus method reduces repeated code; it tells one button it's lost focus and another button that it's gained focus.

Buttons can now be selected, but there is no code to handle buttons being pressed. The VerticalMenu class needs to be modified to detect when the A button on the gamepad or the Enter key on the keyboard is pressed. Once this is detected, the currently selected button delegate is called.

```
// Inside the HandleInput function
  else if(_input.Keyboard.IsKeyPressed(Keys.Up)
    || controlPadUp)
  {
    OnUp();
  }
  else if (_input.Keyboard.IsKeyPressed(Keys.Enter)
    || _input.Controller.ButtonA.Pressed)
  {
    OnButtonPress();
  }
}
```

```
private void OnButtonPress()
{
  _buttons[_currentFocus].OnPress();
}
```

Run the code and use the keyboard or gamepad to navigate the menu. Pressing the exit button will exit the game, but pressing the start button will currently do nothing. The start button needs to change the state to the inner game state. This means that StartMenuState needs access to the state system.

```
private void InitializeGameState()
{
  _system.AddState("start_menu", new StartMenuState(_titleFont,
_generalFont, _input, _system));
```

The StartMenuState constructor will also need to be modified, and it will keep a reference to the state system.

```
StateSystem _system;
public StartMenuState(Engine.Font titleFont, Engine.Font generalFont,
Input input, StateSystem system)
{
  _system = system;
```

This can be used by the start button to change states when it is pressed. The start button is set up in the InitializeMenu method and needs to be modified like so.

```
Button startGame = new Button(
  delegate(object o, EventArgs e)
  {
    _system.ChangeState("inner_game");
  },
  new Text("Start", _generalFont));
```

The inner_game state doesn't exist yet but that's what we'll develop next. For a first pass, the start menu is now complete. Running the program will produce something similar to Figure 10.5.

Subsequent passes can change this menu as needed, adding more animation, demo modes, or whatever you like!

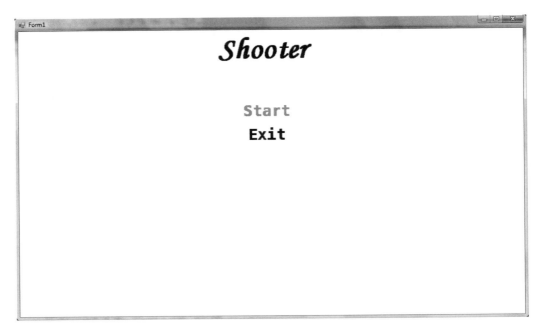

Figure 10.5
First pass of the start game menu.

The Inner Game State

For the first pass, the inner game is going to be as simple as possible. It will wait a few seconds and then change to the game over state. It needs to pass some information over to the game over state to report if the player won or lost the game.

A PersistantGameData class will be used to store information about the player, including if he had just lost or won a game. Eventually the inner game will allow the player to play a shooting game, but not in this first pass.

The inner game level will last for a fixed period of time; if the player is alive when the time is up the player wins. The time a level takes is described by a LevelDescription class. For now, the only thing this class contains is how long the level will last.

```
class LevelDescription
{
  // Time a level lasts in seconds.
  public double Time { get; set; }
}
```

The `PersistentGameData` class will have a description of the current level and information about whether the player has just won that level.

```
class PersistantGameData
{
  public bool JustWon { get; set; }
  public LevelDescription CurrentLevel { get; set; }
  public PersistantGameData()
  {
    JustWon = false;
  }
}
```

The `JustWon` member is set to `false` in the constructor because the player cannot have won a game before the game data is created. The persistent game data class needs to be created in the Form.cs file. Add a new function to be called from the constructor called `InitializeGameData`; it should be called just after `InitializeTextures` and just before the game fonts are created.

```
PersistantGameData _persistantGameData = new PersistantGameData();
private void InitializeGameData()
{
  LevelDescription level = new LevelDescription();
  level.Time = 1; // level only lasts for a second
  _persistantGameData.CurrentLevel = level;
}
```

With this class set up it's now easy to design the `InnerGameState`.

```
using System;
using System.Collections.Generic;
using System.Linq;
using System.Text;
using Engine;
using Engine.Input;
using Tao.OpenGl;

namespace Shooter
{
  class InnerGameState : IGameObject
  {
    Renderer _renderer = new Renderer();
```

```
   Input _input;
   StateSystem _system;
   PersistantGameData _gameData;
   Font _generalFont;

   double _gameTime;

   public InnerGameState(StateSystem system, Input input, Persis-
tantGameData gameData, Font generalFont)
   {
     _input = input;
     _system = system;
     _gameData = gameData;
     _generalFont = generalFont;
     OnGameStart();
   }

   public void OnGameStart()
   {
     _gameTime = _gameData.CurrentLevel.Time;
   }

   #region IGameObject Members

   public void Update(double elapsedTime)
   {
     _gameTime -= elapsedTime;

     if (_gameTime <= 0)
     {
       OnGameStart();
       _gameData.JustWon = true;
       _system.ChangeState("game_over");
     }
   }

   public void Render()
   {
     Gl.glClearColor(1, 0, 1, 0);
     Gl.glClear(Gl.GL_COLOR_BUFFER_BIT);
     _renderer.Render();
   }
```

```
    #endregion
  }
}
```

The constructor takes in the state system and persistent game data. Using these classes the `InnerGameState` can determine when the game is over and change the game state. The constructor also takes in the input and general font as these will be of use when adding the second pass of functionality. The constructor calls `OnGameStart`, which sets the `gameTime` that will determine how long the level lasts. There will be no level content at this time so the level time is set to 1 second.

The `Update` function counts down the level time. When the time is up it and the state changes to `game_over`. The `gameTime` is reset by calling `OnGameState` and because the player is still alive then, the `JustWon` flag is set in the persistent data object. The inner game state `Render` function clears the screen to a pink color so it's obvious when the state change occurs.

The `InnerGameState` class should be used to add another state to the state system in the Form.cs file.

```
  _system.AddState("inner_game", new InnerGameState(_system, _input,
_persistantGameData, _generalFont));
```

That's it for the first pass of the inner game.

The Game Over State

The `gameover` state is a simple state that tells the player that the game has ended and if he won or lost. The state determines if the player won or lost the game by using the `PersistentGameData` class. The state will display its information for a short time and then return the player to the start menu. The player can return to the start menu earlier by pressing a button and forcing the `GameOverState` to finish.

```
%using System;
using System.Collections.Generic;
using System.Linq;
using System.Text;
using Engine;
using Engine.Input;
```

```csharp
using Tao.OpenGl;

namespace Shooter
{
  class GameOverState : IGameObject
  {
    const double _timeOut = 4;
    double _countDown = _timeOut;

    StateSystem _system;
    Input _input;
    Font _generalFont;
    Font _titleFont;
    PersistantGameData _gameData;
    Renderer _renderer = new Renderer();

    Text _titleWin;
    Text _blurbWin;

    Text _titleLose;
    Text _blurbLose;

    public GameOverState(PersistantGameData data, StateSystem system,
Input input, Font generalFont, Font titleFont)
    {
      _gameData = data;
      _system = system;
      _input = input;
      _generalFont = generalFont;
      _titleFont = titleFont;

      _titleWin = new Text("Complete!", _titleFont);
      _blurbWin = new Text("Congratulations, you won!", _generalFont);
      _titleLose = new Text("Game Over!", _titleFont);
      _blurbLose = new Text("Please try again...", _generalFont);

      FormatText(_titleWin, 300);
      FormatText(_blurbWin, 200);

      FormatText(_titleLose, 300);
      FormatText(_blurbLose, 200);
    }
```

```
    private void FormatText (Text _text, int yPosition)
    {
      _text.SetPosition(-_text.Width / 2, yPosition);
      _text.SetColor(new Color(0, 0, 0, 1));
    }

    #region IGameObject Members
    public void Update (double elapsedTime)
    {
      _countDown -= elapsedTime;

      if (  _countDown <= 0 ||
          _input.Controller.ButtonA.Pressed ||

          _input.Keyboard.IsKeyPressed(System.Windows.Forms.Keys.
Enter))
      {
        Finish();
      }
    }

    private void Finish()
    {
      _gameData.JustWon = false;
      _system.ChangeState("start_menu");
      _countDown = _timeOut;
    }

    public void Render()
    {
      Gl.glClearColor(1, 1, 1, 0);
      Gl.glClear(Gl.GL_COLOR_BUFFER_BIT);
      if (_gameData.JustWon)
      {
        _renderer.DrawText(_titleWin);
        _renderer.DrawText(_blurbWin);
      }
      else
      {
        _renderer.DrawText(_titleLose);
        _renderer.DrawText(_blurbLose);
      }
```

```
        _renderer.Render();
    }
    #endregion
  }
}
```

This class needs to be loaded like the rest in the form.cs class.

```
private void InitializeGameState()
{
  // Game states are loaded here
  _system.AddState("start_menu", new StartMenuState(_titleFont,
_generalFont, _input, _system));
  _system.AddState("inner_game", new InnerGameState(_system, _input,
_persistantGameData, _generalFont));
  _system.AddState("game_over", new GameOverState(_persistantGameData,
_system, _input, _generalFont, _titleFont));
  _system.ChangeState("start_menu");
}
```

The `GameOverState` creates a title and message for winning and losing the game. It then uses the persistent data `JustWon` member to decide which message to display. It also has a counter, and the state eventually times out returning the user to the start menu.

The creation of these three states completes the first pass of the game. The game, while currently not very fun, is already in a complete state. The next section will add more detail to the inner game and refine the overall structure to make it look better.

Developing the Inner Game

The inner game currently doesn't allow any interaction and times out after a few seconds. To make the inner game state more game-like, a `PlayerCharacter` needs to be introduced and the player needs to be able to move the character around. This will be the first goal. It's important to create a game in a series of small achievable goals that are well defined; it makes it much easier to write the code. In this case, the `PlayerCharacter` will be some type of spaceship.

Once the first goal is reached then the player needs to feel as though he is advancing through a level. This will be done by scrolling the background texture. The next small goal is to let the player shoot bullets. Bullets need something to hit, so the enemies will also be needed. Each goal is a small step that leads logically on to the next. It's very quick to build up a game in this manner.

Moving the Player Character

The player will be represented as a spaceship created using a sprite and a texture. The spaceship will be controlled by the arrow keys or the left control stick on the gamepad.

The code for controlling the `PlayerCharacter` won't go directly into the `InnerGameState` class. The `InnerGameState` class is meant to be a light, easy to understand class. The bulk of the level code will be stored in a class called `Level`. Each time the player plays a level, a new level object is made and the old one is replaced. Creating a new level object each time ensures that there's no strange error caused by leftover data from a previous play through.

```
using System;
using System.Collections.Generic;
using System.Linq;
using System.Text;
using Engine;
using Engine.Input;
using System.Windows.Forms;
using System.Drawing;

namespace Shooter
{
  class Level
  {
    Input _input;
    PersistantGameData _gameData;
    PlayerCharacter _playerCharacter;
    TextureManager _textureManager;

    public Level(Input input, TextureManager textureManager,
PersistantGameData gameData)
    {
      _input = input;
      _gameData = gameData;
      _textureManager = textureManager;
```

```
        _playerCharacter = new PlayerCharacter(_textureManager);
    }

    public void Update(double elapsedTime)
    {
        // Get controls and apply to player character
    }

    public void Render(Renderer renderer)
    {
        _playerCharacter.Render(renderer);
    }
  }
}
```

This code describes a level. It takes the input and persistent game data in the constructor. The input object is used to move the `PlayerCharacter`. The persistent game data can be used to keep track of such things as the score or any other data that should be recorded over a number of levels. The texture manager is used to create the player, enemies, and background sprites.

The `PlayerCharacter` class will contain a sprite that represents the player spaceship. The CD contains a sprite called spaceship.tga in the Assets directory. This needs to be added to the project and its properties changed so that it is copied into the build directory. Load this texture in the form.cs `InitializeTextures` method.

```
private void InitializeTextures()
{
  // Init DevIl
  Il.ilInit();
  Ilu.iluInit();
  Ilut.ilutInit();
  Ilut.ilutRenderer(Ilut.ILUT_OPENGL);

  _textureManager.LoadTexture("player_ship", "spaceship.tga");
```

Now that the player sprite is loaded into the `TextureManager`, the `PlayerCharacter` class can be written.

```
public class PlayerCharacter
{
```

```
  Sprite _spaceship = new Sprite();

  public PlayerCharacter (TextureManager textureManager)
  {
    _spaceship.Texture = textureManager.Get("player_ship");
    _spaceship.SetScale(0.5, 0.5); // spaceship is quite big, scale
it down.
  }
  public void Render (Renderer renderer)
  {
    renderer.DrawSprite(_spaceship);
  }
}
```

The `PlayerCharacter` class at this stage only renders out the spaceship. To see this is in action a `Level` object needs to be created in the `InnerGameState` and hooked up to the `Update` and `Render` methods. The structure of the level class has its own `Render` and `Update` methods so it's very easy to plug into the `InnerGame` State. The `Level` class makes use of the `TextureManager` class and this means the `InnerGameState` must change its constructor so that it takes in a `TextureManager` object. In the form.cs file the `textureManager` object needs to be passed into the `InnerGameState` constructor.

```
class InnerGameState : IGameObject
{
  Level _level;
  TextureManager _textureManager;
// Code omitted

  public InnerGameState ( StateSystem system, Input input, TextureManager
textureManager,
            PersistantGameData gameData, Font generalFont)
  {
  _ textureManager = textureManager;
// Code omitted

  public void OnGameStart ()
  {
    _level = new Level(_input, _textureManager, _gameData);
```

```
    _gameTime = _gameData.CurrentLevel.Time;
  }

// Code omitted
  public void Update(double elapsedTime)
  {
    _level.Update(elapsedTime);

// Code omitted
  public void Render()
  {
    Gl.glClearColor(1, 0, 1, 0);
    Gl.glClear(Gl.GL_COLOR_BUFFER_BIT);
    _level.Render(_renderer);
```

Run the code and start the game. The spaceship will flash, giving a brief glance of this new player sprite and then suddenly the game will end. To test the `InnerGameState` thoroughly, the level length must be increased. The level length is set in the form.cs file in the `InitializeGameData` function. Find the code and make the length longer; 30 seconds is probably fine.

The spaceship movement is going to be very simple, with no acceleration or physics modeling. The control stick and arrow keys map directly to the movement of the ship. The `PlayerCharacter` class needs a new method called `Move`.

```
double _speed = 512; // pixels per second
public void Move(Vector amount)
{
  amount *= _speed;
  _spaceship.SetPosition(_spaceship.GetPosition() + amount);
}
```

The `Move` method takes in a vector that gives the direction and amount to move the spaceship. The vector is then multiplied by the `speed` value to increase the movement length. The new vector is then added to the current position of the ship to create a new position in space, and the sprite is moved there. This is how all basic movement is done in arcade-style games. The movement can be given a different feel by modeling more physical systems such as acceleration and friction, but we will stick with the basic movement code.

The spaceship is moved around by the values in the `Input` class, which is handled in the `Level` `Update` loop.

```
public void Update (double elapsedTime)
{
  // Get controls and apply to player character
  double _x = _input.Controller.LeftControlStick.X;
  double _y = _input.Controller.LeftControlStick.Y * - 1;
  Vector controlInput = new Vector (_x, _y, 0);

  if (Math.Abs (controlInput.Length ()) < 0.0001)
  {
    // If the input is very small, then the player may not be using
    // a controller; he might be using the keyboard.
    if (_input.Keyboard.IsKeyHeld (Keys.Left))
    {
      controlInput.X = -1;
    }

    if (_input.Keyboard.IsKeyHeld (Keys.Right))
    {
      controlInput.X = 1;
    }

    if (_input.Keyboard.IsKeyHeld (Keys.Up))
    {
      controlInput.Y = 1;
    }

    if (_input.Keyboard.IsKeyHeld (Keys.Down))
    {
      controlInput.Y = -1;
    }
  }

  _playerCharacter.Move (controlInput * elapsedTime);
}
```

The controls are quite simple for the gamepad. A vector is created that describes how the control stick is pushed (The Y axis is reversed by multiplying the value by minus 1 so that the ship will go up when you push up rather than down). This vector is then multiplied by the elapsed time so that the movement will be constant no matter the frame rate. The scaled vector is then used to move the ship. There is also support for the keyboard. The values of the control stick are checked, and if the control stick doesn't seem to have moved, then the keyboard keys are checked. It's assumed if you're not moving the control stick, then you might be playing on the keyboard. The keyboard is less granular than the control stick; it can only give up, down, left, and right as absolute, 0 or 1, values. The keyboard input is used to make a vector so that it can be treated in the same way as the control stick input. `IsKeyHeld` is used instead of `IsKeyPressed` because we assume that if the user is holding down the left key, he wants to continue to move left rather than move left once and stop.

Run the program and you will be able to move the ship around the screen. The movement goal is complete!

Faking Movement with a Scrolling Background

Adding a background is going to be fairly easy. There are two basic starfield textures on the CD in the Assets directory called background.tga and background_p.tga. Add these files to the solution and alter the properties so they're copied to the build directory as you've done for all the other textures. Then load them into the texture manager in the form.cs `InitializeTextures` function.

```
_textureManager.LoadTexture("background", "background.tga");
_textureManager.LoadTexture("background_layer_1",
"background_p.tga");
```

Two backgrounds have been chosen so that they can be layered on top of each other to make a more interesting effect than would be achievable with only one texture.

This background is going to be animated by using UV scrolling. This can all be done by making a new class called `ScrollingBackground`. This scrolling background class could also be reused to make the start and game over menu more interesting, but the priority at the moment is the inner game.

```
using System;
using System.Collections.Generic;
using System.Linq;
using System.Text;
```

```
using Engine;

namespace Shooter
{
  class ScrollingBackground
  {
    Sprite _background = new Sprite();

    public float Speed { get; set; }
    public Vector Direction { get; set; }
    Point _topLeft = new Point(0, 0);
    Point _bottomRight = new Point(1, 1);

    public void SetScale(double x, double y)
    {
      _background.SetScale(x, y);
    }

    public ScrollingBackground(Texture background)
    {
      _background.Texture = background;
      Speed = 0.15f;
      Direction = new Vector(1, 0, 0);
    }

    public void Update(float elapsedTime)
    {
      _background.SetUVs(_topLeft, _bottomRight);
      _topLeft.X += (float)(0.15f * Direction.X * elapsedTime);
      _bottomRight.X += (float)(0.15f * Direction.X * elapsedTime);
      _topLeft.Y += (float)(0.15f * Direction.Y * elapsedTime);
      _bottomRight.Y += (float)(0.15f * Direction.Y * elapsedTime);
    }

    public void Render(Renderer renderer)
    {
      renderer.DrawSprite(_background);
    }
  }
}
```

An interesting thing to note about the scrolling background class is that it has a direction vector (called Direction). This vector can be used to alter the direction of the scrolling. In a normal shooting game, a background usually scrolls right to left. Altering the scrolling direction can cause the background to scroll in any direction desired. This would be useful in a space exploration game where the background could move in the opposite direction to the player's movement.

The scrolling class also has a Speed member; this isn't strictly necessary as the speed of the scrolling could be encoded as the magnitude of the vector, but separating the speed makes it simpler to alter. The direction and speed are used to move the U,V data of the vertices in the Update method.

This background can now be added into the Level class.

```
ScrollingBackground _background;
ScrollingBackground _backgroundLayer;

public Level(Input input, TextureManager textureManager, PersistantGa-
meData gameData)
{
  _input = input;
  _gameData = gameData;
  _textureManager = textureManager;

  _background = new ScrollingBackground(textureManager.Get
("background"));
  _background.SetScale(2, 2);
  _background.Speed = 0.15f;

  _backgroundLayer = new ScrollingBackground(textureManager.Get
("background_layer_1"));
  _backgroundLayer.Speed = 0.1f;
  _backgroundLayer.SetScale(2.0, 2.0);
```

These two background objects are created in the constructor and each is scaled by two. The backgrounds are scaled up because the texture is about half the size of the screen area. The texture is scaled to make the texture large enough to entirely cover the playing area without leaving gaps at the edges.

The two backgrounds scroll at different speeds. This produces what is known as a parallax effect. The human brain understands the 3D world through a number of different cues known as depth cues. For instance, each eye sees a slightly different angle of the world, and the differences between these views can be used to determine the third dimension. This is known as the binocular cue.

Parallax is another one of these cues; simply put, objects further from the viewer appear to move slower than those closer to the view. Think of driving in a car with a large mountain in the distance. The mountain appears to move very slowly, but trees next to the road fly past. This is a depth cue, and the brain knows that the mountain is far away.

Parallax is easy to fake. A fast scrolling star field appears to have stars close to the spaceship; another background moving more slowly appears to have stars far away. The background classes merely need to move at different speeds, and this gives the background a feeling of depth.

The background objects need to be rendered and updated. This requires more code changes.

```
public void Update (double elapsedTime)
{
  _background.Update((float)elapsedTime);
  _backgroundLayer.Update((float)elapsedTime);

// A little later in the code

public void Render (Renderer renderer)
{
  _background.Render(renderer);
  _backgroundLayer.Render(renderer);
```

Run the code and check out the parallax effect. It's quite subtle with the given star fields, so feel free to modify the images or add several more layers.

The ship now appears to be zooming along in space, and everything suddenly feels a lot more game-like. The next task is to add an enemy.

Adding Some Simple Enemies

The enemies will be represented by a sprite and therefore they will use the Sprite class. The enemy sprite should be different from the player sprite so add a new sprite texture called spaceship2.tga from the CD Assets directory. Change its properties so that it will be copied to the \bin directories when the program is built.

This snippet of code loads the texture into the texture manager.

Figure 10.6
Scrolling backgrounds.

```
_textureManager.LoadTexture("enemy_ship", "spaceship2.tga");
```

Once this has been added, a class can be constructed to simply represent the enemy.

```
using System;
using System.Collections.Generic;
using System.Linq;
using System.Text;
using Engine;

namespace Shooter
{
  class Enemy
  {
    Sprite _spaceship = new Sprite();
    double _scale = 0.3;
    public Enemy(TextureManager textureManager)
    {
      _spaceship.Texture = textureManager.Get("enemy_ship");
```

```
      _spaceship.SetScale(_scale, _scale);
      _spaceship.SetRotation(Math.PI); // make it face the player
      _spaceship.SetPosition(200, 0); // put it somewhere easy to see
   }

   public void Update(double elapsedTime)
   {
   }

   public void Render(Renderer renderer)
   {
      renderer.DrawSprite(_spaceship);
   }

   }
}
```

The enemies will be rendered and controlled by the `Level` class. It's very likely we'll have more than one enemy at a time, so it's best to make a list of enemies.

```
class Level
{
  List<Enemy> _enemyList = new List<Enemy>();

  // A little later in the code

  public Level(Input input, TextureManager textureManager, Persis-
tantGameData gameData)
  {
    _input = input;
    _gameData = gameData;
    _textureManager = textureManager;
    _enemyList.Add(new Enemy(_textureManager));

  // A little later in the code

  public void Update(double elapsedTime)
  {
    _background.Update((float)elapsedTime);
    _backgroundLayer.Update((float)elapsedTime);
    _enemyList.ForEach(x => x.Update(elapsedTime));
```

```
// A little later in the code
public void Render (Renderer renderer)
{
  _background.Render(renderer);
  _backgroundLayer.Render(renderer);
  _enemyList.ForEach(x => x.Render(renderer));
```

This code is all pretty standard. A list of enemies is created, and an enemy is added to it. The list is then updated and rendered using the lambda syntax. Run the program now and you should see two spaceships: the player spaceship and an enemy facing it. With the current code, the player can fly through the enemy ship with no reaction. If the player crashes into the enemy ship then the player should take some damage or the state should change to the game over state. Before any of that can happen, the collision needs to be detected.

The collision detection will be the simple rectangle-rectangle collision explored earlier in the book. Before coding the collision it may be useful to visualize the bounding box around the enemy. This is quite simple to code using OpenGL's immediate mode and GL_LINE_LOOP. Add the following code to the Enemy class.

```
public RectangleF GetBoundingBox()
{
  float width  = (float)(_spaceship.Texture.Width * _scale);
  float height = (float)(_spaceship.Texture.Height * _scale);
  return new RectangleF( (float)_spaceship.GetPosition().X - width / 2,
            (float)_spaceship.GetPosition().Y - height / 2,
            width, height);
}

// Render a bounding box
public void Render_Debug()
{
  Gl.glDisable(Gl.GL_TEXTURE_2D);

  RectangleF bounds = GetBoundingBox();
  Gl.glBegin(Gl.GL_LINE_LOOP);
  {
    Gl.glColor3f(1, 0, 0);
    Gl.glVertex2f(bounds.Left, bounds.Top);
    Gl.glVertex2f(bounds.Right, bounds.Top);
```

```
    Gl.glVertex2f(bounds.Right, bounds.Bottom);
    Gl.glVertex2f(bounds.Left, bounds.Bottom);

  }
  Gl.glEnd();
  Gl.glEnable(Gl.GL_TEXTURE_2D);
}
```

C#'s `RectangleF` class is used; therefore, the `System.Drawing` library needs to be added to the `using` statements at the top of `Enemy.cs`. The function `GetBoundingBox` uses the sprite to calculate a bounding box around it. The width and height are scaled according to the sprite, so even if the sprite is scaled, the bounding box will be correct. The `RectangleF` constructor takes in the x and y position of the top-left corner, and then the width and height of the rectangle. The position of the sprite is its center, so to get the top-left corner, half the width and height must be subtracted from the position.

The `Render_Debug` method draws a red box around the sprite. The `Render_Debug` method should be called from the `Enemy.Render` method. This debug function can be removed at any time.

```
public void Render(Renderer renderer)
{
  renderer.DrawSprite(_spaceship);
  Render_Debug();
}
```

Run the code and a red box will be drawn around the enemy, as can be seen in Figure 10.7. Visual debug routines are a great way to understand what your code is really doing.

The `GetBoundingBox` function can be used to determine if the enemy is colliding with anything else. At the moment, the player ship doesn't have a `GetBoundingBox` function, and the principle of DRY (Don't Repeat Yourself) means you shouldn't just copy this code! Instead, a new parent class should be created that centralizes this functionality; then the `Enemy` and `PlayerCharacter` can both inherit from this.

Before the `Enemy` and the `PlayerCharacter` classes are generalized, this `Sprite` class needs to be modified. To make the bounding box drawing functions simpler, the sprite should have some methods to report the current scale.

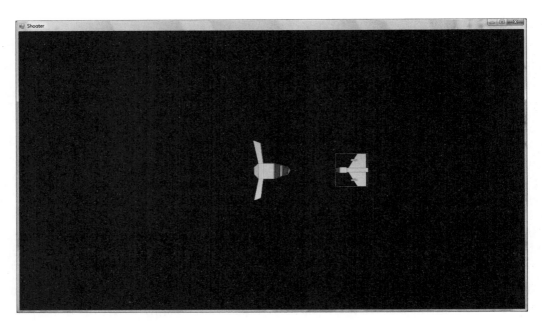

Figure 10.7
An enemy bounding box.

```
public class Sprite
{
  double _scaleX = 1;
  double _scaleY = 1;  public double ScaleX
  {
    get
    {
      return _scaleX;
    }
  }

  public double ScaleY
  {
    get
    {
      return _scaleY;
    }
  }
```

Changing the `Sprite` class is a change to the Engine library, which is a change that shouldn't be taken lightly. In this case, it is a good change that will be beneficial to any future project using the Engine library. With the `Sprite` method updated, the `Entity` class can be created back in the Shooter project.

```
using System;
using System.Collections.Generic;
using System.Linq;
using System.Text;
using Engine;
using Tao.OpenGl;
using System.Drawing;
namespace Shooter
{
  public class Entity
  {
    protected Sprite _sprite = new Sprite();

    public RectangleF GetBoundingBox()
    {
      float width = (float)(_sprite.Texture.Width * _sprite.ScaleX);
      float height = (float)(_sprite.Texture.Height * _sprite.ScaleY);
      return new RectangleF((float)_sprite.GetPosition().X - width / 2,
              (float)_sprite.GetPosition().Y - height / 2,
              width, height);
    }

    // Render a bounding box
    protected void Render_Debug()
    {
      Gl.glDisable(Gl.GL_TEXTURE_2D);

      RectangleF bounds = GetBoundingBox();
      Gl.glBegin(Gl.GL_LINE_LOOP);
      {
        Gl.glColor3f(1, 0, 0);
        Gl.glVertex2f(bounds.Left, bounds.Top);
        Gl.glVertex2f(bounds.Right, bounds.Top);
        Gl.glVertex2f(bounds.Right, bounds.Bottom);
        Gl.glVertex2f(bounds.Left, bounds.Bottom);

      }
```

```
    Gl.glEnd();
    Gl.glEnable(Gl.GL_TEXTURE_2D);
  }


 }
}
```

The `Entity` class contains a sprite and some code to render that sprite's bounding box.

With this entity definition, the `Enemy` class can be greatly simplified.

```
public class Enemy : Entity
{
  double _scale = 0.3;
  public Enemy(TextureManager textureManager)
  {
    _sprite.Texture = textureManager.Get("enemy_ship");
    _sprite.SetScale(_scale, _scale);
    _sprite.SetRotation(Math.PI); // make it face the player
    _sprite.SetPosition(200, 0); // put it somewhere easy to see
  }

  public void Update(double elapsedTime)
  {
  }

  public void Render(Renderer renderer)
  {
    renderer.DrawSprite(_sprite);
    Render_Debug();
  }

  public void SetPosition(Vector position)
  {
  _ sprite.SetPosition(position);
  }
}
```

The `Enemy` is now a type of `Entity` and no longer needs its own reference to a sprite. This same refactoring can be applied to the `PlayerCharacter` class.

```
public class PlayerCharacter : Entity
{
  double _speed = 512; // pixels per second

  public void Move(Vector amount)
  {
    amount *= _speed;
    _sprite.SetPosition(_sprite.GetPosition() + amount);
  }

  public PlayerCharacter(TextureManager textureManager)
  {
    _sprite.Texture = textureManager.Get("player_ship");
    _sprite.SetScale(0.5, 0.5); // spaceship is quite big, scale it down.
  }

  public void Render(Renderer renderer)
  {
    Render_Debug();
    renderer.DrawSprite(_sprite);
  }
}
```

Run the code again, and now both the enemy and player will have appropriate bounding boxes.

For now, the rule will be that if the `PlayerCharacter` hits an enemy, the game ends. This can be refined later by giving the player some health. To get a game working as fast as possible, it will for now be instant death.

The first change is in the `InnerGameState`; it needs to recognize when the player has died and therefore failed to complete the current level.

```
public void Update(double elapsedTime)
{
  _level.Update(elapsedTime);
  _gameTime -= elapsedTime;

  if (_gameTime <= 0)
  {
    OnGameStart();
    _gameData.JustWon = true;
```

```
    _system.ChangeState("game_over");
  }

  if (_level.HasPlayerDied())
  {
    OnGameStart();
    _gameData.JustWon = false;
    _system.ChangeState("game_over");
  }
}
```

Here the `Level` class has been given an extra function, `HasPlayerDied`, that reports if the player has died. In this case, the player's death is checked after the `gameTime`. This means that if the time runs out, but the player died in the last possible second, he still won't win the level.

In the `level` class, the `HasPlayerDied` method needs to be implemented. It's just a simple wrapper around the current `PlayerCharacter`'s state.

```
public bool HasPlayerDied()
{
  return _playerCharacter.IsDead;
}
```

The death flag is contained in the `PlayerCharacter` class.

```
bool _dead = false;
public bool IsDead
{
  get
  {
    return _dead;
  }
}
```

When the player collides with an enemy, this death flag can be set and the game will end with the player losing the level. The level needs some code to process the collisions that happen between the enemy craft and the player. This collision processing is done in the `level` class, which has access to the `PlayerCharacter` and the list of enemies.

```
private void UpdateCollisions
  ()
```

```
{
  foreach (Enemy enemy in _enemyList)
  {
    if (enemy.GetBoundingBox().IntersectsWith(_playerCharacter.
GetBoundingBox()))
    {
      enemy.OnCollision(_playerCharacter);
      _playerCharacter.OnCollision(enemy);
    }
  }
}

public void Update(double elapsedTime)
{
  UpdateCollisions();
```

The collision processing code is called each frame by the level's Update method. The collisions are determined by iterating through the list of enemies and checking if their bounding box intersects with the player. The intersection is worked out using C#'s RectangleF IntersectsWith method. If the bounding box of the player and enemy do intersect, then OnCollision is called for the player and the enemy. The Player.OnCollision method is passed the enemy object. It collides with it and the Enemy.OnCollision is passed the player object. There is no test for enemies colliding with other enemies; it's assumed this is no problem if it happens in the game.

The OnCollision class needs to be implemented for both the Enemy and PlayerCharacter classes. Here is the skeleton method that needs to be added to the Enemy class.

```
internal void OnCollision(PlayerCharacter player)
{
  // Handle collision with player.
}
```

Unlike Enemy, the PlayerCharacter class actually has some functionality. Its implementation is as follows.

```
internal void OnCollision(Enemy enemy)
{
  _dead = true;
}
```

When the player collides with the enemy, its dead flag is set to true, which will cause the game to end. The game is now partially playable with an outcome for losing or winning. From this point on, the refinements to the game will start to make it more fun to play.

Introducing Simple Weapons

Weapons in the game mainly take the form of different types of bullets. A good goal to aim for is to have the player shoot a bullet each time the A button or spacebar is pressed. Eventually the enemies will also be firing bullets, which is important to bear in mind when creating the bullet system.

To experiment with bullets, another texture is needed. Find bullet.tga on the CD in Assets directory and add it to the project, remembering to set the properties as before. Then this texture needs to be loaded into the texture manager.

```
_textureManager.LoadTexture("bullet", "bullet.tga");
```

Once the texture is loaded, the next logical class to create is the `Bullet` class. This will have a bounding box and a sprite so it too can inherit from `Entity`. The class should be created in the Shooter project.

```
public class Bullet : Entity
{
  public bool Dead { get; set; }
  public Vector Direction { get; set; }
  public double Speed { get; set; }

  public double X
  {
    get { return _sprite.GetPosition().X; }
  }

  public double Y
  {
    get { return _sprite.GetPosition().Y; }
  }

  public void SetPosition(Vector position)
  {
    _sprite.SetPosition(position);
```

```
    }

    public void SetColor (Color color)
    {
      _sprite.SetColor(color);
    }

    public Bullet (Texture bulletTexture)
    {
      _sprite.Texture = bulletTexture;

      // Some default values
      Dead = false;
      Direction = new Vector(1, 0, 0);
      Speed = 512; // pixels per second
    }
    public void Render (Renderer renderer)
    {
      if (Dead)
      {
        return;
      }
      renderer.DrawSprite(_sprite);
    }

    public void Update (double elapsedTime)
    {
      if (Dead)
      {
        return;
      }
      Vector position = _sprite.GetPosition();
      position += Direction * Speed * elapsedTime;
      _sprite.SetPosition(position);
    }
  }
}
```

The bullet has three members: the direction the bullet will travel, the speed it will travel, and a flag to tell if the bullet is dead or not. There are also position setters and getters for the bullet sprite. There is also a setter for the color; it makes sense to allow the bullets to be colored. The player bullets will only hurt the enemies and the enemy bullets will only hurt the player. To let the player know which bullets are which, they are given different colors.

You may see the position getter and setter and color setter and wonder if it would be better just to make the `sprite` class public. Then if we wanted to change the position or color, we could just alter the bullet sprite directly. Every situation is different but as a general rule, it's better to keep more data private and provide an interface to the data that needs to be changed. Also `bullet.SetColor()` is more straightforward to read than `bullet.Sprite.SetColor()`.

The constructor takes in a texture for the bullet and sets some default values for the color, direction, and speed. The speed is measured in pixels per second. The final two methods are `Render` and `Update`. The `Update` loop updates the position of the bullet using the direction and speed. The position increase is scaled by the amount of time since the last frame, so the movement will be consistent on any speed of computer. The render is quite straightforward; it just draws the bullet sprite. Both the render and update loops do nothing if the bullet has its dead flag set to true.

A lot of bullets are going to be flying about and there needs to be a certain amount of logic to deal with that. Bullets that leave the screen need to be turned off. A `BulletManager` class is a fine place to put all this logic. There are two ways to write a `BulletManager` class: the simple straightforward way and the memory-efficient way. The `BulletManager` introduced here is the straight-forward type; when an enemy is destroyed on screen its reference is removed from the `BulletManager` and the object is destroyed in code; freeing any memory it was using. Every time the player fires, a new bullet is created. This is basic, but creating and deleting lots of objects in the game loop is a bad thing; it will make your code slow if you do it too much. Creation and deletion of objects tends to slow operations.

A more memory-efficient method of managing the bullets is to have a big list of, say, 1,000 bullets. Most of the bullets are dead; every time the user fires the list is searched and a dead bullet is brought to life. No new objects need to be created. If all 1,000 bullets are alive, then either the player can't fire or a heuristic (such as bullet that's been alive longest) is used to kill one of the current bullets and let the player use that one. Recycling bullets in this way is a better way to write the `BulletManager`. Once you've seen the simple manager in action, you can always have a go at converting it to the more memory-efficient one yourself.

```
using System;
using System.Collections.Generic;
using System.Linq;
using System.Text;
using Engine;

namespace Shooter
{
  public class Bullet : Entity
  {
    public bool Dead { get; set; }
    public Vector Direction { get; set; }
    public double Speed { get; set; }

    public double X
    {
      get { return _sprite.GetPosition().X; }
    }

    public double Y
    {
      get { return _sprite.GetPosition().Y; }
    }

    public void SetPosition(Vector position)
    {
      _sprite.SetPosition(position);
    }

    public void SetColor(Color color)
    {
      _sprite.SetColor(color);
    }

    public Bullet(Texture bulletTexture)
    {
      _sprite.Texture = bulletTexture;

      // Some default values
      Dead = false;
      Direction = new Vector(1, 0, 0);
      Speed = 512; // pixels per second
```

```
    }
    public void Render(Renderer renderer)
    {
      if (Dead)
      {
        return;
      }
      renderer.DrawSprite(_sprite);
    }

    public void Update(double elapsedTime)
    {
      if (Dead)
      {
        return;
      }
      Vector position = _sprite.GetPosition();
      position += Direction * Speed * elapsedTime;
      _sprite.SetPosition(position);
    }
  }

}
```

The `BulletManager` only has two member variables: a list of bullets it's managing and a rectangle representing the screen bounds. Remember to include the using `System.Drawing` statement at the top of the file so that the `RectangleF` class can be used. The screen bounds are used to determine if a bullet has left the screen and can be destroyed.

The constructor takes in a rectangle, `playArea`, describing the playing area and assigns it to the `_bounds` member. The `Shoot` method is used to add a bullet to the `BulletManager`. Once a bullet is added, the `BulletManager` tracks it until it leaves the play area or hits a ship. The `Update` method updates all the bullets being tracked and then checks if any are out of bounds; finally, it deletes any bullets that have the `Dead` flag set to true.

The `CheckOutOfBounds` function uses the rectangle intersection test between the bullet and playing area to determine if it's off-screen. The `RemoveDeadBullets` performs an interesting trick; it iterates through the list of bullets backwards and removes any bullets that are dead. `Foreach` can't be used here and neither can forward iteration; if you were doing forward iteration and removed a bullet, then the list would become shorter by one element, and when the loop got to the end of the list, it would have an out of bounds error. Reversing the iteration of the loop fixes this problem. The length of the list doesn't matter; it will always head to 0.

The Render method is quite standard; it just renders out all of the bullets.

This BulletManager is best placed in the Level class. If you don't have a using System.Drawing statement at the top of the Level.cs file then you will need to add one before you can use the RectangleF class.

```
class Level
{
  BulletManager _bulletManager = new BulletManager(new RectangleF(-1300
/ 2, -750 / 2, 1300, 750));
```

The BulletManager is given a playing area. This is a little bigger than the actual window size. This provides a buffer so that the bullets are totally off-screen before they are destroyed. The BulletManager then needs to be added to the Update and Render methods in the Level class.

```
public void Update(double elapsedTime)
{
  UpdateCollisions();
  _bulletManager.Update(elapsedTime);

// A little later in the code

public void Render(Renderer renderer)
{
  _background.Render(renderer);
  _backgroundLayer.Render(renderer);

  _enemyList.ForEach(x => x.Render(renderer));
  _playerCharacter.Render(renderer);
  _bulletManager.Render(renderer);
}
```

The BulletManager is rendered last so that bullets will be rendered on top of everything. At this point, the BulletManager is fully integrated, but there's no way to test it without giving the player a way to fire bullets. For this to happen, the `PlayerCharacter` class needs access to the manager. In the `Level` constructor, pass the `BulletManager` into the `PlayerCharacter` constructor.

```
_playerCharacter = new PlayerCharacter(_textureManager,
_bulletManager);
```

The `PlayerCharacter` class code then needs to be altered to accept and store a reference to the `BulletManager`.

```
BulletManager _bulletManager;
Texture _bulletTexture;
public PlayerCharacter(TextureManager textureManager, BulletManager
bulletManager)
{
  _bulletManager = bulletManager;
  _bulletTexture = textureManager.Get("bullet");
```

The `PlayerCharacter` constructor also stores the `bulletTexture` that will be used when firing bullets. To fire a bullet, a `bullet` object needs to be created and positioned so that it starts near the player and then passes into the `BulletManager`. A new `Fire` method in the `PlayerCharacter` class will be responsible for this.

```
Vector _gunOffset = new Vector(55, 0, 0);
public void Fire()
{
  Bullet bullet = new Bullet(_bulletTexture);
  bullet.SetColor(new Color(0, 1, 0, 1));
  bullet.SetPosition(_sprite.GetPosition() + _gunOffset);
  _bulletManager.Shoot(bullet);
}
```

The bullet is created using the `bulletTexture` that was set up in the constructor. It's then colored green, but you can choose any color you want. The position of the bullet is set so that it is the same position as the player's ship, but with an offset so that the bullet appears to come from the front of the ship. If there was no offset, the bullet would appear right in the middle of the `ship` sprite and this would look a little weird. The bullet direction isn't altered because forward on the X axis is the default value. The default speed is also fine. Finally, the bullet is given to the `BulletManager` and is officially fired using the `Shoot` method.

The player can now fire bullets, but there is no code to detect input and call the Fire method. All the input for the player is handled in the Level class in the Update method. It's a bit messy to have the input code in the root of the Update method, so I've extracted a new function called UpdateInput; this helps keep things a bit tidier.

```
public void Update(double elapsedTime)
{
  UpdateCollisions();
  _bulletManager.Update(elapsedTime);

  _background.Update((float)elapsedTime);
  _backgroundLayer.Update((float)elapsedTime);
  _enemyList.ForEach(x => x.Update(elapsedTime));

  // Input code has been moved into this method
  UpdateInput(elapsedTime);

}

private void UpdateInput(double elapsedTime)
{
  if (_input.Keyboard.IsKeyPressed(Keys.Space) || _input.Controller.
ButtonA.Pressed)
  {
    _playerCharacter.Fire();
  }
  // Pre-existing input code omitted.
```

Take all the input code out of the Update loop and put it at the end of the new UpdateInput method. This UpdateInput method is then called from the Update method. Some new code has also been added to handle the player firing. If the space bar on the keyboard or the A button on the gamepad is pressed, then the player fires a bullet. Run the program and try the spaceship's new firing abilities.

The new bullets can be seen in Figure 10.8. The bullets are created every time the player hits the fire button. For gameplay reasons, it's probably best to slow this down a little and give the spaceship a small recovery time between shots. Modify the PlayerCharacter class as follows.

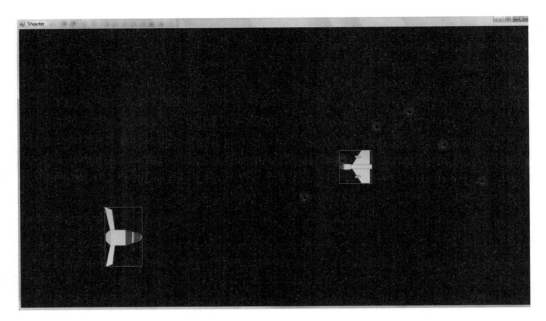

Figure 10.8
Firing bullets.

```
Vector _gunOffset = new Vector(55, 0, 0);
static readonly double FireRecovery = 0.25;
double _fireRecoveryTime = FireRecovery;
public void Update(double elapsedTime)
{
  _fireRecoveryTime = Math.Max(0, (_fireRecoveryTime - elapsedTime));
}

public void Fire()
{
  if (_fireRecoveryTime > 0)
  {
    return;
  }
  else
  {
    _fireRecoveryTime = FireRecovery;
  }

  Bullet bullet = new Bullet(_bulletTexture);
```

```
   bullet.SetColor(new Color(0, 1, 0, 1));
   bullet.SetPosition(_sprite.GetPosition() + _gunOffset);
   _bulletManager.Shoot(bullet);
}
```

To count down the recovery time, the `PlayerCharacter` class needs an `Up-date` method to be added. The `Update` method will count down the recovery time, but it never goes below 0. This is done by using the `Math.Max` function. With the recovery time set, the `Fire` command returns immediately if the spaceship is still recovering from the last shot. If the recovery time is 0, then the ship can fire and the recovery time is reset so it can start counting down again.

The `Level` also needs a minor change; it needs to call the `PlayerChar-acter`'s `Update` method.

```
public void Update(double elapsedTime)
{
  _playerCharacter.Update(elapsedTime);

  _background.Update((float)elapsedTime);
  _backgroundLayer.Update((float)elapsedTime);

  UpdateCollisions();
  _enemyList.ForEach(x => x.Update(elapsedTime));
  _bulletManager.Update(elapsedTime);

  UpdateInput(elapsedTime);
}
```

Run the program again and you won't be able to fire as fast. This is *your* game, so tweak the recovery rate to whatever feels right to you!

Damage and Explosions

The bullets have been added, but they sail right through the enemy inflicting no damage; it's time to change that. The enemy should know when it's been hit and respond appropriately. We'll start by handling the collisions and then create an animated explosion.

The collision code is handled in the `Level` class, in the `UpdateCollisions` function. This function needs to be extended to also handle collisions between bullets and enemies.

```
private void UpdateCollisions()
{
  foreach (Enemy enemy in _enemyList)
  {
    if (enemy.GetBoundingBox().IntersectsWith(_playerCharacter.
GetBoundingBox()))
    {
      enemy.OnCollision(_playerCharacter);
      _playerCharacter.OnCollision(enemy);
    }

    _bulletManager.UpdateEnemyCollisions(enemy);
  }
}
```

One extra line has been added to the end of the for loop. The BulletManager is asked to check any collisions between the bullets and the current enemy. UpdateEnemyCollisions is a new function for the BulletManager, so it needs to be implemented.

```
internal void UpdateEnemyCollisions(Enemy enemy)
{
  foreach (Bullet bullet in _bullets)
  {
    if(bullet.GetBoundingBox().IntersectsWith(enemy.GetBounding-
Box()))
    {
      bullet.Dead = true;
      enemy.OnCollision(bullet);
    }
  }
}
```

The collision between the bullet and enemy is determined by checking the intersection between the bounding boxes. If the bullet has hit the enemy, then the bullet is destroyed and the enemy is notified about the collision.

If a bullet hits an enemy, there are a number of different ways to react. The enemy could be immediately destroyed and explode, or the enemy could take damage, requiring a few more shots to be destroyed. Assigning health levels to the enemy is probably something we'd like in the future, so we may as well do it now. Let's add a `Health` member variable to the enemy and then we can implement the `OnCollision` function for bullets.

```
public int Health { get; set; }
public Enemy (TextureManager textureManager)
{
  Health = 50; // default health value.
  //Remaining constructor code omitted
```

The `Enemy` class already has one `OnCollision` method, but that is for colliding with the `PlayerCharacter`. We will create a new overloaded `OnCollision` method that is only concerned about colliding with bullets. When a bullet hits the enemy, it will take some damage and lower its health value. If the health of the enemy drops below 0, then it will be destroyed. If the player shoots the enemy and causes some damage, there needs to be some visual feedback to indicate the enemy has taken a hit. A good way to present this feedback is to flash the enemy yellow for a fraction of a second.

```
static readonly double HitFlashTime = 0.25;
double _hitFlashCountDown = 0;
internal void OnCollision(Bullet bullet)
{
  // If the ship is already dead then ignore any more bullets.
  if (Health == 0)
  {
    return;
  }

  Health = Math.Max(0, Health - 25);
  _hitFlashCountDown = HitFlashTime; // half
  _sprite.SetColor(new Engine.Color(1, 1, 0, 1));

  if (Health == 0)
  {
    OnDestroyed();
  }
}

private void OnDestroyed()
{
  // Kill the enemy here.
}
```

The OnDestroyed function is a placeholder for now; we'll worry about how the enemy is destroyed a little later. In the OnCollision function, the first if statement checks if the ship is already at 0 health. In this case, any additional damage is ignored; the player has already killed the enemy and the game doesn't need to acknowledge any more shots. Next the Health is reduced by 25, an arbitrary damage number, to represent the damage of a single bullet hit. Math. Max is used to ensure that the health never falls below 0. The ship should flash yellow when hit. The countdown is set to represent how long the flash should take. The ship sprite is set to a yellow color, which in RGBA is 1,1,0,1. Finally, the health is checked, and if it equals 0, then the placeholder OnDestroyed method is called. This is the function where the explosion will be triggered.

To cause the ship to flash, the Update loop will also need to be modified. It needs to count down the flash and change the color from yellow to white.

```
public void Update (double elapsedTime)
{
  if (_hitFlashCountDown != 0)
  {
    _hitFlashCountDown = Math.Max(0, _hitFlashCountDown - elapsedTime);
    double scaledTime = 1 - (_hitFlashCountDown / HitFlashTime);
    _sprite.SetColor(new Engine.Color(1, 1, (float)scaledTime, 1));
  }
}
```

The Update loop modifies the flash color of the enemy spaceship. If the flash countdown has already dropped to 0, then the flash has finished and doesn't need to be updated. If the _hitFlashCountDown doesn't equal 0, then it is reduced by the amount of time that has passed since the last frame. Math.Max is used again to ensure the count doesn't fall below 0. The countdown is then scaled to get a value from 0 to 1, indicating how far through the flash we currently are; 0 indicates the flash has just started and 1 indicates it's finished. This number is inversed by subtracting it from 1 so that 1 indicates that the flash has just started and 0 indicates that it's just finished. This scaled number is then used to move the blue channel of the color from 0 to 1. This will flash the ship from yellow to white.

Run the program and shoot the enemy ship a few times; it will flash yellow a few times and then stop responding because it's been destroyed. Enemy ships shouldn't just stop responding; they should explode!

The easiest way to produce a good explosion is to use an animated sprite. Figure 10.9 shows a keyframe texture map of an explosion. This texture was created using a procedural explosion generator available for free from Positech games (http://www.positech.co.uk/content/explosion/explosiongenerator.html).

Figure 10.9 has 16 frames in total; four frames in height and four frames in length. An animated sprite can be created by reading in this texture and changing the U,V coordinates so that it moves from the first frame to the last frame as time passes. An animated sprite is really just a different type of sprite, so to create it, we can extend the existing Sprite class. An animated sprite is something that can be used by many different games, so it should be created in the Engine project rather than the game project.

```
public class AnimatedSprite : Sprite
{
  int _framesX;
  int _framesY;
  int _currentFrame = 0;
  double _currentFrameTime = 0.03;
  public double Speed { get; set; } // seconds per frame
```

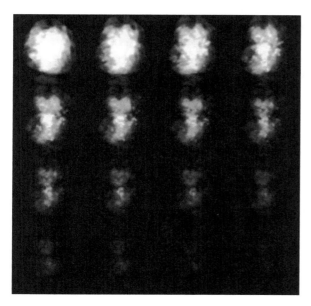

Figure 10.9
Animated explosion texture map.

```
public bool Looping { get; set; }
public bool Finished { get; set; }

public AnimatedSprite()
{
  Looping = false;
  Finished = false;
  Speed = 0.03; // 30 fps-ish
  _currentFrameTime = Speed;
}

public System.Drawing.Point GetIndexFromFrame(int frame)
{
  System.Drawing.Point point = new System.Drawing.Point();
  point.Y = frame / _framesX;
  point.X = frame - (point.Y * _framesY);
  return point;
}

private void UpdateUVs()
{
  System.Drawing.Point index = GetIndexFromFrame(_currentFrame);
  float frameWidth = 1.0f / (float)_framesX;
  float frameHeight = 1.0f / (float)_framesY;
  SetUVs(new Point(index.X * frameWidth, index.Y * frameHeight),
    new Point((index.X + 1) * frameWidth, (index.Y + 1) * frameHeight));
}

public void SetAnimation(int framesX, int framesY)
{
  _framesX = framesX;
  _framesY = framesY;
  UpdateUVs();
}

private int GetFrameCount()
{
  return _framesX * _framesY;
}

public void AdvanceFrame()
{
```

```
    int numberOfFrames = GetFrameCount();
    _currentFrame = (_currentFrame + 1) % numberOfFrames;
  }
  public int GetCurrentFrame()
  {
    return _currentFrame;
  }

  public void Update(double elapsedTime)
  {
    if (_currentFrame == GetFrameCount() - 1 && Looping == false)
    {
      Finished = true;
      return;
    }

    _currentFrameTime -= elapsedTime;
    if (_currentFrameTime < 0)
    {
      AdvanceFrame();
      _currentFrameTime = Speed;
      UpdateUVs();
    }
  }
}
```

This `AnimatedSprite` class works exactly the same as the `Sprite` class, except for the `AnimatedSprite` class can be told how many frames the texture has in X and Y dimensions. When the `Update` loop is called, the frame is changed over time.

This class has quite a few members, but they are mostly used for describing the animation and tracking its progress. The number of frames in X and Y dimension are described by the `_framesX` and `_framesY` member variables. For the Figure 10.9 example, both these variables would be set to four. The `_currentFrame` variable is the frame that the sprite U,Vs are currently set to. The `_currentFrameTime` is the amount of time that will be spent on the current frame before the animation advances to the next frame. `Speed` is a measure of how much time is spent on each frame in seconds. `Looping` determines if the animation should loop, and `Finished` is a flag that is set to true once the animation has ended.

The constructor of the `AnimatedSprite` sets some default values. A freshly created sprite doesn't loop, and has its `Finished` flag set to false, its frame speed set to about 30 frames per second, and the `_currentFrameTime` is set to 0.03 seconds, which will make the animation run at 30 frames per second.

The `GetIndexFromFrame` method takes an index as shown in Figure 10.10 and returns an X,Y coordinate of the index position. For example, index 0 would return 0,0 and index 15 would return 3,3. The index number is broken into an X and Y coordinate by dividing the index by the row length; this gives the number of rows and therefore the Y coordinate of the index. The X coordinate is then whatever is left of the index when the Y rows are removed. This function is very useful when translating, calculating the U,Vs for a certain frame.

`UpdateUVs` uses the current frame index to change the U,Vs so the sprite correctly represents that frame. It first gets the X,Y coordinates of the current frame using `GetIndexFromFrame`. Then it calculates the width and height of

Figure 10.10
Animated explosion texture map with frame index.

an individual frame. As texture coordinates range from 0 to 1, the width and height of a single frame is calculated by dividing the number of frames along the X and the Y by 1. Once the dimensions of a single frame are calculated, the positions of the U,Vs can be worked out by multiplying the frame width and height by the X,Y coordinates of the current frame; this gets the top-left point of the frame on the texture map. The `SetUVs` method requires a `TopLeft` and `BottomRight` point. The `BottomRight` position is calculated from the `TopLeft` position by adding an extra frame width and height.

`SetAnimation` is the method used to set the number of frames along the X and Y of the texture map. It makes a call to `UpdateUVs` so that the sprite is updated to display the correct frame. `GetFrameCount` gets the total number of frames in the animation. The `AdvanceFrame` method moves the animation to the next frame if it comes to the end of the frames; then the frame index wraps around to 0 again. The wrap around is done using modulus—the `%` operator. The modulus operator computes the remainder that results from performing integer division. The best way to understand the use of the modulus operator is to provide an example you are probably already familiar with: time. A clock face has 12 numbers, and it works in modulo 12: 13:00 hours in modulo 12 is 1 o'clock. In our case, the modulo is equal to the total number of frames in the animation.

The `Update` method is responsible for updating the current frame and making the explosion appear to animate. If `Looping` is set to false and the current frame is the last frame, then the `Update` method returns immediately and the `Finished` flag is set to true. If the animation hasn't finished or is looping, then the frame countdown, `_currentFrameTime`, is updated, and if it goes below 0, the frame needs to be changed. The frame is updated by making a call to `AdvanceFrame`, resetting the `_currentFrameTime`, and finally updating the U,Vs.

With the `AnimatedSprite` class added to the Engine project, the explosion animation can be tested. Find the explode.tga file on the CD in the Assets folder and add it to the project, setting the properties as usual. It can then be loaded in the form.cs file with the other textures.

```
_textureManager.LoadTexture("explosion", "explode.tga");
```

A quick way to test the animation is to load it directly into the `Level` as an animated sprite.

```
AnimatedSprite _testSprite = new AnimatedSprite();public Level(Input
input, TextureManager textureManager, PersistantGameData gameData)
{
    _testSprite.Texture = textureManager.Get("explosion");
    _testSprite.SetAnimation(4, 4);

// a little later in the code
public void Update(double elapsedTime)
{
  _testSprite.Update(elapsedTime);

// a little later in the code

public void Render(Renderer renderer)
{
  // Background and other sprite code omitted.
  renderer.DrawSprite(_testSprite);
  renderer.Render();
}
```

Running the program and entering a level will now play the explosion animation once. This confirms everything is working fine (see Figure 10.11).

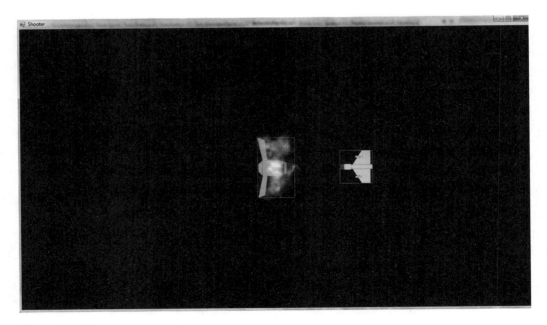

Figure 10.11
The explosion in the game.

Managing Explosions and Enemies

In the last section, we got an example explosion working, but it really needs to be set off only when enemies are destroyed. To this end, two new systems need to be created: one to handle the explosions and general game effects, and one to handle the oncoming enemies.

The explosions should be handled in a similar way to the bullets—creating a dedicated manager that handles the creation and destruction of the explosions. In the future of your project, it's possible you'll want more effects—smokes, sparks, or even power ups—than explosions. The EffectsManager class should be created in the Shooter project.

```
using System;
using System.Collections.Generic;
using System.Linq;
using System.Text;
using Engine;

namespace Shooter
{
  public class EffectsManager
  {
    List<AnimatedSprite> _effects = new List<AnimatedSprite>();
    TextureManager _textureManager;

    public EffectsManager(TextureManager textureManager)
    {
      _textureManager = textureManager;
    }

    public void AddExplosion(Vector position)
    {
      AnimatedSprite explosion = new AnimatedSprite();
      explosion.Texture = _textureManager.Get("explosion");
      explosion.SetAnimation(4, 4);
      explosion.SetPosition(position);
      _effects.Add(explosion);
    }

    public void Update(double elapsedTime)
    {
```

```
  _effects.ForEach(x => x.Update(elapsedTime));
  RemoveDeadExplosions();
}

public void Render(Renderer renderer)
{
  _effects.ForEach(x => renderer.DrawSprite(x));
}

private void RemoveDeadExplosions()
{
  for (int i = _effects.Count - 1; i >= 0; i-)
  {
    if (_effects[i].Finished)
    {
      _effects.RemoveAt(i);
    }
  }
}


}
}
```

This `EffectManager` allows an explosion to be set off, runs the explosion animation until it ends, and then removes the explosion effect. You may notice it's very similar to the `BulletManager` class. These separate managers could all be combined in one generalized manager, but by keeping them separate, the interactions between the game objects can be specific and more efficient. Explosions don't care about collision detection with enemies or players but bullets do. In separate managers, it's easy to separate out the particular requirements of each object; explosions only need to run an animation, whereas bullets need to check for intersection with all of the enemies. Separate managers work great when only a limited number of objects are in the game, but if there are going to be many different entities, then a more generalized entity manager is a better choice.

The `EffectsManager` needs to be initialized in the `Level` class and hooked up to the render and update loops.

```
EffectsManager _effectsManager;
public Level(Input input, TextureManager textureManager, PersistantGa-
meData gameData)
```

```
{
  _input = input;
  _gameData = gameData;
  _textureManager = textureManager;
  _effectsManager = new EffectsManager(_textureManager);

// code omitted

public void Update(double elapsedTime)
{
  _effectsManager.Update(elapsedTime);

// code omitted

public void Render(Renderer renderer)
{
  // Background, sprites and bullet code omitted
  _effectsManager.Render(renderer);
  renderer.Render();
}
```

The ExplosionManager is now hooked up and can be used to launch several explosions at once. For the enemies to launch explosions when they die, they need access to the manager, which can be passed into the constructor.

```
EffectsManager _effectsManager;

public Enemy(TextureManager textureManager, EffectsManager
effectsManager)
{
  _effectsManager = effectsManager;
```

The enemy can now set off an explosion when it dies.

```
private void OnDestroyed()
{
  // Kill the enemy here.
  _effectsManager.AddExplosion(_sprite.GetPosition());
}
```

In the Level.cs file, the EffectsManager needs to be passed into the Enemy constructor. Once this is done, shooting the enemy a couple of times in the game will cause an explosion when the enemy is destroyed.

Next, the enemies will get their own manager; this will be the final manager needed to create a full, working game.

```
public class EnemyManager
{
  List<Enemy> _enemies = new List<Enemy>();
  TextureManager _textureManager;
  EffectsManager _effectsManager;
  int _leftBound;

  public List<Enemy> EnemyList
  {
    get
    {
      return _enemies;
    }
  }

  public EnemyManager(TextureManager textureManager, EffectsManager
effectsManager, int leftBound)
  {
    _textureManager = textureManager;
    _effectsManager = effectsManager;
    _leftBound = leftBound;

    // Add a test enemy.
    Enemy enemy = new Enemy(_textureManager, _effectsManager);
    _enemies.Add(enemy);
  }

  public void Update(double elapsedTime)
  {
    _enemies.ForEach(x => x.Update(elapsedTime));
    CheckForOutOfBounds();
    RemoveDeadEnemies();
  }

  private void CheckForOutOfBounds()
  {
    foreach (Enemy enemy in _enemies)
    {
      if (enemy.GetBoundingBox().Right < _leftBound)
```

```
      {
        enemy.Health = 0; // kill the enemy off
      }
    }
  }

  public void Render(Renderer renderer)
  {
    _enemies.ForEach(x => x.Render(renderer));
  }

  private void RemoveDeadEnemies()
  {
    for (int i = _enemies.Count - 1; i >= 0; i-)
    {
      if (_enemies[i].IsDead)
      {
        _enemies.RemoveAt(i);
      }
    }
  }
}
```

An extra function needs to be added to the Enemy class to check if the enemy has been destroyed.

```
class Enemy : Entity
{
  public bool IsDead
  {
    get { return Health == 0; }
  }
```

The IsDead method of the Enemy class returns true if the enemy's health is equal to 0; otherwise, it returns false. The EnemyManager, like the BulletManager, has an out of bounds check, but it's a little different. Enemies in a scrolling shooter game tend to start off on the far right of the screen and then move past the player exiting to the left. The out of bounds check compares the right-most point of the enemy bounding box against the left-most part of the screen. This removes enemies that the player fails to destroy and that escape off the left of the screen.

The Level class now needs to be modified to introduce this new manager and get rid of the old list.

```
// List<Enemy> _enemyList = new List<Enemy>(); <- Removed
EnemyManager _enemyManager;

public Level(Input input, TextureManager textureManager, PersistantGa-
meData gameData)
{
  _input = input;
  _gameData = gameData;
  _textureManager = textureManager;

  _background = new ScrollingBackground(textureManager.Get
("background"));
  _background.SetScale(2, 2);
  _background.Speed = 0.15f;

  _backgroundLayer = new ScrollingBackground(textureManager.Get
("background_layer_1"));
  _backgroundLayer.Speed = 0.1f;
  _backgroundLayer.SetScale(2.0, 2.0);

  _playerCharacter = new PlayerCharacter(_textureManager,
_bulletManager);

  _effectsManager = new EffectsManager(_textureManager);
  // _enemyList.Add(new Enemy(_textureManager, _effectsManager));
<- Removed
  _enemyManager = new EnemyManager(_textureManager, _effectsMana-
ger, -1300);
}
```

The collision processing needs to change a little as well; it will now use the list of enemies in the EnemyManager when checking for enemy collisions.

```
private void UpdateCollisions()
{
  foreach (Enemy enemy in _enemyManager.EnemyList)
```

To be able to see the enemies, the Update and Render loops need to be modified.

```
public void Update(double elapsedTime)
{
  // _enemyList.ForEach(x => x.Update(elapsedTime)); <- Remove this line
  _enemyManager.Update(elapsedTime);

// Code omitted

public void Render(Renderer renderer)
{
  _background.Render(renderer);
  _backgroundLayer.Render(renderer);

  //_enemyList.ForEach(x => x.Render(renderer)); <- remove this line
  _enemyManager.Render(renderer);
```

Run the program now. Shooting the enemy a couple of times will make it explode and disappear. This has started to become much more game-like. The most obvious failings at the moment are that there is only one enemy and it doesn't move.

Level Definitions

The current level lasts for 30 seconds and has one enemy at the start—this isn't a very interesting level. If there was some system for defining levels, then it would be easier to add a bit more excitement to this level. The level definition is a list of enemies to spawn at certain times. A level definition will therefore need some way to define enemies; the following code is a good starting point. The EnemyDef class should be added to the Engine project.

```
using System;
using System.Collections.Generic;
using System.Linq;
using System.Text;
using Engine;
namespace Shooter
{
  class EnemyDef
  {
    public string EnemyType { get; set; }
    public Vector StartPosition { get; set; }
    public double LaunchTime { get; set; }
```

```
    public EnemyDef()
    {

      EnemyType = "cannon_fodder";
      StartPosition = new Vector(300, 0, 0);
      LaunchTime = 0;
    }

    public EnemyDef(string enemyType, Vector startPosition, double
launchTime)
    {
      EnemyType = enemyType;
      StartPosition = startPosition;
      LaunchTime = launchTime;
    }


  }
}
```

There is a string that describes the enemy type. In the code, we might provide several different types of enemies: small fast ones, big slow ones, etc. The default enemy type is cannon fodder, and that's what we've got now. The start position is off the right of the screen. The launch time is the time at which the enemy will appear in the level. The level time counts down from some large number to 0. If the gameTime goes lower than the launch time, then an enemy object will be created and it will be launched into the level.

The EnemyManager is the class that will handle the enemy spawning. This means the constructor needs to be modified, and a list of upcoming enemies needs to be added.

```
List<EnemyDef> _upComingEnemies = new List<EnemyDef>();
public EnemyManager(TextureManager textureManager, EffectsManager
effectsManager, int leftBound)
{
  _textureManager = textureManager;
  _effectsManager = effectsManager;
  _leftBound = leftBound;
  _upComingEnemies.Add(new EnemyDef("cannon_fodder", new Vector(300,
300, 0), 25));
  _upComingEnemies.Add(new EnemyDef("cannon_fodder", new Vector(300,
-300, 0), 30));
```

```
_upComingEnemies.Add(new EnemyDef("cannon_fodder", new Vector(300, 0,
0), 29));

  // Sort enemies so the greater launch time appears first.
  _upComingEnemies.Sort(delegate(EnemyDef firstEnemy, EnemyDef
secondEnemy)
    {
      return firstEnemy.LaunchTime.CompareTo(secondEnemy.LaunchTime);
    });
}
```

The _upcomingEnemies list is a list of enemy definitions sorted by launch time. The greater the launch time, the higher in the list the definition appears. Each frame the top item of the list is checked to see if it's ready to launch. Only the top enemy definition needs to be checked because the list is sorted. If the list wasn't sorted, then every item in the list would need to be checked to decide which of the enemy definitions had a launch time greater than the current gameTime, and therefore needed to be launched next.

This enemy launching is done in the Update loop of the EnemyManager, which calls the new method UpdateEnemySpawns.

```
private void UpdateEnemySpawns(double gameTime)
{
  // If no upcoming enemies then there's nothing to spawn.
  if (_upComingEnemies.Count == 0)
  {
    return;
  }

  EnemyDef lastElement = _upComingEnemies[_upComingEnemies.Count - 1];
  if (gameTime < lastElement.LaunchTime)
  {
    _upComingEnemies.RemoveAt(_upComingEnemies.Count - 1);
    _enemies.Add(CreateEnemyFromDef(lastElement));
  }
}

private Enemy CreateEnemyFromDef(EnemyDef definition)
{
  Enemy enemy = new Enemy(_textureManager, _effectsManager);
  enemy.SetPosition(definition.StartPosition);
```

```
    if (definition.EnemyType == "cannon_fodder")
    {
      // The enemy type could be used to alter the health or texture
      // but we're using the default texture and health for the cannon
fodder type
    }
    else
    {
      System.Diagnostics.Debug.Assert(false, "Unknown enemy type.");
    }

    return enemy;
}

public void Update(double elapsedTime, double gameTime)
{
  UpdateEnemySpawns(gameTime);
```

The `Update` methods in the `EnemyManager` and `Level` class have been modified to take in a `gameTime` parameter. The `gameTime` is a number that counts down to zero, at which point the level will end. This value is used to determine when to create new enemies. The `InnerGameState` has to pass this `gameTime` value into the `Update` method of the `Level` object, and the `Level` passes it on to the `EnemyManager`.

```
// In Level.cs
public void Update(double elapsedTime, double gameTime)
{
  _enemyManager.Update(elapsedTime, gameTime);
// In InnerGameState.cs
public void Update(double elapsedTime)
{
  _level.Update(elapsedTime, _gameTime);
```

The `gameTime` is passed all the way from the inner game state down to the `UpdateEnemySpawns` function in the `EnemyManager`. `UpdateEnemy-Spawns` first checks if there are any upcoming enemies in the `_upcomingEnemies` list; if there aren't, then the method does nothing. If there are some upcoming enemies, the code checks the top of the list to see if it's ready to be launched. If the enemy definition is ready to be launched, then it's removed from the `_upcomingEnemies` list and the definition is used to make a new enemy object. The newly created enemy is then added to the _enemies list, spawning it in the game world.

CreateEnemyFromDef does pretty much what it says; it takes an EnemyDef object and returns an Enemy object. There's only one type of enemy at the moment so it's quite a simple function, but there's a lot of scope for adding new enemy types.

Run the program now and as the level time ticks down, three enemies will spawn in the level.

Enemy Movement

Enemies in a scrolling shooter should sweep in from the right of the screen and attempt to exit to the right without getting blown up. The enemy advance is shown in Figure 10.12. The player bullets already have movement code so the enemies could reuse that code. This would work, but the enemy movement would be pretty boring; they'd move from right to left in a straight line. Enemy movement should be far more interesting, and the easiest way to do this is to give

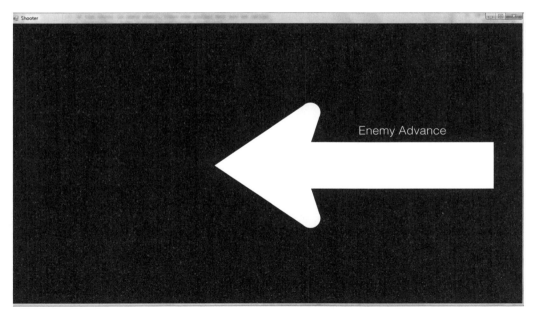

Figure 10.12
The enemy advance.

each enemy a predefined path with a number of way points. The enemy will hit all the way points and then exit to the left.

A path can be described easily as a series of points that lead from the right of the screen to the left of the screen. Figure 10.13 shows a path made up of points that could describe an enemy's path through the playing area.

This path can be joined together to produce something like Figure 10.14. This shows the path the enemy would use, but the corners are very jagged. It would be nice if we could get something smoother. Splines are a nice way of creating smooth paths. Figure 10.15 shows a Catmull-Rom spline; this type of spline is guaranteed to pass through all the control points. Edwin Catmull who worked at Pixar and helped create *Toy Story* co-invented this type of spline with Raphael Rom.

The spline is obviously smoother, but it does require another class to be created. Splines are a mathematical description of a curve.

Catmull-Rom splines are simply a way to get a position, *t*, between any two of the points that make up the spline. In Catmull-Rom splines, the two points on either

Figure 10.13
A path of points.

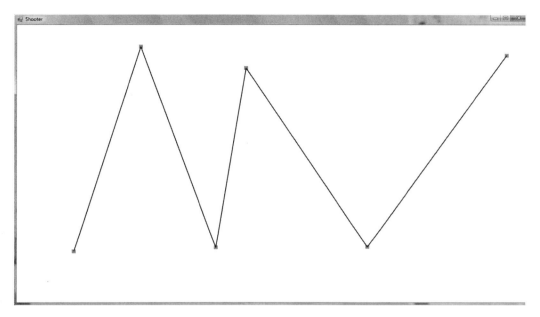

Figure 10.14
Linear interpolation of a path.

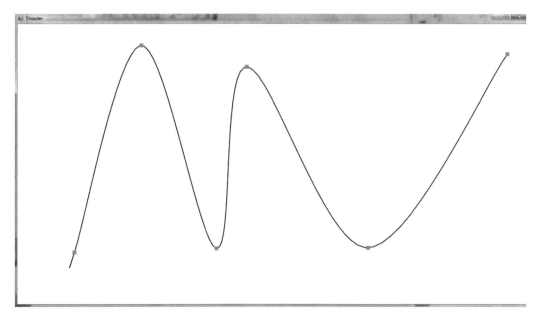

Figure 10.15
Spline path.

side of t are used in the calculation, as are their two neighbors, as shown in Figure 10.16.

Once some position can be obtained for a value of t (0-1) between any two neighboring points, then this can be extended so that t (0-1) can be mapped on to the entire line, not just one section. The calculation to get a position from t and four points is as follows.

$$f(t) = 0.5 \ ^*[t^3 \quad t^2 \quad t \quad 1] \ast \begin{bmatrix} -1 & 3 & -3 & -1 \\ 2 & -5 & -4 & -1 \\ -1 & 0 & 1 & 0 \\ 0 & 2 & 0 & 0 \end{bmatrix} \ast \begin{bmatrix} P0 \\ P1 \\ P2 \\ P3 \end{bmatrix}$$

This looks a little intimidating; three matrices are multiplied by a scalar that weighs all four points and decides how the t value is transformed into a position. It's not important to understand exactly how this works (though you are encouraged to investigate!); it's good enough to know what results will occur when you apply it.

Here is the C# implementation of a Catmull-Rom spline. This class should be added to the Engine project as it will be useful for more than this project. The spline code works in 3D so it can also be useful for tasks such as manipulating cameras or moving 3D entities along a path. The interface for this `spline` class

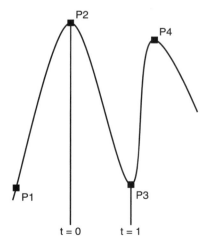

Figure 10.16
Catmull-Rom splines.

is based on Radu Gruian's C++ Overhauser code (http://www.codeproject.com/
KB/recipes/Overhauser.aspx —the Code Project website may require you to
register before it allows you to view the article. Registration is free.).

```
public class Spline
{
  List<Vector> _points = new List<Vector>();
  double _segmentSize = 0;

  public void AddPoint(Vector point)
  {
    _points.Add(point);
    _segmentSize = 1 / (double)_points.Count;
  }
  private int LimitPoints(int point)
  {
    if(point < 0)
    {
      return 0;
    }
    else if (point > _points.Count - 1)
    {
      return _points.Count - 1;
    }
    else
    {
      return point;
    }
  }

  // t ranges from 0 - 1
  public Vector GetPositionOnLine(double t)
  {
    if (_points.Count <= 1)
    {
      return new Vector(0,0,0);
    }

    // Get the segment of the line we're dealing with.
    int interval = (int)(t / _segmentSize);

    // Get the points around the segment
    int p0 = LimitPoints(interval - 1);
```

```
    int p1 = LimitPoints(interval);
    int p2 = LimitPoints(interval + 1);
    int p3 = LimitPoints(interval + 2);

    // Scale t to the current segment
    double scaledT = (t - _segmentSize * (double)interval) / _segmentSize;
    return CalculateCatmullRom(scaledT, _points[p0], _points[p1],
_points[p2], _points[p3]);
  }
  private Vector CalculateCatmullRom(double t, Vector p1, Vector p2,
Vector p3, Vector p4)
  {
    double t2 = t * t;
    double t3 = t2 * t;

    double b1 = 0.5 * (-t3 + 2 * t2 - t);
    double b2 = 0.5 * (3 * t3 - 5 * t2 + 2);
    double b3 = 0.5 * (-3 * t3 + 4 * t2 + t);
    double b4 = 0.5 * (t3 - t2);

    return (p1 * b1 + p2 * b2 + p3 * b3 + p4 * b4);
  }
}
```

This spline class is very simple to use. Any number of points can be added and the spline will join them together. The line is indexed from 0 to 1; a position on the line of 0.5 will return whatever point in space the middle of the line crosses. This makes the spline very easy to use with the earlier tween class. The spline requires all control points to be evenly spaced to give uniform values of t.

Each enemy is given a new Path class that will guide it across the level. This Path class is specific to the shooting game and should be created in the Shooter project.

```
public class Path
{
  Spline _spline = new Spline();
  Tween _tween;

  public Path(List<Vector> points, double travelTime)
  {
```

```
    foreach (Vector v in points)
    {
      _spline.AddPoint(v);
    }
    _tween = new Tween(0, 1, travelTime);
  }

  public void UpdatePosition(double elapsedTime, Enemy enemy)
  {
    _tween.Update(elapsedTime);
    Vector position = _spline.GetPositionOnLine(_tween.Value());
    enemy.SetPosition(position);
  }
}
```

The class constructor takes in a time and a list of points; from this it creates a `spline` and a `tween` object. The `travelTime` determines how long the enemy will take to travel the path defined by the spline. The `UpdatePosition` method updates the tween and gets a new position from the spline, which is used to reposition the enemy. The following code modifies the `Enemy` to use the `Path` class.

```
public Path Path { get; set; }
public void Update(double elapsedTime)
{
  if (Path != null)
  {
    Path.UpdatePosition(elapsedTime, this);
  }
  if (_hitFlashCountDown != 0)
  {
    _hitFlashCountDown = Math.Max(0, _hitFlashCountDown - elapsedTime);
    double scaledTime = 1 - (_hitFlashCountDown / HitFlashTime);
    _sprite.SetColor(new Engine.Color(1, 1, (float)scaledTime, 1));
  }
}
```

Now that all enemies have paths, the `StartPosition` variable from the `EnemyDef` can be removed, as the path will define where the enemy starts. Enemies can move through the level, but to do this they need to be given a path.

In the `EnemyManager`, when an enemy is created, it needs to be given a path. In the following the `cannon_fodder` enemy type is given a path that goes from right to left, veering upwards as it reaches the middle. The time for the enemy to follow the full path takes ten seconds.

```
private Enemy CreateEnemyFromDef(EnemyDef definition)
{
  Enemy enemy = new Enemy(_textureManager, _effectsManager);
  //enemy.SetPosition(definition.StartPosition); <- this line can be
removed
  if (definition.EnemyType == "cannon_fodder")
  {
    List<Vector> _pathPoints = new List<Vector>();
    _pathPoints.Add(new Vector(1400, 0, 0));
    _pathPoints.Add(new Vector(0, 250, 0));
    _pathPoints.Add(new Vector(-1400, 0, 0));

    enemy.Path = new Path(_pathPoints, 10);
  }
  else
  {
    System.Diagnostics.Debug.Assert(false, "Unknown enemy type.");
  }

  return enemy;
}
```

Now a more interesting level can be defined by editing the `EnemyManager` constructor.

```
public EnemyManager(TextureManager textureManager, EffectsManager
effectsManager, int leftBound)
{
  _textureManager = textureManager;
  _effectsManager = effectsManager;
  _leftBound = leftBound;

  _textureManager = textureManager;
  _effectsManager = effectsManager;
  _leftBound = leftBound;
```

```
_upComingEnemies.Add(new EnemyDef("cannon_fodder", 30));
_upComingEnemies.Add(new EnemyDef("cannon_fodder", 29.5));
_upComingEnemies.Add(new EnemyDef("cannon_fodder", 29));
_upComingEnemies.Add(new EnemyDef("cannon_fodder", 28.5));

_upComingEnemies.Add(new EnemyDef("cannon_fodder", 25));
_upComingEnemies.Add(new EnemyDef("cannon_fodder", 24.5));
_upComingEnemies.Add(new EnemyDef("cannon_fodder", 24));
_upComingEnemies.Add(new EnemyDef("cannon_fodder", 23.5));

_upComingEnemies.Add(new EnemyDef("cannon_fodder", 20));
_upComingEnemies.Add(new EnemyDef("cannon_fodder", 19.5));
_upComingEnemies.Add(new EnemyDef("cannon_fodder", 19));
_upComingEnemies.Add(new EnemyDef("cannon_fodder", 18.5));

    // Sort enemies so the greater launch time appears first.
    _upComingEnemies.Sort(delegate(EnemyDef firstEnemy, EnemyDef
secondEnemy)
    {
        return firstEnemy.LaunchTime.CompareTo(secondEnemy.LaunchTime);

    });
}
```

The enemies now use paths to describe how they move through the level so a
start position for each enemy definition is no longer required. This means the
EnemyDef class needs to be rewritten.

```
public class EnemyDef
{
    public string EnemyType { get; set; }
    public double LaunchTime { get; set; }

    public EnemyDef()
    {
        EnemyType = "cannon_fodder";
        LaunchTime = 0;
    }

    public EnemyDef(string enemyType, double launchTime)
    {
```

```
      EnemyType = enemyType;
      LaunchTime = launchTime;
   }
}
```

Run the code again, and you will see a stream of enemies arcing through the top half of the screen, as shown in Figure 10.17.

At this point, it might be nice to add a few more enemy types to spice up the level.

```
private Enemy CreateEnemyFromDef(EnemyDef definition)
{
   Enemy enemy = new Enemy(_textureManager, _effectsManager);

   if (definition.EnemyType == "cannon_fodder")
   {
      List<Vector> _pathPoints = new List<Vector>();
      _pathPoints.Add(new Vector(1400, 0, 0));
      _pathPoints.Add(new Vector(0, 250, 0));
      _pathPoints.Add(new Vector(-1400, 0, 0));
```

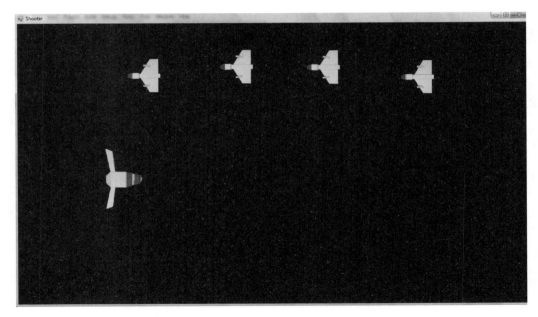

Figure 10.17
More interesting levels.

```
  enemy.Path = new Path(_pathPoints, 10);
}
else if (definition.EnemyType == "cannon_fodder_low")
{
  List<Vector> _pathPoints = new List<Vector>();
  _pathPoints.Add(new Vector(1400, 0, 0));
  _pathPoints.Add(new Vector(0, -250, 0));
  _pathPoints.Add(new Vector(-1400, 0, 0));

  enemy.Path = new Path(_pathPoints, 10);
}
else if (definition.EnemyType == "cannon_fodder_straight")
{
  List<Vector> _pathPoints = new List<Vector>();
  _pathPoints.Add(new Vector(1400, 0, 0));
  _pathPoints.Add(new Vector(-1400, 0, 0));

  enemy.Path = new Path(_pathPoints, 14);
}
else if (definition.EnemyType == "up_1")
{
  List<Vector> _pathPoints = new List<Vector>();
  _pathPoints.Add(new Vector(500, -375, 0));
  _pathPoints.Add(new Vector(500, 0, 0));
  _pathPoints.Add(new Vector(500, 0, 0));
  _pathPoints.Add(new Vector(-1400, 200, 0));

  enemy.Path = new Path(_pathPoints, 10);
}
else if (definition.EnemyType == "down_1")
{
  List<Vector> _pathPoints = new List<Vector>();
  _pathPoints.Add(new Vector(500, 375, 0));
  _pathPoints.Add(new Vector(500, 0, 0));
  _pathPoints.Add(new Vector(500, 0, 0));
  _pathPoints.Add(new Vector(-1400, -200, 0));
  enemy.Path = new Path(_pathPoints, 10);
}
else
{
  System.Diagnostics.Debug.Assert(false, "Unknown enemy type.");
```

```
    }

  return enemy;
}
```

Each of these enemies has an interesting path and can be put together to form a more interesting level. Here is some new Level set up code for the EnemyManager constructor.

```
public EnemyManager(TextureManager textureManager, EffectsManager
effectsManager, int leftBound)
{
  _textureManager = textureManager;
  _effectsManager = effectsManager;
  _leftBound = leftBound;

  _upComingEnemies.Add(new EnemyDef("cannon_fodder", 30));
  _upComingEnemies.Add(new EnemyDef("cannon_fodder", 29.5));
  _upComingEnemies.Add(new EnemyDef("cannon_fodder", 29));
  _upComingEnemies.Add(new EnemyDef("cannon_fodder", 28.5));

  _upComingEnemies.Add(new EnemyDef("cannon_fodder_low", 30));
  _upComingEnemies.Add(new EnemyDef("cannon_fodder_low", 29.5));
  _upComingEnemies.Add(new EnemyDef("cannon_fodder_low", 29));
  _upComingEnemies.Add(new EnemyDef("cannon_fodder_low", 28.5));

  _upComingEnemies.Add(new EnemyDef("cannon_fodder", 25));
  _upComingEnemies.Add(new EnemyDef("cannon_fodder", 24.5));
  _upComingEnemies.Add(new EnemyDef("cannon_fodder", 24));
  _upComingEnemies.Add(new EnemyDef("cannon_fodder", 23.5));

  _upComingEnemies.Add(new EnemyDef("cannon_fodder_low", 20));
  _upComingEnemies.Add(new EnemyDef("cannon_fodder_low", 19.5));
  _upComingEnemies.Add(new EnemyDef("cannon_fodder_low", 19));
  _upComingEnemies.Add(new EnemyDef("cannon_fodder_low", 18.5));

  _upComingEnemies.Add(new EnemyDef("cannon_fodder_straight", 16));
  _upComingEnemies.Add(new EnemyDef("cannon_fodder_straight", 15.8));
  _upComingEnemies.Add(new EnemyDef("cannon_fodder_straight", 15.6));
  _upComingEnemies.Add(new EnemyDef("cannon_fodder_straight", 15.4));
  _upComingEnemies.Add(new EnemyDef("up_1", 10));
  _upComingEnemies.Add(new EnemyDef("down_1", 9));
```

```
_upComingEnemies.Add(new EnemyDef("up_1", 8));
_upComingEnemies.Add(new EnemyDef("down_1", 7));
_upComingEnemies.Add(new EnemyDef("up_1", 6));
// Sort enemies so the greater launch time appears first.
_upComingEnemies.Sort(delegate(EnemyDef firstEnemy, EnemyDef
secondEnemy)
{
  return firstEnemy.LaunchTime.CompareTo(secondEnemy.LaunchTime);

});

}
```

Try out the level; you may find it a little challenging so this is a great time to play around with the code and balance the game a little. Try increasing the player firing rate or the spaceship speed.

Enemy Attacks

Enemies move in interesting ways across the level, but they're still quite passive. The player can blast away at them and they do nothing! The enemies should have some kind of recourse, so in this section we'll look at turning the tables a little.

There's already a `BulletManager`, and this currently handles only the player bullets. The enemy bullets will only affect the player, and the player bullets will only affect the enemies. For this reason, it's easiest to have separate lists of bullets. This means a few of the functions need to be generalized to accept a list of bullets.

```
public class BulletManager
{
  List<Bullet> _bullets = new List<Bullet>();
  List<Bullet> _enemyBullets = new List<Bullet>();

// Code omitted

  public void Update(double elapsedTime)
  {
    UpdateBulletList(_bullets, elapsedTime);
    UpdateBulletList(_enemyBullets, elapsedTime);
  }
```

```
public void UpdateBulletList (List<Bullet> bulletList, double
elapsedTime)
  {
    bulletList.ForEach(x => x.Update(elapsedTime));
    CheckOutOfBounds(_bullets);
    RemoveDeadBullets(bulletList);
  }

  private void CheckOutOfBounds (List<Bullet> bulletList)
  {
    foreach (Bullet bullet in bulletList)
    {
      if (!bullet.GetBoundingBox().IntersectsWith(_bounds))
      {
        bullet.Dead = true;
      }
    }
  }

  private void RemoveDeadBullets (List<Bullet> bulletList)
  {
    for (int i = bulletList.Count - 1; i >= 0; i-)
    {
      if (bulletList[i].Dead)
      {
        bulletList.RemoveAt(i);
      }
    }
  }

  internal void Render (Renderer renderer)
  {
    _bullets.ForEach(x => x.Render(renderer));
    _enemyBullets.ForEach(x => x.Render(renderer));
  }
```

The above code introduces a second list for enemy bullets; it now requires a function that will let the enemy shoot bullets and a function to check if any of them hit the player.

```
public void EnemyShoot (Bullet bullet)
{
```

```
      _enemyBullets.Add(bullet);
}

public void UpdatePlayerCollision(PlayerCharacter playerCharacter)
{
  foreach (Bullet bullet in _enemyBullets)
  {
    if(bullet.GetBoundingBox().IntersectsWith(playerCharacter.
GetBoundingBox()))
    {
      bullet.Dead = true;
      playerCharacter.OnCollision(bullet);
    }
  }
}
```

The `UpdatePlayerCollision` is quite similar to the existing `UpdateEne-myCollision` method and eventually they should be combined, but for this iteration of the game development, it's easier if they stay separate. The `PlayerCharacter` class needs a new `OnCollision` method that takes in a bullet object.

```
internal void OnCollision(Bullet bullet)
{
  _dead = true;
}
```

The `PlayerCharacter` now has two collision methods: one for bullets and one for enemies. The `PlayerCharacter` dies if he touches an enemy or a bullet so these methods are redundant. The reason they have been written this way is to make extending the game easier. It's important to know what the player is colliding with. If the player is given a health value, then colliding with an enemy may cause more damage than a bullet. If missiles, mines, or various types of power-up are added, they too can have an extra collision method to deal with that case.

Shooter is a very strict game. If the player hits an enemy, he immediately loses. The same is true if he hits a bullet. The `BulletManager` now needs an extra call in the `Update` loop of the `Level` class to test if an enemy bullet has hit the player.

```
private void UpdateCollisions()
{
  _bulletManager.UpdatePlayerCollision(_playerCharacter);
```

For the enemies to use their newfound shooting powers, they need access to the `BulletManager` class. This can be passed into the `EnemyManager` and into each individual enemy from there. Here it's passed into the `EnemyManager` from the `Level` class constructor.

```
public Level(Input input, TextureManager textureManager, Persistant
GameData gameData)
{
  _input = input;
  _gameData = gameData;
  _textureManager = textureManager;
  _effectsManager = new EffectsManager(_textureManager);
  _enemyManager = new EnemyManager(_textureManager, _effectsManager,
_bulletManager, -1300);
```

In the following code, the `EnemyManager` stores a reference to the `Bullet-Manager` and uses it when constructing enemies.

```
BulletManager _bulletManager;
public EnemyManager(TextureManager textureManager, EffectsManager
effectsManager, BulletManager bulletManger, int leftBound)
{
  _bulletManager = bulletManger;

// Code omitted

private Enemy CreateEnemyFromDef(EnemyDef definition)
{
  Enemy enemy = new Enemy(_textureManager, _effectsManager,
_bulletManager);
```

The enemies now have the `BulletManager` and with it the power to start shooting bullets. The question now is when should the enemies shoot? They can't shoot every frame or the game would be far too hard. The enemies shouldn't all fire at the same time or it will be far too difficult. The trick is to set the firing times randomly for each enemy.

```
public double MaxTimeToShoot { get; set; }
```

```
public double MinTimeToShoot { get; set; }
Random _random = new Random();
double _shootCountDown;

public void RestartShootCountDown()
{
  _shootCountDown = MinTimeToShoot + (_random.NextDouble() *
MaxTimeToShoot);
}

BulletManager _bulletManager;
Texture _bulletTexture;
public Enemy(TextureManager textureManager, EffectsManager
effectsManager, BulletManager bulletManager)
{
  _bulletManager = bulletManager;
  _bulletTexture = textureManager.Get("bullet");
  MaxTimeToShoot = 12;
  MinTimeToShoot = 1;
  RestartShootCountDown();

// Code omitted
public void Update(double elapsedTime)
{
  _shootCountDown = _shootCountDown - elapsedTime;
  if (_shootCountDown <= 0)
  {
    Bullet bullet = new Bullet(_bulletTexture);
    bullet.Speed = 350;
    bullet.Direction = new Vector(-1, 0, 0);
    bullet.SetPosition(_sprite.GetPosition());
    bullet.SetColor(new Engine.Color(1, 0, 0, 1));
    _bulletManager.EnemyShoot(bullet);
    RestartShootCountDown();
  }
}
```

When the enemy is created, it sets a timer for the next time it will shoot. The timer is set using C#'s Random class and a minimum and maximum time. The timer will be set somewhere in between these minimum and maximum values. All ships will shoot at different times. The RestartShootCountDown method sets the random time when the enemy will shoot. Math.NextDouble returns a random number from 0 to 1, which is scaled between the MinTime-ToShoot and MaxTimeToShoot member variables.

The Update loop ticks down the _shootCountDown, and once it is equal to or below 0 the enemy fires a bullet. The bullet is made to be slower than the player bullets and it's shot in the opposite direction. The enemy bullets are also colored red so it's obvious they're different from the players. Once the enemy shoots, the _shootCountDown timer is reset.

The enemies shoot towards the left of the screen. You may want to make it a little harder and have the enemies aim at the player. To do this, the enemies must have a reference to the PlayerCharacter. Then it's a simple matter of working out the direction of the player in reference to the enemy ship. If you decide to add aiming to the enemies, here's a little snippet of code that might help.

```
Vector currentPosition = _sprite.GetPosition();
Vector bulletDir = _playerCharacter.GetPosition() - currentPosition;
bulletDir = bulletDir.Normalize(bulletDir);
bullet.Direction = bulletDir;
```

This concludes this second refinement of the game. The enemies can fire on the player and move about in interesting ways. The enemies can be destroyed and will explode in a satisfying ball of flame.

Continuing Iterations

After two basic iterations of development, we have a wonderful but basic side-scrolling shooter. There is massive scope for developing this project into something totally individual. The project is yours now and you can develop it as you want. If you feel a little lost, here are some suggestions.

- A very simple first step is to introduce a new enemy type; just add an extra else if and perhaps modify a path or the health. Once you've done that, consider making a new enemy texture and changing the new enemy to use this texture. This will suddenly make the game a lot more interesting.

- A score is important in scrolling shooters. The score can be displayed using the Text class. The score should increase every time the player destroys an enemy.

- Sound is also very simple to add. A sound manager needs to be created as it was earlier in the book, and a number of suitable sounds could be generated for shooting, exploding, and taking damage. Then you just need to find the places where explode, damage, and shoot events occur and make a call to the sound manager to play the correct sound. The main bulk of the work is passing the sound manager through all the objects so that it can be used where it's needed.

- Regarding the code, there is a large number of managers and a few scattered functions with similar code. The code could be made tighter and easier to extend if these managers were generalized and any repeated code was removed. A good starting point is to see what similar methods each of the managers use and then consider extending the `Entity` class so one general `EntityManager` could be created.

- The game's single level is defined in the `EnemyManager` constructor. This isn't very extendable. A good starting project might be to define the level definitions in a text file. On load-up the program can read the text and load the level definition. The level definition could be very simple, such as

```
cannon_fodder, 30
cannon_fodder, 29.5
cannon_fodder, 29
cannon_fodder, 28.5
```

- Each line has an enemy type and a launch time separated by a comma. This is very easy to parse and read into a `Level` definition class. The level data should probably be stored in a `PersistantGameData` class.

- Once you have one level loaded, it's easy to make a new level file, and then suddenly you have the potential for a multi-level game. When one level is successfully finished, instead of returning the `StartGameState`, the state could return to the `InnerGameState` but using the next level. If the game has multiple levels, then it would good if the game was able to save the player's progress through these levels. A very simple way to save the game data would be to write out the score and current level to a text file.

- Instead of having a linear level progression (1,2,3,4), the user could be presented with an overworld map to select which levels he'd like to complete next. An overworld map generally indicates all the levels as nodes linked by paths. Such a system has been used in some of the *Super Mario* games. An overworld map makes it very easy to introduce secret paths and levels that are discovered by doing particularly well in the previous level.

- If the player is hit by an enemy spaceship or bullet, the `PlayerCharacter` dies and it's game over. It would be preferable to give the player some margin for error, perhaps by giving the spaceship some health—allowing it to take damage like the enemies. The health could be represented by a health bar on screen that goes down each time the ship takes a hit. You may also want to introduce the concept of lives—the player starts with several lives, each allowing one more go at the level before the game is lost.

- As levels progress, they tend to get more difficult. To help the player, you could give him better weapons and items to repair any damage to his ship. In scrolling shooting games, power-ups and other items tend to be dropped by enemies. A new `item` class needs to be created, and it can be added to the scene (possibly via the `EffectsManager`) to be picked up by the player. A health pack can repair some amount of the damage the player has received. New weapons can deal more damage or perhaps there can be two bullets every time the player shoots instead of one.

- You could also add alternate weapons that are triggered by different buttons. Bombs or lasers, for instance, could be secondary weapons that have a limited number of shots.

- RPG elements are a very popular way to add a greater degree of depth. Enemies could drop money (or scrap that could later be sold for money). After each level the player could buy new weapons, upgrade existing ones, or even buy a new type of ship. You may even want to allow players to place weapons at different locations on the ship by altering the `PlayerChar-acter`'s `_gunOffset` member.

- The RPG elements could be taken even further by adding a layer of narrative to the game. This could be done during the level with text boxes and scrip-ted movements of enemies and the player. Story elements could also be added to an overworld map or after each level.

- Large boss enemies at the end of the level are also a staple of the side-scrolling shooter. You could make the boss enemy an aggregate of several different types of enemies. Then parts of the boss can be destroyed, but the `PlayerCharacter` only wins when all the boss parts are destroyed.

- The scrolling space backgrounds are quite dull and could be made more lively with animated space debris, far away supernova, and planets. The scrolling background can be altered at any time, so with a little work it would be easy to give the impression the spaceship was traveling toward the surface of a planet.

- As a final suggestion, you could add a local multiplayer mode. This is pretty easy to do. A second game controller or the keyboard would need its input to be redirected to a second `PlayerCharacter`. Some logic would also need to be changed so that if one player died the other could keep on playing.

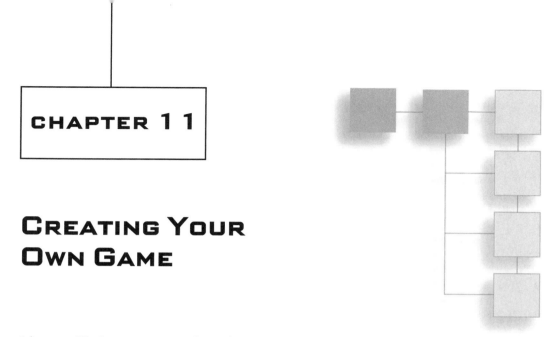

CHAPTER 11

CREATING YOUR OWN GAME

It's very likely you are reading this book because you have some great ideas for games and want to learn how to turn those ideas into programs. This chapter offers general advice on game creation and covers some challenges that particular game genres experience and how to approach them.

This is a very broad whirlwind tour of game creation, touching on some of the more interesting problems you'll encounter as you start programming. There are some suggested steps for writing games, code snippets for algorithms, and on the CD, you'll find a list of resources and further reading for all the game types listed here.

Project Management

Writing games is fun and rewarding, but finishing a game project is much harder. This section will cover the approach to take when developing a project. It's important to know when to abandon a game project and when to soldier on and finish it.

A game can't start without an idea, so consider carrying a small notebook around with you and jotting down any sudden bolt of inspiration that strikes you during the day. A second tip for generating game ideas is to take a critical look at the games you enjoy playing; try to break down the games into systems and note any gameplay features that you like. If you see a nice GUI, special effect, puzzle, or game interaction, try to re-create it. Re-creating parts of existing games is an excellent way to improve your skills.

When you get your great game idea, then it's time to move on to the next stage: the feasibility test. Do you have the resources to create this game? If it requires hours of full-motion video, hundreds of hours of gameplay, and thousands of fully animated monsters, then unless you are surrounded by some extremely talented friends or are very well-funded, you may have to tone down your ambition. The ideal game will be something that pushes your abilities but is still achievable. If you are very new to game development, start with small projects that can be achieved in a few days (such as *Pong* or *Space Invaders*) and slowly work your way up to more demanding projects.

Once you've decided on a game idea that's passed your feasibility test, it's time to break it down into manageable chunks. This is the fun, high-level design bit. You have a vague idea of this great game, but now you need to solidify the idea and work out how it's going to fit together. A good idea is to sketch out the classes and systems of the game on paper with boxes and then indicate relationships and interactions with arrows. This rough high-level plan is a great thing to pin to a wall or keep in your development area. It's a map that will help guide you as you starting digging into the details of the project. If you still don't feel you're quite at the boxes and arrows stage, then try playing your vision of the game in your head using your imagination. What happens when you first start the game? When you begin the first level? What actions can you perform? How does the world respond to those actions?

Let's say you want to create a game in which you must sing different songs to make characters on the screen perform actions and interact with the environment. When breaking down this design, the first big system that jumps out is the player input; being able to detect if the player is singing and then determine which song the player is singing is an area that will require research. The singing section needs a small project all to itself. At the very least, one system will have to get the voice input from the player via the microphone, and another system will have to be able to identify the different songs the player is singing. Each creature will have to be checked to see if the current song being sung is important to them. The actions the creatures can perform need to be defined. The win/lose state of the game needs to be defined. How the world is represented needs to be defined. These are some of the questions this one line game design brings up. By the time you're done thinking through your game on paper, you should have many questions that need to be answered and a list of items to research.

The next phase is prioritizing the questions and tasks that this early design phase has uncovered. Not every game will have features that require researching, but if there are any research tasks that the game relies on then they need to be done first; this might be as simple as a quick Google search or it may require asking people who are better informed or reading books and articles on the subject. Small toy programs are a great place to try out different research ideas, which if successful can be cleaned up and incorporated into the final project.

Once you think you have finished all the research, ask yourself "What is the very least I can do to get a basic working game?" Then do that and if possible try to do it in one sitting. Once you have a first iteration of your game, it's much easier to come back to it and slowly refine it. A half finished game is harder to pick up if you've had a few days break from development.

Game programming requires time; usually a period of four or so hours is required for a minimum session, especially if you want to get into that state of flow when you stop noticing the passage of time and become entirely focused on the task at hand. To-do lists are a good way to direct your development efforts. A good tip is to write the to-do item and then just below it, write the smallest step you need to do to start this to-do item, for example.

1. Set up the development environment and get a basic window and game loop up

    – Open Visual Studio, create a new project and call it "Project Minstrel"

2. Build Simple Song Classifier skeleton class

    – Add SongClassifier.cs file and add System.Speech library

The little sentence after the to-do point is something you can do right now; it's almost easier to take that first step than not, and once you've taken the first step, you're obliged to finished the full to-do point. Don't collect a backlog of un-finished to-do items each time you begin developing your project, then throw away the last to-do list and start again. Anything that's super-important you can copy across.

Don't be afraid to stop working on a project if it doesn't seem to be going any-where. Every project, even those that don't get completed, imparts some kind of lesson (even if that lesson is of the "Well, I won't do that again" variety, it's still useful!). You will get a lot more done on a project you want to work on than a project you feel obligated to work on just because you've invested a lot of time in it.

If you are looking for feedback or help, there are lots of game programming communities on the Internet that will be happy to try out your game and offer suggestions and advice (such as The Independent Game Source `http://forums.tigsource.com/index.php`. For other communities please see the accompanying CD). Online communities also host regular game programming competitions and usually have services if you wish to find another programmer or artist to team up with.

Display Methods

Games, for the most part, fall neatly into two categories: 2D games like *Super Mario, Tetris,* and *Pokémon* and 3D games like *Quake, Fallout 3,* and *Grand Theft Auto.* 2D games tend to be easier to program.

2D Games

2D games have been covered quite extensively in this book so you should already have a good head start if your game idea is 2D based. 2D games often suggest pixel art style graphics, but this doesn't have to be the case; there is still a lot of room for innovation in presenting a 2D game. The graphics could appear like cut-out pieces of paper, crayon drawings, vector graphics (using OpenGL's `GL_LINE` drawing mode), abstract, or silhouette graphics. (Silhouette graphics have the great advantage that they are much easier to draw.) The math involved with 2D games tends to be simpler than a 3D game, but it really depends on the specific game. Most programmers experiment with 2D games before learning about 3D game programming, and a lot of game development knowledge is independent of whether the game is developed in 3D or 2D.

3D Games

One of most important skills for a game programmer is the ability to independently research and learn about new programming and development techniques. Sometimes a game idea demands a new unfamiliar technology (for instance you may wish to have a rope in your game in which case you need to research a way for this to be simulated); other times you may learn a new technology just for the fun or the challenge and in so doing, you discover a new idea for a game. The vast majority of big budget modern games are 3D and this alone makes learning 3D game development appealing.

3D graphics programming is a vast, intimidating heap of mathematics, techniques, and terminology, and it's important to approach it in a measured, achievable manner. To aim to compete with the latest FPS shooter with your first project is only setting yourself up for disappointment. A better goal is something that can be achieved quite quickly and is a stepping stone to more ambitious projects. For 3D graphics, getting a box to display on the screen is an achievable first step–even better if the box rotates. A later intermediate step might be to re-create the side-scrolling shooter game covered in the last chapter, but use 3D models instead of sprites.

The code examples in this book have often made use of a function called `Setup2DGraphics` in the Form.cs file. It's quite trivial to write an equivalent `Setup3DGraphics`.

```
private void Setup3DGraphics(double width, double height)
{
  double halfWidth = width / 2;
  double halfHeight = height / 2;
  Gl.glMatrixMode(Gl.GL_PROJECTION);
  Gl.glLoadIdentity();
  Glu.gluPerspective(90, 4 / 3, 1, 1000);
  Gl.glMatrixMode(Gl.GL_MODELVIEW);
  Gl.glLoadIdentity();
}
```

This code is nearly identical to the `Setup2DGraphics` call, but it uses the function `gluPerspective` instead of `glOrtho`. The `gluPerspective` function takes in a field of view as the first argument, the aspect ratio as the second, and the near and far planes as the last two arguments. This describes something similar to the lens of a camera for viewing the 3D scene.

If `Setup3DGraphics` is called instead of `Setup2DGraphics` then that's nearly all that's needed to start 3D game programming. Here's a game state that renders a pyramid in 3D using OpenGLs immediate mode producing an image similar to Figure 11.1. Make sure that you have replaced all `Setup2DGraphics` calls with `Setup3DGraphics` calls before running this state.

Figure 11.1
A 3D pyramid.

```
class Test3DState : IGameObject
{
  public Test3DState(){}
  public void Update(double elapsedTime){ }

  public void Render()
  {
    Gl.glDisable(Gl.GL_TEXTURE_2D);
    Gl.glClearColor(1, 1, 1, 0);
    Gl.glClear(Gl.GL_COLOR_BUFFER_BIT);

    // This is a simple way of using a camera
    Gl.glMatrixMode(Gl.GL_MODELVIEW);
    Gl.glLoadIdentity();
    Vector cameraPosition = new Vector(-75, 125, -500); // half a meter back
      on the Z axis
    Vector cameraLookAt = new Vector(0, 0, 0); // make the camera look at the
      world origin.
    Vector cameraUpVector = new Vector(0, 1, 0);
```

```
Glu.gluLookAt(cameraPosition.X, cameraPosition.Y,
  cameraPosition.Z,
              cameraLookAt.X,    cameraLookAt.Y,
  cameraLookAt.Z,
              cameraUpVector.X, cameraUpVector.Y,
  cameraUpVector.Z);

Gl.glBegin(Gl.GL_TRIANGLE_FAN);
{
  Gl.glColor3d(1, 0, 0);
  Gl.glVertex3d(0.0f, 100, 0.0f);

  Gl.glColor3d(0, 1, 0);
  Gl.glVertex3d(-100, -100, 100);

  Gl.glColor3d(0, 0, 1);
  Gl.glVertex3d(100, -100, 100);

  Gl.glColor3d(0, 1, 0);
  Gl.glVertex3d(100, -100, -100);

  Gl.glColor3d(0, 0, 1);
  Gl.glVertex3d(-100, -100, -100);

  Gl.glColor3d(0, 1, 0);
  Gl.glVertex3d(-100, -100, 100);
}
  Gl.glEnd();
 }
}
```

The function call to Glu.gluLookAt is new and it sets up the positioning of a 3D camera to view the scene through. The position of the camera is made of three vectors: the first is the position of the camera in the world, the second is the position of what the camera should point at, and the final vector points upwards. If the up vector were reversed by setting the Y component to −1 then the scene shown in Figure 11.1 would appear upside down.

If you wish to learn more about using 3D graphics in games, then I suggest the following steps.

- Set up a 3D scene and draw a cube using OpenGL's immediate mode and GL_QUADS.

- Write out the vertices of the box to a file and then load them in. This is your first simple file format.

- Update the code so that it uses vertex buffers and not immediate mode.

- Research index buffers and update the code and your file format to use these index buffers.

- Research the .obj file format. It's a plain text format. Write a simple program to load .obj files into a set of index and vertex buffers. Ignore the materials and parametric surface information. (Tip: Remember that OpenGL expects surfaces to come in clockwise order.)

Those steps are enough to get started with 3D game programming. Once you can load simple .obj files then you can move and transform them using the existing matrix class.

When you are ready to move on to animating 3D models, start with the .MD2 file format. This is the file format used by Quake II to store its enemies and characters. There are hundreds of free test files available to download from the internet that can be used to test your loader. Once you get to this stage, you will probably have a much better idea of what part of 3D graphics programming you want to learn next.

Types of Games

Games come in many different shapes and sizes, which can be roughly categorized into genres. Games in the same genre will generally need to be programmed in a similar way.

Text Games

Text games are some of the simplest games to get started with as no graphics are required. The programmer can focus entirely on the story. There are a large variety of different text games but the most common are interactive fiction games. Here is a sample of an interaction with a simple interactive fiction game.

```
You are in a dark room, you can see nothing.
>Search
You search around in the dark, your fingers brush against something
   metallic.
>Examine metallic thing
It's hard to make out in the dark but it seems to be a flashlight.
>Turn on flashlight.
The flashlight flickers to life.
```

An interactive fiction game has two main parts: a data structure holding the description of the world and a parser that interprets the users input. The data structure describing the world can be quite simple.

```
class Room
{
  public string Description {get; set;}
  public List<Room> Exits{get; set;}
  public Room(string description, List<Room> exits)
  {
    Exits = exits;
    Description = description;
  }
}
```

The Room class is a single place in the game world; it has a string of text that describes it and a list of exits to different rooms. The player can be given a description of each room and use the exits to travel around the map. Exits can be added and removed as puzzles are solved.

The parser is a piece of code that matches patterns. The user might type "Look" into the console and then press enter to look around a room; in code this would be handled like so:

```
if (_input == "look")
{
  // The look function writes the description to the console.
  _currentRoom.Look();
}
```

A more complicated statement would require more parsing; for example, "use hammer on doorstep." The following code is a little idealized but gives an idea of how the user commands could be broken down.

```
if (_input.StartsWith("use"))
{
  _input = _input.RemoveSubstring("use")
  int result = _input.Find("on")

  if ( result == -1) break; // pattern not recognized

  string firstParameter = input.SubString(0, result)
  string secondParameter = input.SubString(result + "on".Length(),
    input.Length());

  // the use function will use these strings to look up objects
  Use(firstParameter, secondParemeter);
}
```

This code snippet assumes that all the input text is lowercase; if the player capitalizes any letter then the function won't work! A fix for this is to process the input string like this:

```
_input = _input.ToLower()
```

To begin a Visual Studio project for a text-adventure game, choose Console Application rather than Windows Form Application, as is shown in Figure 11.2.

Once the console project is started, input can be read from the console using `Windows.Console.ReadLine()` and output to the console using `Windows.Console.WriteLine()`.

A good resource for creating interactive fiction is the Inform Programming language `http://inform7.com/`. It allows the user to type in almost natural English to describe an interactive fiction world.

Puzzle Games

Puzzle games are a good choice for a first game; they tend to need only a few resources and they are usually relatively simple to understand. Popular puzzle games include games such as a jigsaw, Sudoku, Boggle, Tetris, and Bejeweled. A lot of very popular games are based around collections of puzzle games such as the PC game 7th Guest, the Professor Layton games on the DS, and even Brain Training. All these games are simple to understand and play but are still challenging and fun to create.

Figure 11.2
Creating a console application.

Tetris is a good first game to program; at first glance it appears simple, but when you start to break it down you will find some interesting challenges. In case you are not familiar with *Tetris* the aim is to create a horizontal line of blocks without gaps. Once such a line is created, the line disappears and the blocks above drop down to replace the line. Different colored and shaped blocks fall from the top of the game area and the player must rotate and move the blocks to maximize the number of lines completed. As the game progresses, the speed of the falling blocks increases.

A first goal for creating a *Tetris* is to make small 1x1 blocks fall from the top of the playing area to the bottom and then stop. Additional blocks should stack up on top of the ones that have fallen before them. This starting goal can be seen in Figure 11.3. Once you've got this code working, then you've really broken the back of writing a *Tetris* game.

The next stage in developing the game is to detect when the game is lost. This is when the number of blocks stacks so high it reaches the top of the playing area. Basic player input should be implemented next allowing the blocks to be moved

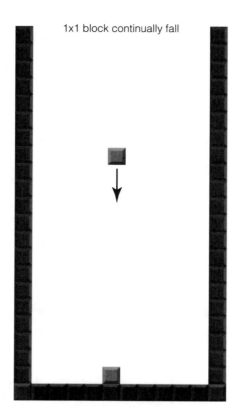

1x1 block continually fall

Figure 11.3
A first step towards a *Tetris* game.

a unit left or right. The player shouldn't be able to move the block once it's finished falling and neither should they be able to move the block outside of the playing area. *Tetris* has no end game, it's one of those classic era games where you can never win but only hope to delay your inevitable failure. There is no explicit win state to model but one of the major goals in *Tetris* is to get a complete row of bricks. Your program should detect completed rows and remove the row. Any blocks above the row should drop down a level. This is also a good point to introduce a scoring system and display the player's score on screen.

The next step is to make the *Tetris* pieces, which are called tetrominoes; I would suggest designing them so they are a collection of the smaller 1x1 blocks that have been used in the earlier stage. The user must be able to rotate these te-trominoes but rather than try to rotate all the sprites 90° around the center of the tetrominoe, I would just cheat and store four versions of each tetrominoe for each direction it can be rotated. When the player presses the rotate button, the current tetrominoe can be replaced with another new tetrominoe piece that is its next rotation. Instead of 1×1 blocks continually falling from the top of the play area to the bottom, random tetrominoes should be created.

The final challenge regarding *Tetris* is the chain reaction rule. This rule is shown in Figure 11.4. Sometimes completing a row in *Tetris* leaves some blocks immediately above the row hanging in space. These blocks need to fall down. When these blocks do fall down they, in turn, may trigger the completion of another row and this may cause a chain reaction.

The chain rule can be quite tricky; after a row is completed, the *Tetris* board needs to be searched for any free pieces that can move down. All free pieces are then moved down, and before the game resumes, all the rows need to be checked to see if any have been completed. If you follow this rough road map, you should have a reasonable *Tetris* without too much hair pulling.

First-Person Shooter Games

First-person shooter games may seem a little intimidating as they require familiarity with a lot of complex mathematics. A lot of the complexity of 3D games

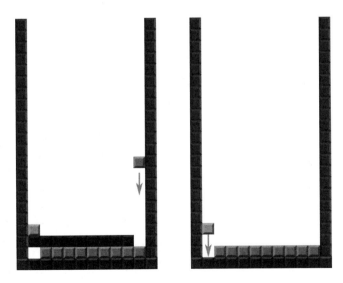

Figure 11.4
A first step towards a *Tetris* game.

comes from the algorithms that work out what the player can currently see. If the program knows what the player can see, then it doesn't need to render any objects that are hidden. This can produce massive speed improvements. These algorithms are usually a type of space partitioning, but you only need to learn about them if you've already got to the stage where you can write a basic FPS.

Here is a list of steps to start you on your way to FPS game creation.

- Create a simple 3D scene with a camera class (use `Glu.gluLookAt`) that can change its position.

- Draw a large quad under the camera so that it appears like a floor. Optionally, texture this quad.

- Make it so the arrows keys move the position and look-at position of the camera.

If you successfully follow these steps, you will have something that feels like an FPS game, but you can't move the camera around with the mouse, and there is no real level. To develop the game further than this requires quite a lot more mathematics; here are some of the major formulas to research.

Ray-Triangle, Ray-Plane, Ray-Sphere, and Ray-Quad collision checks need to be researched and implemented. Each of these checks should return one or more positions where the intersection occurred. (A Ray is a position and a direction. It's useful for representing lasers and determining if the character's feet are currently touching the floor.)

Line-segment-Triangle, Line-segment-Plane, Line-segment-Sphere, and Line-segment-Quad intersection checks can be created from the Ray checks. Line segments are used to check if the player or player's bullet has passed through a wall or enemy. A line segment is made by drawing a line from the player's position in the last frame to the player's position in the current frame. If the line segment crosses a wall, that means the player is trying to walk through the wall. Walking through walls is a bad thing, so the player's position needs to be pushed back along the line segment until the player is no longer passing through the wall.

For the camera movement, you may wish to research polar coordinates because they are usually used to translate the movement of the mouse to the movement of the camera in the game world. You may also wish to investigate BSP (Binary Space Partitioning) trees as these render the 3D levels more efficiently. The best way to research this type of game is to take each element on its own and create a simple test program to make sure that everything is working as you expect. Once you have all of the technology down, you can bring all the elements together to make a more complicated game.

Strategy Games

Strategy games come in two general types: turn-based games that have a close relationship with traditional tabletop war games, and real-time games, which have a far more distant relationship to tabletop games. Turn-based games are easier to program. The player has a number of possible actions he can carry out each turn, and once no more actions can be done, the turn can end. Real-time games allow the player to perform as many actions as fast as he can, but each action takes a certain amount of time before it completes. Turn-based games tend to favor 2D representational graphics, sticking close to their board game roots, whereas real-time games usually use 3D graphics.

Strategy games tend to favor a top-down view, allowing the player to view as much of the game world as possible. If the graphics are 2D, then tiles and sprites are often used to represent the different types of land, unit, and characters. 3D games usually use a 3D height map. In the `Engine` class, a sprite was a 2D quad; imagine if that quad was subdivided many times so its surface was more like a grid. An example height map can be seen in Figure 11.5. Each of the vertices can be moved up or down on the Y axis to give the impression of terrain, as can be seen in Figure 11.5. Height maps are often specified by grayscale images. Each pixel of the image corresponds to each vertex in the grid-mesh, the height depending on the intensity of the pixel. A gray pixel value halfway between black and white might represent no movement of the vertex; a black pixel would move the vertex negative one, and a white pixel would move the vertex positive one.

The advantage of using a bitmap to represent the height is that it allows the height map to be painted in a paint package. Height maps get a lot of use in computer games, and after reading this description, they will probably be very easy to spot! Real-time strategy games often use height maps for the terrain and 3D models for each of the units in the game.

The difficulty with strategy games, especially strategy games that are war-based, is the artificial intelligence. There are two different AI systems: the first is the AI

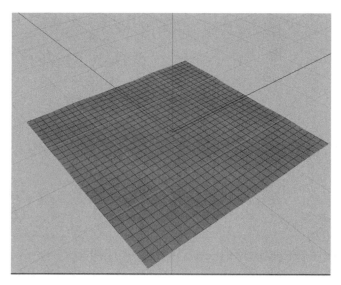

Figure 11.5
A grid of vertices.

of your own units; if you tell a tank to go from one location to another, it should take the shortest route and avoid running over civilians. This type of problem is generally known as path finding, and the easiest solution is to research the A-Star algorithm and implement a suitable variant of it. Not all games use A-Star for path finding, but it is a very popular method that is quite easy to understand.

The second type of AI in real-time strategy games is the AI that controls the computer component. This AI must provide a challenge to the player, but it shouldn't appear to cheat, and it should be beatable. There are all sorts of novel solutions to this problem using exotic sounding things like neural networks, but the usual solution is the slightly more mundane state machine and a few rules. A strategy game AI might have a number of states such as `build-up-units`, `attack`, and `defend`. Each state has some associated rules; for instance, the `build-up-units` state might have a rule "if the numbers of units are greater than ten, then move to the `attack` state." The `attack` state might have rules such as "if the offensive unit isn't near enemy base, then move to enemy base." It may also have rules about what should be attacked first and what priorities certain targets should be given. These rules can usually be defined in a data file, and then they are refined with a lot of tweaking and play testing.

Role-Playing Games

Role-playing games are very popular with game developers, but they are also very challenging. Role-playing games have many items, locations, enemies, and characters; these all require text and art. There are also several systems that need to be developed to create a full game: the conversation system, world exploration, inventory management, a leveling system, and combat.

Roguelike Games

Roguelike games get their name from their similarity to an early dungeon crawling game called *Rogue*. Roguelikes nearly always use the ASCII characters instead of graphics. Like text games, this means more of the programmer's time can be focused on the game instead of developing graphics. Some of the more popular Roguelikes are *ADoM* (http://www.adom.de/), *Nethack* (http://www.nethack.org/), and *Crawl* (http://crawl.develz.org/wordpress/). ASCII is also used for *Dwarf Fortress* (http://www.bay12games.com/dwarves/), a large-scale generic fantasy world creator and simulator that allows the user to control a number of dwarves as they build an underground lair. ASCII games do not have to be simple; *Dwarf Fortress* includes a detailed weather simulator, fluid physics, psychological models, and much more.

Creating an ASCII game in C# is similar to creating a text-based game. A console application should be created. Unlike the text game, ASCII games need a game loop. Each update, the world is output as text to the console. After the world is printed, the console cursor needs to be moved back to the start of the console window. The console cursor is a position that dictates where text will be printed when the program writes to the console. The next world update is printed over the earlier one, updating it. Here is some code that renders a small ASCII map with an @ character representing the player.

```
static void Main(string[] args)
{
  int _mapWidth = 10;
  int _mapHeight = 10;
  int _playerX = 0;
  int _playerY = 0;
  bool _playerIsAlive = true;
  while (_playerIsAlive)
  {
    for (int i = 0; i < _mapHeight; i++)
```

```
        {
          for (int j = 0; j < _mapWidth; j++)
          {
            if (j == _playerX && i == _playerY)
            {
              Console.Write('@');
            }
            else
            {
              Console.Write('.');
            }
          }
          Console.WriteLine();
        }
          Console.WriteLine();
        }
        Console.SetCursorPosition(0, 0);
      }
}
```

Even though this code snippet is quite short, it demonstrates the basics of a Roguelike. The next step is to read the input from the arrow keys and move the character around the small world.

Tile-Based Role-Playing Games

Tile-based games build a 2D world from small sprites called tiles. Tiles are used in all sorts of different games, not just role-playing, but they were a very popular technique with the early Japanese-style RPGS such as the *Final Fantasy* games (prior to the seventh), *Chrono Trigger*, the early *Zelda* games, and many other titles. Tiled graphics are still very common on handheld devices such as the DS and PlayStation portable. An example of a tile-based game can be seen in Figure 11.6. All the tiles describing the world are packed together in one or more textures called a tilemap. The tilemap used to build Figure 11.7 can be seen in Figure 11.8.

A good starting point for a tile-based game is to create a text file that represents the world. For example:

```
############
#          #
#          #
#S        E#
############
```

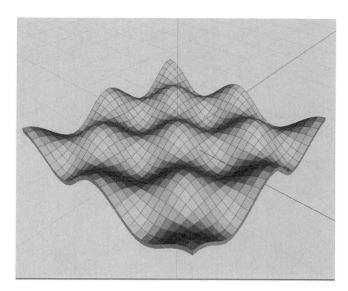

Figure 11.6
A grid with vertices displaced making a height map.

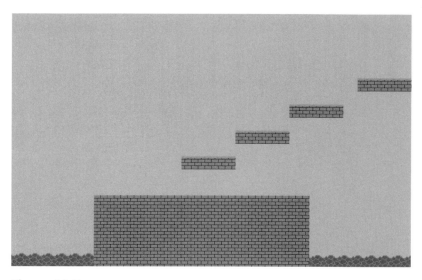

Figure 11.7
A tile-based game.

Figure 11.8
A tile map.

Here each pound sign represents a wall that blocks the character. The S character represents the start of the level, and the E represents the end. Here is some rough code to demonstrate how a level could be built up.

```
double startX = 0;
double startY = 0;
double tileWidthHeight = 32;

Dictionary<char, TileData> tileLookUp = LoadTileDefinitions();
string levelDef =
    "############\n" +
    "#          #\n" +
    "#          #\n" +
    "#S        E#\n" +
    "############\n";
```

```
TileMap tileMap = new TileMap();
double currentX = startX;
double currentY = startY;
int xPosition = 0;
int yPosition = 0;
foreach (char c in levelDef)
{
  if (c == '\n')
  {
    xPosition = 0;
    yPosition = yPosition + 1;
    currentX = startX;
    currentY -= tileWidthHeight;
    continue;
  }
  Tile t = tileLookUp[c].CreateTile();
  t.SetPosition(currentX, currentY);
  tileMap.AddTile(xPosition, yPosition, t);
  xPosition++;
  currentX += tileWidthHeight;
}
```

The text-based tile definition is iterated through, and each character is transformed into a tile. Each tile is a type of sprite and is carefully positioned so it is flush with its neighboring tile. ASCII characters are used to index a dictionary that contains a set of tile definitions containing tile data. This tile data will probably contain a texture; it will also have some flags that determine if the player can walk on the tile, and it may have some special properties such as ending the game when the player steps on it. The tile definition is used to create a tile, which uses a sprite to draw itself. Once the tile is created, it's positioned and added to the tilemap. In the game loop, the tilemap is used to render all the tiles. The player is rendered after the tiles and is free to walk around.

A common feature for tile-based games is to layer the tiles. Several tilemaps are created and laid on top of each other. This can be used to provide a parallax effect, where the background moves slowly compared to the progress of the player. It also allows the player to pass behind certain elements on the map.

3D Role-Playing Games

There is a wide variety of ways to make a 3D role-playing games, *Fallout 3, Oblivion,* and *Bioshock* use an FPS approach. Other 3D games emulate the more traditional tile-based approach by using an overhead camera that looks down on the players and game world. *Diablo 3* and *Twilight* are two good examples of this style. The third option is the third-person camera that one might see in *Zelda* since the N64 era, or the Mass Effect games.

The FPS-based approach puts you inside the eyes of the character, encouraging immersion in the game world. To start this kind of game, you would first need to be able to make a simple FPS game. FPS games tend to take place in tight buildings separated into missions or levels; RPGs tend to have big open areas and a large game world. Open worlds that allow a character to seamlessly walk from one city to another are very hard to program; data must be loaded and unloaded dynamically as the character walks around the world. This is very hard in an FPS game because if the player manages to climb somewhere quite high, then he expects to be able to look out onto the world and see where he has come from. This means a low-detail version of the world needs to be present in memory most of the time, and areas need to become more detailed as the player approaches. If this kind of algorithm interests you, then I suggest searching for papers on ROAM (Real-time Optimally Adapting Meshes). As with other games, it's a good idea to start small and simple and take small steps to something more complicated.

An easier approach to the open-world problem is to confine the player to small areas that can be loaded in memory all at once. Games such as *System Shock* and *Bioshock* use this limitation to drive the story. In *System Shock,* you are confined to a space station, and you can only move to different levels using a central elevator. While the elevator is moving, the old level is unloaded and the new level is loaded in. *Bioshock* works in a very similar way, but it's an underwater base.

Third-person games are very similar to FPS games, but the camera is pulled back allowing the player character to be seen on screen at all times. There are still the same problems with representing a vast dynamic world on only a limited amount of memory and computer resources. The Mass Effect games split up the world by scattering the levels over different planets. While the player is disembarking from his ship to the planet surface, the level is loaded. Zelda games have either an explicit loading screen as one area is loaded and another unloaded, or sometimes a dog leg is used. A dog leg is a stretch of level where nothing can be seen apart from the narrow corridor the player is walking down. The shape of the corridor is roughly like a dog's leg, or a very relaxed L shape. The corridor is long enough that it gives just enough time for the new level to be loaded before the player emerges from it. Dog legs don't have to be corridors; they can also be mountain passes or a narrow alleyway between tall buildings.

A top-down camera doesn't suffer as much from the vast world problems as an FPS or third-person camera view, because the camera only looks at a small chunk of the world. A player with an FPS camera can look to the horizon and see vast trails of the land; this is not the case with the top-down camera. There is always quite a small fixed area around the player. This makes loading and unloading chunks of a level easier. Top-down views also do quite well with a tile-based approach, but instead of each tile being a sprite, each tile is a 3D mesh that matches its surrounding 3D tiles. This makes it much faster to make levels; a few chunks can be modeled and then attached together to form a level fairly quickly.

Platform Games

Platform games are very popular for amateur and independent game developers. There is a little math involved, but it tends to be quite simple, and there are a lot of different gameplay ideas that can be explored in the 2D platformer world. Most platformer games use a tile approach quite similar to the approach discussed in the role-playing section.

Platform games usually require a small degree of physics modeling; gravity nearly always needs modeling. The physics can be written using the basic equations for velocity and acceleration, or by using a third-party physics library, such as a Box2d (there is a C# port called Box2dx). If you decide to code everything by hand, then you can get something up and running quite quickly with the sprite classes and simple rectangle-rectangle collision tests.

Here is a very simple game state that moves a red square around with the arrow keys, and it can be made to jump with the up arrow key.

```
class PlatfomerTestState : IGameObject

{
  class PlatformEntity
  {
    const float _width = 16;
    const float _height = 16;
    RectangleF bounds = new RectangleF(-_width, -_height, _width,
      _height);
```

```
    public void Render()
    {
      Gl.glBegin(Gl.GL_LINE_LOOP);
      {
        Gl.glColor3f(1, 0, 0);
        Gl.glVertex2f(bounds.Left, bounds.Top);
        Gl.glVertex2f(bounds.Right, bounds.Top);
        Gl.glVertex2f(bounds.Right, bounds.Bottom);
        Gl.glVertex2f(bounds.Left, bounds.Bottom);

      }
      Gl.glEnd();
      Gl.glEnable(Gl.GL_TEXTURE_2D);
    }

    public Vector GetPosition()
    {
      return new Vector(bounds.Location.X + _width, bounds.Location.
        Y + 16, 0);
    }

    public void SetPosition(Vector value)
    {
      bounds = new RectangleF((float)value.X - _width, (float)value.
        Y - _height, _width, _height);
    }
  }

  PlatformEntity _pc = new PlatformEntity();
  Input _input;
  double _speed = 1600;
  Vector _velocity = new Vector(0, 0, 0);
  bool _jumping = false;
  double _gravity = 0.75;
  double _friction = 0.1;

public PlatfomerTestState(Input input)
    {
      _input = input;
    }
    #region IGameObject Members
```

```
public void Update(double elapsedTime)
{
  if (_input.Keyboard.IsKeyHeld(Keys.Left))
  {
    _velocity.X -= _speed;
  }
  else if (_input.Keyboard.IsKeyHeld(Keys.Right))
  {
    _velocity.X += _speed;
  }

  if (_input.Keyboard.IsKeyPressed(Keys.Up) && !_jumping)
  {
    _velocity.Y += 500;
    _jumping = true;
  }

  _velocity.Y -= _gravity;
  _velocity.X = _velocity.X * _friction;

  Vector newPosition = _pc.GetPosition();
  newPosition += _velocity * elapsedTime;

  if (newPosition.Y < 0)
  {
    newPosition.Y = 0;
    _velocity.Y = 0;
    _jumping = false;
  }
  _pc.SetPosition(newPosition);
}

public void Render()
{
  Gl.glDisable(Gl.GL_TEXTURE_2D);
  Gl.glClearColor(1, 1, 1, 0);
  Gl.glClear(Gl.GL_COLOR_BUFFER_BIT);

  Gl.glEnable(Gl.GL_LINE_SMOOTH);
  Gl.glLineWidth(2.0f);
```

```
    Gl.glPointSize(10.0f);
    Gl.glColor3d(0, 0, 0);
    _pc.Render();
  }
  #endregion
}
```

There is a small class here called `PlatformEntity`, and this draws a simple red line box and provides methods to move it about. There is some very simple cartoon-like physics modeling in the `Process` loop. The new position for the entity is calculated and then it's checked to see if the entity has fallen below zero on the Y axis; if so, it's pushed back up. This is a good starting point to play around with different control methods, and sprites can be added to give the scene much more character. Additional collision code needs to be added to handle free hanging platforms

Final Words

By now, you should not only have some great game ideas, but also know how to realize these ideas. Remember to start small, create a rough working version as early as possible, and then refine it. If you follow these steps, you will soon have a fun game that you are proud of and eager to release into the world! Good luck and happy coding!

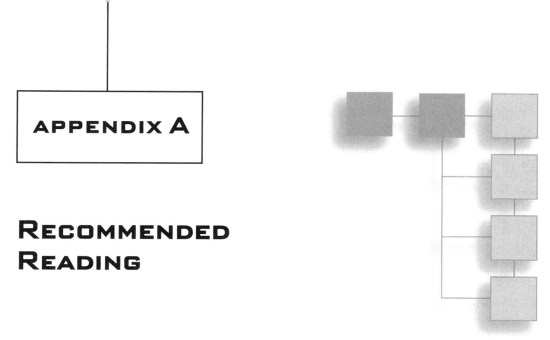

APPENDIX A

RECOMMENDED READING

This appendix suggests excellent books that are useful when creating a game project or improving your skills and knowledge. This section only covers books, but the CD has an HTML file with links to useful websites and papers online.

The Practice of Programming

The *practice of programming* is about the journey—an initial spark of an idea to finished project. These books give some guidelines for how development should be done and what steps need to be taken to painlessly create a great finished program. They are not game specific as the lessons apply to all software development projects, but they're still very much worth reading.

***The Pragmatic Programmer: From Journeyman to Master* (ISBN 0-201-61622-X) by Andrew Hunt and David Thomas**

The Pragmatic Programmer is a relatively short book that describes how to complete software projects. It's not about any language in particular; instead, it is about the process of software development. Despite being very short, it is packed with useful information and I highly recommended it if you want to improve your craft.

***Code Complete Second Edition: A Practical Handbook of Software Construction* (ISBN-13: 978-0735619678) by Steve McConnell**

Code Complete is another book that encourages a pragmatic programming style, but unlike *The Pragmatic Programmer,* this book goes into much greater detail.

It covers how to write tight, clean code that is easy to extend and debug. There is a slight C++/C focus, but the vast majority of the book is applicable to C# or any other programming language.

The C# Language and Software Architecture

Readers of these books are assumed to be familiar with C# or a similar language; therefore, their suggested aim is to provide a deeper understanding. Software Architecture is a term used to describe the design and structure of computer programs; how the code is broken up into parts and how those parts communicate.

CLR via C#, 3rd Edition (ISBN-13: 978-0735627048) **by Jeffrey Richter**

The focus of this book isn't C#; rather, it's the virtual machine that C# runs on. Understanding this virtual machine will help greatly when you desire to improve the speed and efficiency of your C# programs.

Head First Design Patterns (ISBN-13: 978-0596007126) **by Eric T Freeman, Elisabeth Robson, Bert Bates, and Kathy Sierra**

The usual recommended book for design patterns is *Design Patterns : Elements of Reusable Object-Oriented Software,* but it is a very dry book. *Head First Design Patterns* is much more readable and entertaining. Design patterns are small descriptions of how to write code to solve some common challenges in software development. It's worth understanding these patterns to see how other people are approaching design problems and also to be able to understand what is being referenced when people are criticizing the overuse of the Singleton pattern or suggesting the use of a Decorator pattern. The book uses Java to explain the patterns, but it is quite simple to convert the examples to C#.

Math and Graphics Programming

If you want to expand your knowledge of mathematics and graphics programming, these two books are a good starting point.

3D Math Primer for Graphics and Game Development (ISBN-13: 978-1556229114) **by Fletcher Dunn and Ian Parberry**

I've worked with and visited quite a number of different game development studios, and it's quite common to see this book lying on top of somebody's desk. The book covers all the mathematics needed to understand how the fundamentals of 3D games work. It is more approachable than nearly any other equivalent book, but it is still a high-level math text and requires a lot of work by the reader to understand everything. It's also a good reference book with lots of C++ code, which isn't hard to convert to C# code. There are plenty of exercises for the reader as well.

Computer Graphics: Principles and Practice in C (2nd Edition) (ISBN-13: 978-0201848403) **by James D. Foley, Andries van Dam, Steven K. Feiner, and John F. Hughes**

If you wanted to write your own version of OpenGL, this would be the book to follow. It's an excellent reference book with a very broad scope, and code examples are provided in C. It covers principles such as the different ways to represent color, how monitors work, line drawing algorithms, how to write a rasterizer, and so on. The principles of computer graphics are unchanging, but the book is starting to show its age. It has little to say on shaders and modern graphics hardware, but quite a lot to say on systems that are no longer heavily used such as PHIGS (an API that OpenGL overtook).

OpenGL

There are two major books that cover OpenGL, and they're known as the Red Book and the Orange Book. The red book covers the standard OpenGL library, and the orange book covers shaders using the OpenGL shading language GLSL.

OpenGL Programming Guide: The Official Guide to Learning OpenGL (ISBN-13: 978-0321552624) **by Dave Shreiner**

This is the red book, and it covers all the OpenGL basics, noting which parts of OpenGL have changed in the latest versions. The examples are in C++, but nearly all the OpenGL calls are the same in C# and therefore can be copied over.

OpenGL Shading Language 3rd Edition **by Randi J. Rost, Bill Licea-Kane, Dan Ginsburg, John M. Kessenich, Barthold Lichtenbelt, Hugh Malan, and Mike Weiblen**

This is the orange book, and it covers the more modern shader-driven approach to OpenGL. The book uses GLSL, but once you understand one shading language, it's very easy to move to another as they are all quite similar.

INDEX

415

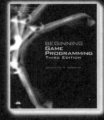

License Agreement/Notice of Limited Warranty

By opening the sealed disc container in this book, you agree to the following terms and conditions. If, upon reading the following license agreement and notice of limited warranty, you cannot agree to the terms and conditions set forth, return the unused book with unopened disc to the place where you purchased it for a refund.

License:

The enclosed software is copyrighted by the copyright holder(s) indicated on the software disc. You are licensed to copy the software onto a single computer for use by a single user and to a backup disc. You may not reproduce, make copies, or distribute copies or rent or lease the software in whole or in part, except with written permission of the copyright holder(s). You may transfer the enclosed disc only together with this license, and only if you destroy all other copies of the software and the transferee agrees to the terms of the license. You may not decompile, reverse assemble, or reverse engineer the software.

Notice of Limited Warranty:

The enclosed disc is warranted by Course Technology to be free of physical defects in materials and workmanship for a period of sixty (60) days from end user's purchase of the book/disc combination. During the sixty-day term of the limited warranty, Course Technology will provide a replacement disc upon the return of a defective disc.

Limited Liability:

THE SOLE REMEDY FOR BREACH OF THIS LIMITED WARRANTY SHALL CONSIST ENTIRELY OF REPLACEMENT OF THE DEFECTIVE DISC. IN NO EVENT SHALL COURSE TECHNOLOGY OR THE AUTHOR BE LIABLE FOR ANY OTHER DAMAGES, INCLUDING LOSS OR CORRUPTION OF DATA, CHANGES IN THE FUNCTIONAL CHARACTERISTICS OF THE HARDWARE OR OPERATING SYSTEM, DELETERIOUS INTERACTION WITH OTHER SOFTWARE, OR ANY OTHER SPECIAL, INCIDENTAL, OR CONSEQUENTIAL DAMAGES THAT MAY ARISE, EVEN IF COURSE TECHNOLOGY AND/OR THE AUTHOR HAS PREVIOUSLY BEEN NOTIFIED THAT THE POSSIBILITY OF SUCH DAMAGES EXISTS.

Disclaimer of Warranties:

COURSE TECHNOLOGY AND THE AUTHOR SPECIFICALLY DISCLAIM ANY AND ALL OTHER WARRANTIES, EITHER EXPRESS OR IMPLIED, INCLUDING WARRANTIES OF MERCHANTABILITY, SUITABILITY TO A PARTICULAR TASK OR PURPOSE, OR FREEDOM FROM ERRORS. SOME STATES DO NOT ALLOW FOR EXCLUSION OF IMPLIED WARRANTIES OR LIMITATION OF INCIDENTAL OR CONSEQUENTIAL DAMAGES, SO THESE LIMITATIONS MIGHT NOT APPLY TO YOU.

Other:

This Agreement is governed by the laws of the State of Massachusetts without regard to choice of law principles. The United Convention of Contracts for the International Sale of Goods is specifically disclaimed. This Agreement constitutes the entire agreement between you and Course Technology regarding use of the software.